JOURNAL FOR THE STUDY OF THE OLD TESTAMENT
SUPPLEMENT SERIES
84

BIBLE AND LITERATURE SERIES
24

Almond Press
Sheffield

"It is a fearful thing to fall
into the hands of the living God"

Hebrews 10:31

Dedication:

To Gloria, Cole, & Amanda

Into the Hands of the Living God

Lyle Eslinger

The Almond Press · 1989

Bible and Literature Series, 24

Published by Almond Press
Editorial direction: David M. Gunn
Columbia Theological Seminary
P.O. Box 520, Decatur
GA 30031, U.S.A.
Almond Press is an imprint of
Sheffield Academic Press Ltd
The University of Sheffield
343 Fulwood Road
Sheffield S10 3BP
England

Typeset by Sheffield Academic Press
and
printed in Great Britain
by Billing & Sons Ltd
Worcester

British Library Cataloguing in Publication Data

Eslinger, Lyle M. *1953-*
Into the hands of the living God
1. Bible, O.T. Deuteronomy. Critical studies
I. Title II. Series
222′.1506

ISSN 0260-4493
ISSN 0309-0787

ISBN 1-85075-212-5

CONTENTS

PREFACE

This book, written over several summers and during a one year fellowship at The Calgary Institute for the Humanities, offers a new perspective on the "Deuteronomistic History." Drawing on key concepts from modern literary theory and a sub-discipline, narratology, my studies of these books have led me to an unorthodox (some might say eccentric) reading of these narratives. Studies of selected passages in this part of the Bible—the "great orations" identified by Martin Noth—lead me to reject historical-critical hypotheses about the literary history of these books. A consequent agnosticism about the literary history of the books—at least about the supposed history sketched in existing suggestions—leads me back to a traditional-looking assumption of unitary authorship, a single Deuteronomist if you will. The same view is fostered by purely technical study of the formal voice structures in these narratives: there is nothing in the conventional literary ontology of these stories that could lead any reader to assume that more than one author, one voice, is expressing itself. But even the appearance of having settled for one rather than several "Deuteronomists" is misleading. As my reading of the story of Solomon will show (chapter five), I have not so much settled for the school of Noth as for the school of nought since I do not find much in these stories that convinces me of Deuteronomic fideism on the part of the unknown author(s) of this, the Bible's most extended narrative piece. The book of Deuteronomy remains a key to unlocking the story's meaning, but seems not the key to the author's own ideology.

Thanks for research support from the following agencies: The Calgary Institute for the Humanities (1986–87); The University of Calgary, Research Grants Committee (1985–88); The Social Sciences & Humanities Research Council of Canada (1986–87). Last, but not least, thanks to David Gunn for accepting the book for the Bible & Literature Series and to David Orton, editor at Sheffield Academic Press, for suggested improvements.

ABBREVIATIONS

AB	Anchor Bible
AnOr	Analecta orientalia
AOAT	Alter Orient und Altes Testament
ARW	*Archiv für Religionswissenschaft*
ATD	Das Alte Testament Deutsch
BAR	*Biblical Archaeology Review*
BASOR	*Bulletin of the American Schools of Oriental Research*
BDB	F. Brown, S. R. Driver, C. A. Briggs, *Hebrew and English Lexicon of the Old Testament*
BHK	R. Kittel, *Biblia Hebraica*
BHS	*Biblia Hebraica Stuttgartensia*
Bib	*Biblica*
BKAT	Biblischer Kommentar: Altes Testament
BLS	Bible & Literature Series
BO	*Bibliotheca orientalis*
BZAW	Beihefte zur *Zeitschrift für die alttestamentliche Wissenschaft* (Giessen), Berlin.
CBQ	*Catholic Biblical Quarterly*
CBQMS	Catholic Biblical Quarterly Monograph Series
BSOAS	*Bulletin of the School of Oriental (and African) Studies*
FRLANT	Forschungen zur Religion und Literatur des Alten und Neuen Testaments
GKC	Gesenius, Kautsch, Cowley, *Gesenius' Hebrew Grammar*
HALAT	W. Baumgartner et al., *Hebräisches und aramäisches Lexikon zum Alten Testament*
HAT	Handbuch zum Alten Testament
HKAT	Handkommentar zum Alten Testament
HSM	Harvard Semitic Monographs
HTR	*Harvard Theological Review*

HUCA	*Hebrew Union College Annual*
JAAR	*Journal of the American Academy of Religion*
JSS	*Journal of Semitic Studies*
ICC	International Critical Commentary
IDBSup	Supplementary volume to *IDB*
IEJ	*Israel Exploration Journal*
Int	*Interpretation*
JANESCU	*Journal of the Ancient Near Eastern Society of Columbia University*
JETS	*Journal of the Evangelical Theological Society*
JNSL	*Journal of Northwest Semitic Languages*
JSOT	*Journal for the Study of the Old Testament*
JSOTSS	*Journal for the Study of the Old Testament–Supplement Series*
JSS	*Journal of Semitic Studies*
JTS	*Journal of Theological Studies*
KAT	Kommentar zur Alten Testament
KHAT	Kurzer Hand-Commentar zum Alten Testament Tübingen
KAT	E. Sellin (ed.), Kommentar zum A.T.
KJV	*King James Version*
NAB	*New American Bible*
NASV	*New American Standard Version*
NCB	New Century Bible
NEB	*New English Bible*
NIV	*New International Version*
OTL	Old Testament Library
OTS	*Oudtestamentische Studien*
RB	*Revue Biblique*
RHR	*Revue de l'histoire des religions*
RSV	*Revised Standard Version*
RV	*Revised Version*
SAT	*Die Schriften des Alten Testaments*
SBLDS	SBL Dissertation Series
SBT	Studies in Biblical Theology
SH	*Scripta Hierosolymitana*
TDOT	Theological Dictionary of the Old Testament

TWAT	G. J. Botterweck and H. Ringgren (eds.), *Theologisches Wörterbuch zum Alten Testament*
VT	*Vetus Testamentum*
VTSup	Vetus Testamentum, Supplements
WBC	Word Bible Commentary
WMANT	Wissenschaftliche Monographien zum Alten und Neuen Testament
ZAW	*Zeitschrift für die alttestamentliche Wissenschaft*
ZTK	*Zeitschrift für Theologie und Kirche*

CHAPTER 1

NARRATORIAL SITUATIONS IN THE BIBLE

Historical Criticism and Literary Criticism

Between modern and traditional biblical interpretation there is one primary difference: the critical stance of the former. The critical method was developed to organize knowledge about the Bible, unhindered by the trammels of faith. As we all know, the movement that resulted was historical criticism. It has taken hold of academic biblical study and established a monopoly that has, for a time, successfully rebuffed all competition.

As its name suggests, the organizing principle of historical criticism—a name that has become synonymous with biblical criticism—is history. By reorganizing the data of biblical literature within a historical framework, the historical critic creates a logical, non-contradictory representation of the events described in biblical narrative. Through this process the critic also generates another narrative about the literary history of the biblical narratives. That is, the historical critic creates two historical frameworks to explain biblical narrative because the critic perceives two different kinds of data requiring organization. The primary concern, at least in the beginning, is with the participants, actions, and events described in the narrative; historical organization of this plane of the Bible's narrative literature culminates in a history of Israel. But to write accurate histories of Israel, the historical critic must also take into account another level in biblical narrative: the compositional plane of the author. This plane intervenes between the critic and the events described in the narrative; historical organization of it results in histories of Israelite literature.[1]

The binocular analytical framework of historical criticism is the product of two factors, one methodological, the other a generic feature of narrative writing. It is a fundamental rule of history writing that one must be circumspect about one's sources. One must always be aware, when using documents as sources, of the influence of the author's own historically conditioned situation on his composition. This awareness is encouraged by the appearance of narrative itself, which is typically a story related by someone, a narrator. As the narrator tells his story he leaves traces of his attitudes and opinions about the subject matter of his story in his narrative account. These traces reflect the author's[2] own existential and historical situations and it is these traces that allow the circumspect critic to take a literary source's biases into account.

Such traces vary in the degree of information that they reveal about the teller. The scale extends from the simple phenomenon of tagged speech, "he said"—which only allows us to

---

1 Roman Ingarden makes similar observations about the analysis of literature in general:

> "In fact, in reading a work, our attention is likewise directed primarily at represented objectivities. We are attuned to them, and our intentional gaze finds in them a certain peace and satisfaction; whereas we pass by the other strata with a certain degree of inattention, and, at any rate, we notice them incidentally, only to the extent that this is necessary for the thematic apprehension of objects. Some naïve readers are interested solely in the vicissitudes of represented objects, while everything else is nearly nonexistent for them. In works in which represented objects are engaged in the function of representation, such readers wish only to *find out* something about the *represented* world. And since the represented world, usually the real world, which then constitutes the main focus of interest, is conceived as something existing only for itself and performing no function, the world represented in a literary work of art is also conceived in the same sense. It is quite in keeping with this that works of literary history on the whole deal mainly with represented objects and, after some analysis of the properties of the "language" or of the nature of "images" used by the author, go into various problems of the work's genesis" (1973:288–89).

2 Though it is common enough, in the study of narrative literature, to make a distinction between the narrator of a narrative and the author of a narrative, historical criticism has been unaware of the importance of this distinction the comprehension of meaning in narrative literature. Biblical critics have mostly assumed that all statements, especially evaluative assertions, in the narrative are the expressions of an author's own views or beliefs. No distinction is made between character voices or that of the narrator: all, democratically, are vehicles for the direct expression of the author's own views. In the study of most biblical narrative, one need observe only one distinction: between the voices of the author/narrator and the characters. This claimed univocality of author and narrator will be demonstrated later in this essay.

know that there is a teller—to seemingly forthright, evaluative comments about the story (e.g. "Notwithstanding they would not hear, but hardened their necks, like to the neck of their fathers, that did not believe in the Lord their God," 2 Kgs 17:14, *KJV*). Here a vivid reflection of the teller's values seems to appear, though irony is common enough in the Bible that one must be careful about accepting face values too easily. But for historical critics such traces of supposed authorial bias are consistently treated as reliable revelations into the compositional circumstance in which the work was written. The note of disapproval in Gen 25:34, for example, seems to betray the narrator's allegiance to Jacob, prompting a historical critical reader such as Herman Gunkel to comment, "*Die Sage lacht den dummen Esau aus, der seine ganze Zukunft um ein Linsengericht verkauft hat; und jubelt über den klugen Jacob in dem die Erzähler ihr eigenes Bild wiedererkennen*" (1902:264).

Whichever of the two levels the historical critic addresses, the ultimate goal of historical reconstruction absolutely depends on literary analysis.[3] To get at the actual history (the history of Israel) lying behind the events recorded in the biblical stories, the historical critic must get past any authorial/narratorial bias. To neutralize the influence of authorial distortion on our perception of the events described, the critic must place the author and his story in the relativizing framework of literary history. To write literary history the critic must isolate and consolidate all traces of authorial self-revelation in the narrative. And to decide which of the multitudinous evaluations and statements in

3 "Historic and literary study are equal in importance: but for priority in order of time the literary treatment has the first claim. The reason of this is that the starting point of historic analysis must be that very existing text, which is the sole concern of the morphological study. The historic inquirer will no doubt add to his examination of the text light drawn from other sources; he may be led in his investigation to alter or rearrange the text; but he will admit that the most important single element on which he has to work is the text as it has come down to us. But, if the foundation principle of literary study be true, this existing text cannot be truly interpreted until it has been read in the light of its exact literary structure. In actual fact, it appears to me, Biblical criticism at the present time is, not infrequently, vitiated in its historical contentions by tacit assumptions as to the form of the text such as literary examination might have corrected" (R.G. Moulton 1908:ix). Moulton and others who voiced similar warnings went unheeded in the early part of this century. Historical criticism's triumphs over traditional literalist readings of the Bible allowed it the unfortunate liberty of ignoring all opposing claims, regardless of their validity. Only more recently has the sentiment expressed by Moulton been able to gain an audience, mainly because the passage of time has allowed the deficiencies in the historical-critical method to come to light and so to criticism more willingly heard (e.g. Polzin (1980:6), who voices a similar caution to Moulton's).

a narrative are to be attributed to the author, the critic must engage in literary analysis and more particularly in analysis of the question of point of view. Therein lies the problem that plagues all historical criticism and, from the perspective of the new biblical narratology, vitiates most existing historical-critical readings of biblical narrative.

In its hasty, but enlightened pursuit of the historical truth about the events described in Bible stories, historical criticism paused only briefly—did it pause at all?—to develop crude, makeshift tools for literary analysis of the variety of phenonema bearing on the complex of narrative phenomena collectively known as "point of view." Unfortunately, the literary theory that supported these rudimentary tools was frequently a product of critics' casual acquaintance with the literary works of their contemporaries or with literary theories developed to explain modern European literature. Certainly there are many parallels between ancient and modern literature—we "moderns" are not that distant from the literate cultures that have preceded us in human history—but the theories derived from the study of contemporary European literature require, as we know now, adaptation to the peculiarities of ancient Hebrew narrative style. Some features of narrative literature such as manipulation of narrative ontology and "point of view" are common; others, such as Hebrew narrative's manipulation of redundancy and repetition are less so.[4] Without a constant view to adaptation and an inductive approach to the study of biblical literary technique, anachronistic analysis was inevitable and many of the conclusions drawn were hampered by it.

Narrative Ontology

The attempt to relativize authorial distortion in description of events is a good example of what I am talking about. Every

---

4 Even with many good literary studies of repetition in Hebrew literature in existence, some historical critics seem unable to turn more than a blind eye to an inductive appreciation of the Bible's foreign literary conventions. B. Halpern, for example, can only caricature modern studies of biblical repetition: "... these [literary studies] assume that the author was free to say what he wanted in any way he wanted to say it: he wrote doublets and created contradictions—he stuttered and stammered—by *choice*" (1988:199). Halpern begs exactly the point: that repetition can be intentional and significant. And historical-critical perceptions of contradiction frequently depend on inattention to subtle differences in supposed reiterations of "the same thing." The biblical authors did not stutter and stammer; they repeated themselves on purpose, sometimes because it takes people more than once to catch on to what is being said.

narrative is a combination of a story that is told and a teller that relates it. Franz Stanzel identifies this literary trait—"mediacy of presentation"—as the distinguishing generic characteristic of all narrative literature (1984:4). The author of a narrative creates both a story and a narrating voice or view that mediates the story. Depending on the manner in which an author chooses to frame this relationship between narrator and story world, there is frequently (almost always in biblical narrative) a hierarchy of authority within the fictive literary cosmos. Only the reader who understands the nature of this hierarchy will be able to draw valid conclusions about an author's views.

The implications for historical criticism's unremitting focus on the biblical authors' socio-historically bound discourse are tremendous. If one is concerned to understand the view of the author of the Deuteronomistic narrative (Joshua–2 Kings) so as to reach a correct assessment of the document's date and the socio-historical context within which it came to expression, it is obvious that one must first be certain that one is reading the author's views and not the pilloried quotation of a view in fact opposed by the author and his narrative (cf. Polzin's discussion of "ultimate semantic authority" 1980:20).

Most biblical narrative is rendered using one common "narrative situation,"[5] which can be sketched as follows:

5 "Narrative situation" is a term coined by Stanzel (*Narrative Situations in the Novel*) to describe the variety of narrative ontologies and epistemologies from which an author may choose to frame his story. Stanzel tries to summarize all possible narrative situations in three categories (1984:xvi).

Narrative Ontology

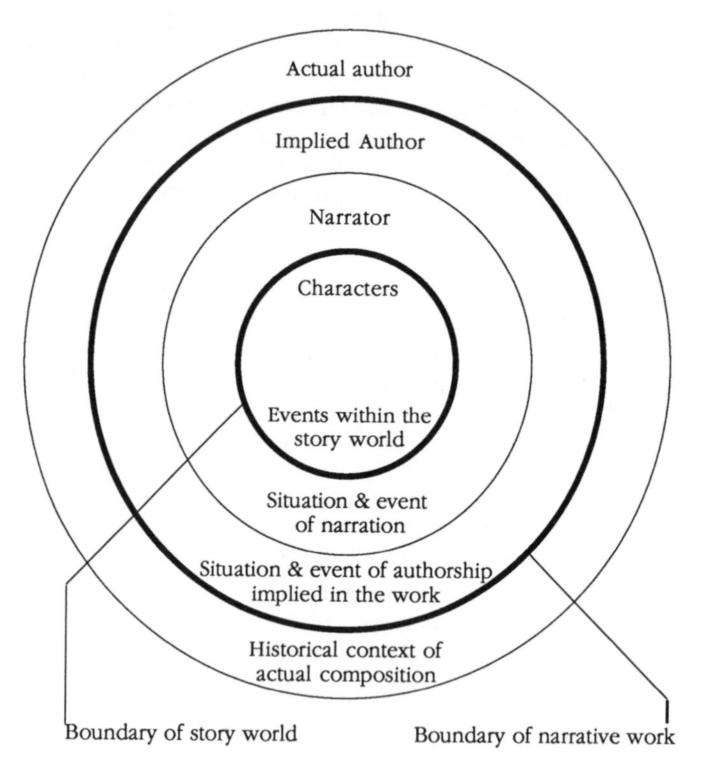

Concerned to know the historical truth about the events described in the story, historical critics must relativize at least three levels of literarily (characters, narrator) or historically (actual author) conditioned perception before they can even begin to evaluate the historical value of the story.[6] If they do not relativize either the literary or historical tiers that bar them from the history for which they search, their reconstructions are predestined to certain delusion.

---

6 The actual events that the story is based on are not represented in the diagram. Imagine them as lying in the paper of the page upon which the diagram is printed. You may catch a direct glimpse of them if you look at the page edgewise. The edgewise view though slim, is about as close as we can come to a view not conditioned by the multiple levels of relativized perception in biblical narrative.

In fact, however, historical-critical analyses have run roughshod over the hierarchical narrative ontology. The complex narrative layering of varying views of characters, the comments of narrators, and the overarching structural and thematic implications of the implied author have all been lumped together in a literary-historical hypothesis that sees the narrative literature as a flat, two dimensional mass of opinions from the long line of actual authors who have contributed to these stories. The third dimension, that of the hierarchical narrative ontology, is entirely overlooked in conventional historical-critical treatments. And aspects of the narrative that are, without presupposing anything beyond the generic conventions of narrative literature, part of the third dimension—the narrative's vertical ontology—have been mistaken for the products of compositional production through time.

A prime example of the danger of the two dimensional historical interpretation of biblical narrative is the treatment of 1 Samuel 8–12, in which historical critics have seen the hands of numerous authors and redactors of varying opinions about the value of a monarchy. No matter whether it is Samuel, God, or the people speaking in the narrative, all statements are directly ascribed to a real author[7] who stands immediately behind the voice in the narrative and voices his own dissenting views over against the other authors of this text, whose contrary voices are heard directly through the other characters or the narrator's own voice. But when one pays some attention to the hierarchy of perspectival levels within the narrative, it is not difficult to see correlations between particular views expressed in the narrative and particular characters or perspectival levels (Eslinger 1983; 1985). The dissonant voices can be heard and understood within the framework of the story world and the ontology of that particular narrative. Samuel, for example, criticizes the proposed monarchy because he stands to lose his pre-eminent position of authority (Eslinger 1985:260–2).

If historical critics had seen the existential matrix that conditioned Samuel's view, which is relative to his personal situation in the story world, I doubt that they would have posited the existence of a dissenting author behind this character. That hypothesis was, after all, supposed to resolve a literary conflict in

---

7 I use the noun "author" to describe all authorial roles, variously described by biblical scholars as "redactors" (editors), compilators, glossators, and sources.

the narrative that could not be resolved except by resort to literary history. The hypothetical explanation of historical-criticism, in which contrary perspectives are explained by recourse to the inference of varying authorial opinions that now find expression in one conglomerate narrative, is a second-order interpretation whose complexity and conjectural foundation makes it easy prey for a literary explanation in terms of narrative ontology.[8] The elegance of the narratological explanation is best appreciated after hearing the multitude of hypothetical literary histories promoted as explanations of the perspectival layers in 1 Sam 8–12. Like phlogiston, the pro- and anti-monarchic sources (or traditions, or redactions) are a plausible, if unverifiable explanation of a literary phenomenon. Now that a first-order alternative presents itself such conjectures should, if one subscribes to Occam's dictates, be put aside. There can be no easy peace between the two reading strategies.

Excursus: Historical & Literary Criticisms

Despite calls for a rapprochement between the new literary studies and historical criticism the contest has hardly begun. Critical interaction between the two perspectives so far has been extremely limited—engagements from the historical-critical side, such as John Emerton's recent articles in *Vetus Testamentum*, are the exception not the rule—with most historically oriented work simply ignoring the criticisms of the literary critics or passing off their theory, methods, and work as inappropriate to biblical literature.

Baruch Halpern's new book (1988) on the deuteronomistic narratives is a case in point. Halpern begins from the assumption—he calls it an intuition (p. xvii)—that biblical narratives are historical, are intended to be taken as histo-

---

8 Moulton (1908:ix) provides the following early example of an elegant obviation of a second order explanation:

"In the latter part of our Book of Micah a group of verses (vii. 7–10) must strike even a casual reader by their buoyancy of tone, so sharply contrasting with what has gone before. Accordingly Wellhausen sees in this changed tone evidence of a new composition, product of an age different in spirit from the age of the prophet: "between v. 6 and v. 7 there yawns a century." What really yawns between the verses is simply a change of speakers .... At this point the Man of Wisdom speaks, and the disputed verses change the tone to convey the happy confidence of one on whose side the divine intervention is to take place .... I submit that in this case a mistaken historical judgment has been formed by a distinguished historian for want of that preliminary literary analysis of the text for which I am contending."

riography. He spends a lot of time (pp. 3–15) trying to legitimate his effort to get at authorial intention, surely a wasted effort as methodological history repeats itself on the question of "the intentional fallacy." (Halpern suggests that some [all?] literary critics "transmogrify the Intentional Fallacy ... from an esthetic into a historical principle. They deny that readers can construe what the Israelite historian meant ..." (p. 5). Anyone who has read the New Critical debate over authorial intention knows that this is a bad case of straw-manning. The point was and is that we simply have no better access to the author's intention than the text that conveys his thoughts. And biblical literary critics are more justified than their New Critical ancestors in applying this view to the Bible, for which so little external data is available to temper our perceptions of authorial intent.)

Authorial intention aside, however, Halpern wants his readers to believe that the central dispute is the question of whether or not it is legitimate to treat biblical narrative as historiography. Attacking literary critics—Halpern calls them "Pyrrhonists"—for rejecting this possibility, he distracts attention onto this subordinate question, away from the real issue. The real dispute is with the faultiness of historical-critical literary theory and the consequent reading on which all of its historical considerations rest. Whether or not any given text or passage ought to be regarded as historiography is a second order generic question rarely addressed by literary critical analyses of biblical narrative. It is a neglected question precisely because it is, for most such analyses, a matter of indifference to the primary task: the careful reading of biblical literature in sympathy with its own conventions. Most literary critics would agree, I think, that *after* a careful reading of the text the question of its generic status, historiographic or otherwise, is fair and legitimate game. Genre, after all, is not a tag pre-defined and readily accessible—it is a product of our reading apprehensions of a text. The literary strategies that a good close reading uncovers may lead one to suppose that, yes, it looks like good history writing should. My reading of narratorial objectivity in the deuteronomistic narratives, though I am inclined to see it as a rhetorical strategy and hence to regard it with some suspicion, might be quite amenable to a reading as a historian's controlled objectivity. Halpern could, I think, use it to buttress his plea for a reconsideration of the author's status as historian (e.g. pp. 275–78). On the other hand, a contrived plot such as is found in the story of King Josiah's discovery of the law book in the Temple (2 Kgs 22-3) might *after careful analysis* lead me to think, no, this cannot be a self-conscious effort to reproduce accurately the facts of the matter (see Eslinger 1986).

Having struck what he seems to consider a mortal blow to the new literary critical approach to biblical literature, Halpern seems also to assume that it is a safe course for one interested in the deuteronomistic narratives as historiography to ignore literary critical readings. Aside from a few passing jabs at Robert Alter's *introductory* work, Halpern does not engage in debate with the many detailed literary critical readings of the texts with which he concerns himself. As a result his reading of the deuteronomist as historian is based on the same well-trodden historical-critical reading paths worn through the material: two redactors—this time H(Dtr) and E(Dtr)—whose own differences are only the last layers of contradicting views first apparent in their recalcitrant source material. (e.g. pp. 181–83). Nowhere do we see a defence of this hypothesis of authorial multiplicity against the existing detailed readings of this same material by such scholars as J.P. Fokkelman, D.M. Gunn, or R. Polzin. The new reading thus birthed is congenitally defective, in-bred historical-criticism talking to itself.

Both sides of the dispute have ignored the opposition, though historical critics have had the luxury of being the status quo and this has perhaps led to the greater laxity. Only through methodological engagement will the weaknesses of each position be exposed and corrected and only then should the desired rapprochement occur.[9]

Biblical Narratology

To improve the state of literary affairs in the study of biblical narrative biblical scholars are beginning to devise a literary theory and method that accounts for the multi-leveled mediation of events. To the good fortune of biblical studies a rich source of

---

9 Having made this plea I find myself in the unfortunate position of being guilty of insufficient engagement with historical-critical readings in this set of essays. In defence, I have done a fair job of debating the issues, which are the same, in my first book on these narratives (1985). If I had had the time, I would have extended each of these essays in the same measure and written a series rather than a monograph. But the book is already much delayed and the reader will have to look to the detailed study of 1 Samuel 1–12 for the bulk of the methodological debate.

theory about narrative is already available in the field of literary criticism now known as narratology.[10] Just as the founding fathers of historical criticism frequented the domains of folklorists and historians, contemporary biblical scholars are beginning to explore the field of narratology to gain new insights into biblical narrative.

Narratology is the organized study and description of the characteristic features of the narrative genre in the western literary tradition. Based on the distinguishing generic characteristic, "mediacy of presentation," (Stanzel 1979:15) that distinguishes narrative from other kinds of literature, narratology focuses on the mechanics of narrative composition. Narrative has two primary components, a tale and a teller; narratology analyses the two parts as *story*, the events, actions, and characters that are described, and *discourse*, the means of communicating the content to the reader (Chatman 1978:19). An important aim of narratology is to describe how authors can manipulate discourse as a tool to affect the meaning of story. Narratology often devotes greater attention to the discourse that relates story because it is the only medium in narrative literature that is directly aimed at the reader.[11] No voice within the story world of the narrative can address the reader directly without breaking the conventions that govern this literary form.

In developing a biblical narratology, then, one takes the theoretical developments of narratology and combines them with an on-going inductive study of Hebrew narrative, its idiomatic style and devices. Because narratology has been developed within a cross-cultural, generically defined field, its theories and analyses are well-suited to an interdisciplinary study of biblical literature. In addition to the inherent adaptability of the discipline of narratology, which tends on the whole toward the study of narrative as a genre rather than specific instances of narrative technique, the consciousness of all would-be biblical narratologists that they are primarily students of Hebrew narratology and that their best teacher is Hebrew narrative should

---

10 Curiously, English speaking historical-critical scholars sometimes react negatively to the mention of this study, feigning innocent exasperation at another neologistic "-ology." It is difficult to understand how such academics, who usually know Greek, have any more difficulty with narrato-logy than they do with bio-logy, cosm-ology, or the-ology.

11 According to G. Genette it is also more appropriate for narratology to study discourse, since that is the distinctive modal character of this genre alone (see the comments of Gerald Prince (1984:867).

protect this promising new approach to biblical narrative against the imperialistic tendencies that have sometimes accompanied methodological developments in biblical studies.

Just how suitable is narratology as a tool for biblical study? Approximately 64% of biblical literature is prose. Of that 64% only the pentateuchal legal texts appear to stand outside the narrative genre, but even the laws are enclosed within a narrative context. And even those seemingly anti-literary texts have narrative qualities the literariness of which can be appreciated when the conventions within which they were written are understood.[12]

All biblical narrative is mediated by a narrator. The narrator is the reader's guide, a medium for the duration of the story. The reader is closer to the narrator than to any of the characters in the story. The narrator intervenes between the reader and the world of the story just as our own senses and conceptual faculties intervene between us and our own world (K. Friedemann 1910:26). As readers, all that we can know about the fictional story world is already filtered and interpreted for us by our ears, eyes, and nose—the biblical narrator.

There are many different types of narrator, each uniquely prominent and influential on the reader's perception of the story. In the Bible the scale of narratorial prominence is unevenly balanced. Narrators such as those of Ezekiel of the revelations, prominent in self-references using the first person pronoun "I," are in the minority; the majority are impersonal observers who report only what they see and rarely draw attention away from the story onto themselves or the existential situation from which they tell their story. The resulting semblance of unconditioned objectivity is a literary convention of great utility to the biblical authors. Given the extreme prejudice with which their readers were (are) accustomed to viewing the subject matter of biblical narrative, it was expedient for the authors to endow their narrators with every available bit of credibility; if their renditions of the age old stories were to be heard

---

12 David Damrosch (1987:66-77) has offered one such reading of the book of Leviticus. According to Damrosch, "Rather than a sterile opposition between law and narrative, the text shows a complex but harmonious interplay between two *forms* of narrative. Law and history meet on a common ground composed of ritual, symbolic, and prophetic elements."

at all, appearances of partisan bias had to be carefully concealed behind a veil of impartiality.

The qualities of narrator visibility and personalization, or depersonalization as is the case in the Bible, are produced by more fundamental choices that each author makes about the type of narrator that he employs. The are two primary variables to manipulate in the narratorial situation.[13] They are the ontological and temporal vantage from which the descriptions of the story world and its characters are described (cf. Stanzel 1971:23; Visser 1977:81–93; Genette 1980:185–94, 215–37). A narrator can be situated in being and/or time either within the world of the story, or outside it. The narrator's existential/temporal stance is visible in his pronominal usages—"I" tending to include the narrator in, or relate him to the story world; "he" tending to exclude or separate him from it—and in the tenses of his verbal descriptions—the present associating the narrator with the story world and the preterite separating him from it. The combination of first person pronominal self-references and the present tense usually defines a narrator standing squarely in the story world, while the preterite and third person references to characters in the story are indications of a narrator speaking from outside the spatio-temporal bounds of the story world.[14] These pronominal and verbal manifestations of the narrator's spatio-temporal stance are supported by his usage of demonstratives and temporal adverbs. The internal narrator's here and now is the external narrator's then and there.

The single most important difference between these two narratorial situations is their variable perceptual and epistemological potentialities. The narrator who shares or has shared space and time with his characters is subject (or was when he

---

13 The "narratorial situation" is the perspectival, existential situation from which the narrator speaks.

14 Both Stanzel (1979:108–47) and Genette (1980:243–52) provide detailed discussion of pronominal indications of narratorial situation. Mieke Bal (1985:120–34) offers many detailed observations about the differences that are roughly categorized here by means of pronominal indications of narratorial stance vis-a-vis the story world. W.J.M. Bronzwaer (*Tense in the Novel* [Groningen: Wolters-Noordhoff, 1970:41–80]) describes the variation of verb tense to create different temporal distances between narratorial situation and story world (cf. Stanzel, 1971:22–37; Chatman 1978:79–84; Genette, 1980:215–27). In ancient narrative one must also take prophetic and predictive temporal modulations into account (Genette 1980:216). In the biblical examples, the prophetic and apocalyptic books, the verbal descriptions usually maintain the separation of narratorial situation and story world at the time of narration, but also allow for increasing contact between the two with the passage of time.

experienced the events he describes) to the same environmental constraints and existential limitations as they. Everything he says is relative to his ontological ties to the story world and his motivation to narrate is also conditioned by the bond (cf. Stanzel 1979:121–27; Bal 1985:124). His perceptions are conditioned and relative to the story world.

In contrast the external narrator is untouched by the limitations that the story world imposes on all its inhabitants. His existential immunity makes for more potential reliability in objective perception and description of events and characters within the story.[15] Of course this seemingly superhuman ability to know the truth of things, unhindered by the common misperceptions and ignorance attendant on mankind, is only a literary convention. But like all artistic conventions we tend to forget the fictionality that inheres, allowing ourselves the aesthetic luxury of accepting conventional fictions as actual, if fleeting, facts. The doctrine of scriptural inspiration may be seen, in part, as an attempt to dogmatize and prolong the illusion produced by the convention. The "truths" revealed by means of the literary convention of an external narrator who has unconditioned access to the truth are enshrined as real, enduring, and guaranteed by God himself.

A good illustration of the privilege that the external narrator owes to his narratorial position is his exemption from the physical limitations that attend life within the story. The external, unconditioned narrator can shift about in space and time as it suits his narratorial purpose, the sole determinant of his represented momentary perceptions. The narrator of Job flaunts such unlimited mobility. In 1:1–5 he describes the land of Uz from an unnamed position with an unrestricted view. In vv. 4–5, which take a maximum of 20 seconds of narrating time, he covers the entire yearly cycle of Job's family activity. Suddenly in v. 6, without apology or explanation, he shifts his focus to heaven to look in on the heavenly council. By way of contrast the first person narrator who lives in the story world in the

---

15 Cf. Dorrit Cohn, "The Encirclement of Narrative," *Poetics Today* 2:2 (1981) 164, "first person narration posits a relationship of existential contiguity between discourse and story, authorial [third person] narration posits a merely mental, cognitive relationship between these two functional spheres."

book of Nehemiah takes four verses (2:12–15) just to describe his nocturnal tour of the walls of Jerusalem.[16]

Related to the perceptual characteristics of the two major narratorial situations are their epistemological properties. A narrator's access to information is a matter of degree. The possibilities extend from the conditioned, limited knowledge of an ordinary human witness who can tell his reader only as much as any other attendant person could (cf. N. Friedman 1955:1174–5), to the unconditioned knowledge of the narrator who seems to know about all times and places (e.g. Gen 1:1–26, prior to the creation of the first human being) and can even tell us what God himself thinks and feels (e.g. Gen 6:6, "And the Lord repented that he had made man ..."). As a rule external narrators sit on the unconditioned end of the scale and internal narrators are epistemologically limited in keeping with their station in human life (cf. Stanzel 1984:90).

Aside from the two narratorial situations of external and internal narrators there is a third possibility in which the prominence of the narratorial situation all but disappears and the events of the story are told as reflected in the mind and senses of one or several of the characters (cf. Chatman 1978:166–95; Genette 1980:185–94; Bal 1985:105, "internal focalization"). Such a narrative situation is by definition limited and incomplete, the logical extension of the direction taken with a first person internal narrator. The decision to use such a narrative mode constitutes a statement about access to meaning and order in human existence; it stands in opposition to that made by the author who chooses an external narrator who can know anything and tells a tale similarly complete and meaningful.

Biblical Narrative Situations

What, then, are the narratorial situations in the Bible? A survey reveals a preference for external, unconditioned narrators. Such a narratorial situation extends through the Pentateuch, the Deuteronomistic narrative (Joshua – 2 Kings), and the books Jonah, Haggai, Ruth, Esther, Daniel, Ezra, and Chronicles. It also appears briefly in the poetic collection in Jeremiah 32–45 and in

---

[16] Cf. Bal (1985:109), "The way in which a subject is presented gives us information about that object itself and about the focalizer [viewer]." We know that the narrator in the book of Nehemiah was bound, as he tells his story, to the physical constraints of the story world and we know that the narrator of the book of Job is not.

the narrative brackets in the book of Job. Remaining is approximately 11% of biblical narrative, all mediated by a "first person" internal narrator (Nehemiah, retrospective; Ezekiel, prophetic). The Bible does not contain any lengthy continuous narrative representation of events seen solely through the eyes of a character in the story (a so-called "reflector" character, cf. Stanzel 1984:59).

Genesis 1

As a rule the opening sentence or paragraph of a narrative reveals the type of narratorial situation used throughout, though as Bal points out, there can be a switch in situations mid-way through (1985:105–6). The introduction also provides some indications as to why this type of narration was chosen to mediate the story (cf. Stanzel 1981:9).

The introduction to biblical narrative is no exception. Genesis 1:1 begins "In the beginning." This is an ultimate beginning at the dawn of creation, before any human observer was created. Yet here is our narrator telling us what happened then. Obviously he is not limited to any position in space and time, especially not to the singularity of place and time that governs all normal human existence. The fact that he can tell us something that no human character within the story could (humans are not created for another 26 verses) shows that he is existentially immune to conditions that will govern characters within the story world and readers in the real. But it is not only what the narrator tells that separates him from the story, it is also how he tells it. The Genesis narrator reveals his temporal separation from the event by describing God's action with a preterite verb—"In the beginning God created ..." He stands subsequent to the event of creation, as do all other human beings both inside and outside the story, yet he is able to see back to that primeval event. What an extraordinarily perceptive fellow!

The narrator's distinctive vision is made more so by his failure to identify the source of his knowledge. He does not say, "In the beginning I saw," or "I dreamt that in the beginning," or even "God told me that in the beginning"; he simply says "In the beginning." His superhuman ability is unapologetically unconditioned. He just knows. The content of this first disclosure suggests that there is little if anything to do with the cosmos that this narrator could not know.

The narrator continues to display his unconditioned knowledge in v. 2 by describing physical conditions prior to God's imposition of law and order on the cosmos. The human characters within the story all depend on this very created order for all facets of their existence. But the narrator is free of such dependence and knows about things outside that order and prior to it; his unconditioned knowledge puts a wide existential and epistemological gap between him and his characters. As his readers we are temporarily privileged to rise above our limitations to share his unobstructed perspective and insight. In reading, the reader gains an Olympian overview of the story world. This perspective is unavailable to any of the human characters in the story and normally unavailable to the reader who seeks to understand his own world, which is at least analogous to the story world. The overview is freed from the human limitations of viewing the world from within. With this narrator we stand outside looking in.

In vv. 3–4 the narrator's dispassionate neutrality towards the world of the story contrasts with God's affection. When God calls light into existence the narrator reports objectively, "There was light." God, on the other hand, "saw that the light was good," an evaluation that implicates him in the story world. And, at the very moment when the narrator is revealing God's involvement in the story world he is also demonstrating his own separation from it by displaying his ability to know the minds of the characters who inhabit that world, including even the mind of God. Moreover while God sees that the light is good the narrator's knowing of God's mind is not even represented by a cognitive verb let alone a perceptual one. God, however supreme and omnipotent compared to the human denizens of the story world, is definitely implicated and subordinated by his involvement to the all-seeing wisdom and insight of the external unconditioned narrator.[17] The contrast illumines the extreme

---

[17] On this point I disagree with the position that seems to be shared by three notable commentators on biblical narrative: Robert Alter, Robert Polzin, and Meir Sternberg. All three authors seem to believe that the biblical narrator consciously subordinates his perspective and views to the deity also known as the character Yahweh or God in the narrative. Sternberg is most explicit on this point: "The very choice to devise an omniscient narrator serves the purpose of staging and glorifying an omniscient God" (1985:89).

God's omniscience and his power are certainly "staged" in the narratives of the Bible. But it is often an exposition of which the character in the narrative would disapprove. Many times the insights that the narrator's own unlimited access to information

ontological separation between this narratorial situation and the story world; it also reveals the insufficiency of the conventional description of this narrator as "omniscient." The epistemological adjective is an inaccurate exaggeration. The narrator never claims he knows all, nor does his creator, the author, make that claim for him. At the same time the adjective falls short of complete description. For the sorts of observations the Genesis narrator makes, his detachment from the story world is as important as his wide ranging cognitive powers. A more accurate description of this narrator is that he is external and his ability to know about events or characters is unconditioned, not subject to the constraints attendant on normal human observers or even on the involved divine participant in his story.

Nehemiah 1

Genesis 1 introduces the biblical story and the dominant narrative situation in the Bible. The fact that the majority of biblical authors chose this mode of narrative mediation suggests

---

provide expose attitudes, thoughts, or practises of the deity that he clearly hides from his human partners in the drama of human history. In the narrative God is secretive precisely because his, as anyone's, hidden motives or actions might be reprehensible from the point of view of interpersonal interactions and fidelities. God, for example, may in fact learn from his experience in interacting with his human creatures, as 1 Sam 15 suggests (cf. Eslinger 1988). But he does not want his human counterpart to know that. So he chides Samuel for the reasonable assumption that because he chose a big fellow for his first king that God would be likely to do the same in the case of the second. Another important example, which will be studied in detail in ch. 3 below ("A New Generation In Israel"), is the uncomplimentary difference between the actual reason for the failure of total conquest (Judg 2:23, a narratorial revelation), and what God wants to believe is the reason (Judg 2:21) and what he tells Israel, in public, is the reason (Judg 2:3). Although such insights into the machinations of the divinity in the Bible are not condemnations, neither are they laudatory; they are certainly not, in any ordinary sense, "glorifying."

Sternberg's view seems less a reflection of the perspective presented by the external, unconditioned narrator than an assumption about the ideological biases and motivations of the ancient authors of "sacred writ" (cf. M. Bal [1986:72], "The biblical narrator duplicating God's omniscience, thanks to divine inspiration, is, he [Sternberg] claims, not a religious dogma ... This way of putting it is, however, symptomatic of the critic's ideological commitment to the text and his use of poetics to support it, if not to impose it"; N. Segal [1988:249], "How is it possible, except by complacency, to avoid reading the author/narrator as controlling his chief character, as more god than God?")

Instead of ideological commitment supporting the deity that he describes acting in his story world, the external unconditioned narrator is neutral, his interests being to reveal the hidden workings of divine-human interaction and to understand. Understanding: that is central. The simple fact that so many of these insights expose what God would keep hidden does, however, evoke, at least initially, a certain sense of shock and repugnance from the reader who shares this view for the first time.

that they found it most advantageous as a vehicle for probing the ways of God and man. The availability of other narrative modes is shown by the existence of books such as Nehemiah and Ezekiel, which are narrated from an entirely different narratorial situation. A brief glance at the introduction of Nehemiah will illustrate the difference.[18]

In Nehemiah 1:1 the narrator also employs preterite description of events within the story. There is an indeterminate temporal gap between the events in the story and the event of narration. But the suggestion of any existential separation between the narrator and the world of the story is canceled by his inclusion in that world by means of the emphatic self-reference, "and *I* was in Shushan." The narrator's ties to the story world are made even more concrete when he gives the exact date and location of his past involvement in it. Here preterite narration provides only temporal separation between events in the story and the event of narration. Both the actions of the character referred to as "I" and the narrator's act of narrating take place on the same existential plane; both are subject to the same limitations and conditions. Only temporally external to the story world, this narrator presents an ontologically internal view it. He remains in and of the world he describes.

The former existence of the narrator in the story world is the single most important difference between the discourse of Nehemiah and that of Genesis, with its absolute separation of story world and narratorial situation. The two different situations create radically different epistemological possibilities, which in turn result in distinct portraits of human existence. Especially important are the differences in the presentation of man's interaction with God, the dominant biblical theme. The internal narrator can only give the reader a common, limited view of the interaction. His narratorial view is superior to the characters' view only by advantage of hindsight. The external narrator obviously has a much better opportunity of presenting a new perspective on the history of divine-human interaction.

In vv. 2–3 the narrator of Nehemiah reveals just how conditioned his narration by means of his own past first person experiences will be. The narratorial view is limited to the "then

---

18 The introductory superscription, "The words of Nehemiah, son of Hacaliah," are not part of the narrative. Rather, they function as a descriptive title for the subsequent narrative.

and there" of his former spatio-temporal position. Knowledge of other times or places necessarily comes to the narrator through the communications of other characters in the story. We learn about the conditions in Jerusalem while the narrator was in Shushan only through some characters who have come from Jerusalem. They describe the situation in Jerusalem in response to a query from our narrator. By way of contrast the external, unconditioned narrator of 2 Kings 24–5 shifts his focus back and forth several times between scenes in Babylon and the plundered city of Jerusalem without once explaining how he knows about what is happening in either city.

The internal narrator's knowledge of the divine character is even more restricted; hindsight is no advantage in this respect. In vv. 4–11 the narrator describes his prayer about the bad turn that Israel's state affairs have taken, but he cannot tell us what God thought or did in response to his prayer. Hindsight is no advantage this time and God's response can only deduced later from the course that events later take (2:8, 18). Unlike the external narrator of Genesis, who discloses nothing about himself but much about God, the internal narrator/character of Nehemiah bares his soul to the reader of his prayer but can say nothing about God who is a closed book both to the praying character, the retrospective narrator, and so also to the reader.

The internal narrator's prominent display of his past existence in the story world is the exact opposite of the ghostly presence of the non-incarnate, external narrator.[19] By confining his representations strictly to the limited view point of his principal character (himself), the narrator forces his reader to view the other characters and the events in which all were caught up through his own eyes. The reader can see things only through the biased view of the narrator at that time but subject to additional self-justifying qualifications. Consequently, all of the narrator's actions are supplied with rationales or rationalizations but other characters' acts are unjustified, inexplicable, and even reprehensible. The conditioned, internal narrator gives his side of the story and in giving it exclusively so, tries to coerce his reader's acceptance (cf. Booth 1961:155). Whether or not the reader accepts this narrator's evaluative norms or not will de-

---

19 Stanzel (1979:126) describes the internal first person narrator as "*Ich mit Leib*," a characterization well suited to this conditioned and limited narratorial situation.

pend on individual readers' idiosyncrasies; but beyond them no one can go with any certainty.

The restricted view is a product of the narrator's ties to the principal character; his motivation for telling his story is existentially conditioned (cf. Stanzel 1979:126–27). In fact the internal narrator of Nehemiah exposes his narratorial strategies by repeatedly asking his intended reader, God, to remember all his good deeds and reward him for them (13:14, 22, 31), and to remember the bad deeds of other characters and punish them (13:29). Obviously the first person internal narratorial situation meets this narrator's needs perfectly.

If the narratorial motivation of the internal narrator is the product of his entanglement in the conditions of his story, what motivates the external, unconditioned narrator of books like Genesis? And what affect does his external perspective have on his story? The external, unconditioned, narratorial situation draws the reader away from entangling involvements on the level of the characters within the story world. The detached objectivity of this vantage is a rare perceptual mode unavailable in the reader's real world where the biblical traditions were/are charged with religious and existential significance. The reader's interest is re-focused on the larger horizon rather than on localized details. Though the narrator can override the inherent neutrality of his external viewpoint with explicit commentary, he almost never does. An example from 1 Samuel will illustrate.

1 Samuel 8–12

In 1 Samuel 8 a crucial moment in Israel's convenantal relationship with Yahweh is described. The future of Israel's theocratic government is at stake. Here, if anywhere, we might expect the narrator to supply his reader with some commentary to guide the reader in the way he ought to go.

A crisis arises when Israel asks for a human to replace God as king (v. 5, cf. vv. 7–8; 10:19; Boecker 1969:32–3). The request is a radical rejection of the theocracy established at Sinai, a denial of Isra-el's identity as the "God-ruled" (שׂרר אל) people. Both God and his servant Samuel denounce the request (vv. 6–8) but the narrator remains silent. He does balance out the denunciation by describing the circumstances that provoked the request (vv. 1–3), a provocation also validated by the chain of events previously described in chs. 2–7. But just as he does not explicitly support the denunciation, he does not say, in so many words, "the request is just." Instead he maintains the neutrality afforded by his external perspective and presents characters and events from a non-partisan viewpoint. He even promotes the objectivity of his external view by using his unlimited access to enter the minds of characters on both sides of the issue. The reader is privileged with an overview of the misunderstandings, the cross-purposes, and the genuine, laudable motivations on each side of the dispute. The narratorial perspective is a synthetic view with its centre focused on the problem of divine-human relationship and interaction within a political framework, not on the pedestrian question of who is right and who is wrong. From the normal human perspective the answer to that question is all too obvious.

The example from 1 Samuel is characteristic of the external, unconditioned narrator's treatment of evaluation. Instead of directly evaluating the actions of characters he uses his privileged access to reveal the often unpublished thoughts or words of one character about another. Even in the saying repeated throughout the deuteronomistic history that "Israel did evil," the apparent directness of the evaluation is removed by the concluding ascription to a character: "in the sight of the Lord." Obviously the neutrality of the external narratorial situation is amenable to the unconditioned narrator who uses his situation and power to achieve a single end. But why did the biblical authors want to present such a perspective on a subject—God and man, or more to the point, God and Israel—that history had made so volatile?

The answer that is suggested by my reading—I do not believe we are yet at the point, in our study of biblical narratology, where we can make anything more than working suggestions about such large conceptual domains—is that this narratorial situation is aimed precisely at the emotional piety and prejudice with which these traditions were/are approached by the normal, conditioned consciousness of the reader. Whether or not the view presented by the external narrator is neutral or not, it is made to appear so and the reader is invited to explore this otherwise unavailable perspective on the old, well-worked traditions. The reader is asked to step across the usual bounds of human understanding about God's motives, to cross over the theological barrier described by God in the well known passage from Isaiah (55:8-6). God's motives can be known and they are not always the most complimentary (e.g. Exod 7:3–5 in the light of Exod 5, especially vv. 22–3; 1 Samuel 2:25). For the biblical God, the end does justify almost any means.

Similarly the reader is asked to transcend conventional views about human suffering, in which the combination of piety and human ignorance about divine motives leads to a theodicy based on man's universal feeling of guilt. Job does not suffer because he sinned; he suffers because God made a bet with Satan that Job feared God out of pure motives (1:8–12). Job suffers for God's honour. This example might seem to reveal a narratorial bias against God because of the biblical reader's usual piety towards the biblical God, but the narrator never once criticizes God for the bet.[20] It is simply a case of the actual state of affairs being presented by the narrator to the shocked chagrin of the pious reader.

Judges 2

One final example gives a more characteristic view of the effect that this narrative mode has on the meaning of the biblical traditions. Israel's repeated political disasters are piously attributed to Israel's idiotic disobedience throughout the prophetic books (e.g. Hos 7:2, 8–16). The external, unconditioned narrator of Judges suggests a revision. The exodus from Egypt was the divine act of benefaction upon which the call to convenantal obedience at Sinai was based. By the time Israel entered the promised land, however, there remained only two individuals, Joshua and Caleb, who had seen that event (Num 14:6–38, especially vv. 22–3). In spite of the fact that nobody but these two men had seen the deed upon which the demand of obedience to the law was based, Israel served God while the witnesses were alive (Judg 1:7). It was only when Joshua died and a new generation arose that did not know Yahweh or the works he did for Israel (Judges 2:10), that Israel "did evil in the

20 Frequently readings such as I present here (cf., e.g. the readings of D.M. Gunn 1980; 1982) are mistaken for a dark, perverted misreading of biblical narrative. It is only against the ponderous sanctimony that has characterized so much of the pious apologetic that passes for exegesis that descriptions of the objective narration of the Bible seems bleak. But as Herbert Schneidau has pointed out, the Bible is a book that constantly challenges and provokes the reader; it is an alienating literature that constantly exposes established dogmas to new searching and criticism. " ... what the Bible offers culture is neither an ecclesiastical structure nor a moral code, but an unceasing critique of itself" (Schneidau 1976:16). I, for one, would apply this to the biblical narrator's critique of the theological dogmas contained within biblical narratives.

sight of the Lord" (v. 11). Moreover the subsequent cycle of apostasy and punishment was not exclusively the product of Israel's ignorance of the exodus. God has his own share in the ignorance and misunderstanding that fuels Israel's history. The narrator grants the reader a privileged audition of a divine monologue through which we learn that God is punishing Israel not for ignorance of the exodus event, but for disobedience to the covenant that he imposed on the fathers (2:20–2). God does not seem to know that Israel does not know about the exodus without which he has no claim to Israel's loyalty.

The narrator blames neither God nor Israel. He simply reports the problem using the tools provided by his external, unconditioned viewpoint. And to the reader he offers a fresh insight into the problem of God and Israel. Existing as they do on two different levels of being, God and Israel constantly misunderstand each other. Divine omniscience may be a reality for the uninvolved God but for the one that has chosen to mix with man in history it seems to cloud the resulting confusion. The history of Israel, traced in the deuteronomistic narratives, is a history of misunderstanding and cross-purposes that ends, as it must, in failure.

It is this existential gap between God and man that is the mainspring of much biblical narrative and it is the genius of biblical authors to have developed a narratorial vehicle—the external unconditioned narrator—to explore what otherwise remains a no-man's land of misconception and ignorance. The key to understanding biblical narrative, it seems to me, is neither history nor literary history, but an appreciative acceptance of the revelations of these extraordinary narrators. Without them and in the measure that we cannot be what they are, we will fail just as miserably as the human characters in their stories to understand the way of God with man.

CHAPTER 2

THESE NATIONS THAT REMAIN

Behold, I have divided unto you by lot these nations that remain, to be an inheritance for your tribes, from Jordan, with all the nations that I have cut off, even unto the great sea westward (Joshua 23:4).

It is widely reported that there is a gross discrepancy between the books of Joshua and Judges regarding the success of the Israelite conquest. A standard manual on the history of Israel reads, "in striking contrast to the sweeping claims of numerous passages in the book of Joshua which insist that Joshua conquered the whole land of Canaan and virtually wiped out its indigenous population (see especially Josh 10:42; 11:16–20, 23; 12:7–24; 21:43–5), Judges 1 ends with a long list of cities (twenty in all) whose inhabitants we are told the various tribes either did not or could not drive out (Judg 1:21, 27–33)" (J.M. Miller 1977:215).

On the whole the response to this literary state of affairs has been to see it as a manifestation of the diverse literary history of these two books of the Bible. "The biblical account of the conquest in Numbers 13–Judges 1 reflects certain internal inconsistencies. Moreover, critical literary analysis has revealed that this account is composite, based on various ancient traditions which represent different literary genres and which have undergone changes during the process of transmission from ancient times" (Miller 1977:213).

The perceived differences between the two accounts are usually traced to the different purposes of each book. Joshua is supposed to glorify the conquest as a success; Judges, to trace the history of Israel's failure as Yahweh's covenant partner. Generally speaking, more credence has been granted to the portrait of the book of Judges as a historical account: this has been called the "classical position" on the historicity of the conquest in the book of Joshua (G.E. Wright 1982:73).[1]

But a careful reading of the book of Joshua soon raises doubts about the conventional notion that the dominant theme of the book of Joshua is the fulfilment of the promises to the fathers through the conquest of the land. B.S. Childs says, for example, "Few would contest the assertion that the main purpose of the book of Joshua was to show the fulfilling of the promises to the fathers regarding the gift of the land ... Joshua 23:14 summarizes this theme: 'not one thing has failed of all the good things which Yahweh your God promised concerning you ...' (cf. 21,45)," (1979:244; cf. J.A. Soggin 1972:19). But as G.E. Wright (1946:106–7) has pointed out, there are descriptions of failures in the conquest within the narratives of the book of Joshua, e.g. 13:1–6.[2] A quick survey of the book reveals as many separate descriptions of failure as of success:

Success	*Failure*
1. Jericho 6:20–21	1. Ai 7:4–5
2. Ai 8:19–29	2. (Gibeon 9:14–27)
3. Five kings 10:10–43: Makkedah v. 28 Libnah v. 30 Lachish vv. 32–33 Eglon v. 35 Hebron v. 37 Debir v. 39.	3. Anakim in Gaza, Gath, and Ashdod 11:22b.
4. Coalition: 11:8–22a Hazor vv. 10–11 all other cities v.12 (Summary: 31 kings ch.12).	4. Geshurites, Maacathites 13:13.

1 J.M. Miller (1977:215–17) summarizes the inconsistencies between the accounts that sparked the scholarly debate.

2 Needless to say Wright, following Albright's historical suggestions (1939:11–23), also presents arguments from archaeological studies to support the historicity of Judges 10–11 (1946:109–14).

5. Sons of Anak (by Caleb) 15:14.	5. Jerusalem 15:63.
6. Kiryath-Sepher 15:17.	6. Canaanites in Gezer 16:10.
7. Leshem 19:47.	7. Canaanite cities 17:11–12 Beth-Shean and towns Ibleam and towns Dor and towns En-dor and towns Taanach and towns Megiddo and towns Napeth.
8. —	8. Seven tribes of undivided inheritance 18:2.

As far as the literary world presented to us in the book of Joshua is concerned, these descriptions of the results of the conquest present us with the facts about described events in the story world; here is the concrete reality, by literary convention totally reliable, against which all evaluative pronouncements, especially those of characters within the same story world, must be measured.[3] On the basis of what, in story fact, happened it

3 The historian may dispute the historicity of the narrative description of events but cannot reject the narrator's description as the reality of the story world without also rejecting the story that is being told. Cf. L. Doležel (1980:24, cf. 11–12) who says that the facts, the reality of the story world "are constructed by the speech acts of the authoritative source—narrator in the broadest sense; the narrator's ability to call individuals, objects, events etc. into fictional existence is given by his authentication authority [which is conferred on the external unconditioned narrator [Doležel's anonymous *Er*–form narrator] by the author who relies on the conventions associated with this narrative model]."

The reader knows about the events in the story solely through the agency of narratorial description, which creates and determines the sequence of related events. Though the story may seem more or less realistic and hence encouraging of historical interpretation, we must remember that first it is a construction, a fictional world. Barbara Herrnstein–Smith's discussion of mimesis pin-points the slippery distinction between the fictional story world and the real world:

> Thus when we speak of mimesis or representation in an artwork, we recognize that it does not constitute the imitation or reproduction of existing objects or events, but rather the fabrication of fictive objects and events of which there are existing or possible instances or types—whether they be rural landscapes, star–crossed lovers, or laments for dead friends. In other words to say that an artist has represented a certain object or event is to say that he has constructed a fictive member of an identifiable class of natural ("real") objects or events (1978:25).

Of course, the option of rejecting the story that is being told is not a new one nor one that historical criticism has shied away from. What is frequently done is to recreate another story, which the historian finds more plausible and perhaps less contradictory. But then, one is no longer reading the book of Joshua, but re–envisioning what one believes the book of Joshua represents, usually a portion of ancient Israel's history.

seems that the conquest was a mixture of success and failure. Though the goal at the outset of the book was total conquest and victory (1:2–5) the story draws to a close with nations yet being allotted to the tribes for conquest (23:4).

What, then, is the reader to make of the statements situated at key points in the book of Joshua that suggest that the conquest was a complete success, as for example 21:41–43 does:

> So the Lord gave Israel all the land which he had sworn to give to their fathers, and they possessed it and lived in it.
>
> And the Lord gave them rest on every side, according to all that he had sworn to their fathers, and no one of all their enemies stood before them; the Lord gave all their enemies into their hand.
>
> Not one of the good promises that the Lord had made to the house of Israel failed; all came to pass.

If such statements are not supported by the narrative reality founded in the narratorial description of events and actions, how should we take them?

An attractive option has been suggested by Robert Polzin (1980). He has proposed that the evaluations are presented ironically. The reader who understands and agrees with the narrative presentation of the conquest up to 21:43 can only take such an incongruous evaluation as ironic. "Utterly to be rejected in the Deuteronomist's retelling of the Israelite occupation of the land are simplistic statements of fulfilment by man of God's law and by God of his own promises—statements like Joshua 21:43–45 which are deeply ironic, given the literary context in which the Deuteronomist places them" (Polzin 1980:208). As always, the exposure of any statement or viewpoint to irony within a narrative aims to unmask the views expressed therein. As a result of this intentional over-exposure to the light of narrated reality the assertions about the total success of the conquest are transformed into pale shadows of what the ironist believes happened in the conquest.

If indeed the narrator's evaluations in 21:43–5 are ironic then the consensus of scholarly opinion about the book's promotion of a successful conquest is a simple but serious case of naive misreading of irony. Instead of accepting the subversion given in the narrator's description of events, of such assertions about the conquest's total success, that is, instead of accepting narrated reality, readers have mistaken the proffered ironic evaluations for straightforward assertions. Their perceptions of the narrative and the events described therein are, thereafter, exactly the views pilloried by the ironic narrator.

Of course this misperception, if it is such, is greatly aided by historical-critical reading strategies, which allow the reader to avoid thinking about contradiction between explicit evaluation and narrated reality by recourse to hypothetical literary history.[4] If evaluations and descriptions in a text contradict all the historical–critical reader needs do to resolve the contradiction is to recreate the historical development of the text in a manner that explains the contradiction. As the history of biblical scholarship shows, such explanations are readily available and virtually unlimited in number.

Misreading aside, the failure of the bid for total conquest is a surprising outcome because it is Yahweh himself who guarantees victory in 1:2–6. The reader who follows the mixed successes and failures that follow on Yahweh's promise of total conquest naturally expects some explanation of the discrepancies offered in this complex narrative, discrepancies between Yahweh's promise and its nonfulfillment and between the narrator's corresponding positive evaluation of the success of the conquest and its failure to correspond with the reality of events in the story world.

The puzzled reader is gratified by no less than six explicit evaluations of the success of the conquest: three from the narrator (11:23; 21:43–45; 23:1), three from Joshua (22:4; 23:1; 23:4–5), and one from Yahweh (13:1–6). Whether those evaluations are ultimately satisfying as explanations of the conquest's course or as avenues of insight into the contradictions between the evaluations themselves and narrated reality is entirely another matter. And it will be obvious already from the proposed ironic voice of the narrator's evaluation in 21:43–5 that the evaluations do not offer a master key to understanding the complexities of the narrative; if anything, they add to it.

Yahweh's Evaluation

Oddly, of all the evaluations in the narrative only Yahweh's assessment is in complete accord with the facts. In 13:1–6 he says that much land remains to be possessed, implying that some

---

4 Kurt Möhlenbrink's statement (1938:239) is characteristic of such strategies, "*Zu den gewonnenen grundlegenden Erkenntnissen der Kritik ist gewiss die Beobachtung zu zählen, dass der Ausgangspunkt des Verständnisses der Texte bei der Einzelsage, nicht bei der heutigen Gesamtkomposition zu nehmen ist.*"

has been conquered and some not. Yahweh's assessment includes neither excuses nor blame; he simply indicates where things stand. As an interpretive key to the failure of total conquest and of Yahweh's promise Yahweh's summary evaluation is of little use. But it is extremely valuable, both to the reader and the narrator, as a buttress supporting the factuality of the narrator's descriptions of a failed total conquest. Yahweh's candid admission of the failure of the total conquest comes as confirmation from within the story that the reality of the situation, which the reader must presuppose, is presented in the narrated description of events, notwithstanding any statements to the contrary. That this evaluation should come from Yahweh himself, by far the most cognizant character in the story, strengthens its support for the narrated reality of a failed total conquest.

Joshua's Evaluations

Joshua vacillates. When he sends the Reubenites, Gadites, and the half-tribe of Manasseh off to their trans-Jordanian territories (22:4) he claims that Yahweh has given their cis-Jordanian brethren "rest" (*hēnîaḥ*). His use of this word suggests, by allusion to Deut 3:20,[5] that the possession of the land is complete. Later, however, just after the narrator has made an identical assertion (*hēnîaḥ*, 23:1) Joshua apportions "these nations that remain as an inheritance" (23:4) for Israel. The irony of Joshua's "choice," or rather the choice made for him by the author, of the word "inheritance" (*naḥ*ᵃ*lâ*) to describe the remaining nations would not have been lost on the assembled Israelites. To the reader who has just read the word thirty–nine times in chs. 13–21:3—all about the land—it screams. Israel's promised inheritance was supposed to be the land, not the remaining nations (Deut 4:21, 38; 12:9–10; 15:4; 19:10,14; 20:16; 21:23). The irony undercuts Joshua's previous assertion about attained "rest" as well as the narrator's assertion in 23:1, if it is mistaken at face value.[6]

In his final statement on the subject (23:14) Joshua returns again to a dogmatic assertion that all Yahweh's promises to Is-

---

5 Deut 3:20 states that when the conquest is complete Yahweh will give Israel "rest" (*hēnîaḥ*) (cf. von Rad 1962:304).

6 It is my opinion, however, that the narrator's positive assessments of the conquest must, as Polzin claims (1980:132, 208), be taken as consciously ironic.

rael have been fulfilled, implying that the possession of the land is complete. Obviously Joshua's perceptions (if he speaks in simplicity) or assertions (if he speaks with duplicity) are the product of his existential situation in the story. He offers this bald contradiction of events as the elderly representative of Yahweh rehearsing what has been accomplished during his term in office. Even when he does admit the contradictory fact that nations remain he tries to ameliorate the difficulty by bequeathing this remnant to Israel as an "inheritance." From the purely theoretical perspective of narratology, of course, all characters' evaluations are contextualized within the story and cannot possibly compete with the authoritative perspective of the narrative as a whole.

The Narrator's Evaluations

The narrator's assessments of the conquest are especially puzzling. Since he is, at once, the source of the narration in which the descriptions of failure are found and the source of the positive explicit evaluations of the conquest's total success, his evaluations present the reader with the most jarring contradiction. On the one hand the narration of events presents only a partial success; on the other the narrator says that the endeavour was a complete success (11:23; 21:43–5). Presuming that the explicit evaluations come from the same individual, the narrator—the so-called deuteronomist—who wrote the descriptions of mixed success, and the onus of proof lies on those who wish to question this primary narrative convention, one must read the explicit evaluation as ironic, with Polzin, or conclude that the narrator is unreliable in his assessments. Given that unreliability is a characteristic foreign to the narratorial situation from which the story is narrated—that of the external, unconditioned narrator[7]—and given that the unreliable narrator is a development of modern narrative, Polzin's conclusion seems justified.

The contradictory combination of what the narrator says happened and what the narrator says about what happened

---

7 Cf. Rimmon–Kenan (1983:103), "A covert, extradiegetic narrator [my external, unconditioned narrator], especially when he is also heterodiegetic, is likely to be reliable." She summarizes the sources of unreliability as the narrator's limited knowledge [access to information], personal involvement [conditionedness], and his problematic value–scheme (100–101).

opens two logical possibilities for the reader. Either one must reject the factuality of the description of events in the story, which would mean rejecting the story (cf. above, note 3) or one must reject the apparent meaning of the evaluation as either wrong or ironic. There is but one reading option: if the reader is to continue reading the narrative as a coherent document, the evaluation must be taken as ironic in tone.[8]

To say that the narrator of the book of Joshua makes ironic statements about the events of the story is to introduce a much greater complexity into one's understanding of the narrative. "Irony carries an implicit compliment to the intelligence of the reader, who is invited to associate himself with the author and the knowing minority who are not taken in by the ostensible meaning" (Abrams 1981:90). The problem, tactically speaking, with suggesting that the narrator presents the conquest from an essentially ironic perspective is that irony is always an implicit device that cannot appear directly on the surface of the narrative. To place it on the surface of the narration, of course, would destroy it as irony; remaining would be a narrative with an obviously different perspective than the one that now exists.

From the vantage of the conventional interpretation of the book of Joshua, however, it is a lame critique that attacks an established interpretation on the basis of a literary device that is said to be implicit and needful of subtle perception to appreciate the irony.[9] The ironic interpretation of Joshua would benefit greatly from some specific examples or more tangible evidence of the narrator's effort to place his own and the characters' positive evaluations of the conquest in an ironic light. Such examples must demonstrate that the context of the supposed ironic narratorial evaluations supports an ironic inter-

---

8 Polzin's proposal of an ironic meaning is preferable to weak historical–critical harmonizations such as Wenham's (1971:143; Wenham cites Kaufmann (1953:84) in support): "The passage at the end of ch. 11 requires careful study, for on first reading it looks as though the editor is guilty of crass self–contradiction. On the one hand he says that he took (vss. 16, 20) all the land; yet some of the big towns were not burnt and some of the earlier population was left (vss. 13, 22). Though possibly in the early sources of Joshua the situation was seen differently, the deuteronomic editor probably understood the taking of the land to mean the gaining of control without eliminating all the opposition."

9 Note E. Vogt's strong reaction even to the lesser suggestion of a unitary narrative. "*Man wollte die Erzählung als einheitlich verstehen, etwa mit Berufung auf semitische Erzählungsweise, aber es ist sicher keine glatte Erzählung, auch nicht für einen Semiten*" (1965:126). Of course Vogt's reaction to apparent obscurantist refuge in a supposed Semitic mentality is laudable.

pretation.[10] Polzin has already made advances in this direction with respect to chs. 13–21 of the book (e.g. 1980:132). But there are two prominent episodes in the first half of the book that illustrate even more clearly how the narrator can seem to present a successful conquest all the while undermining that portrait with exquisite indications of its questionable foundations.

The Case of Rahab

The well known story in Josh 2–6 of Rahab the harlot "who by faith did not perish along with those who were disobedient," (Heb 11:31) raises large questions about the actions of both Yahweh and Israel and so about the state of affairs—the conquest—that issues from their actions. Why was a non-Israelite allowed to make a treaty with the invading Israelites when it was clearly stated in the covenant (Deut 7:2; cf. 20:17) that such contracts were forbidden? Stranger yet, why was such a blatant disregard for the regulation of Deut 7:2 (cf. 20:17) overlooked by God? And why was the later campaign against Jericho nevertheless successful?[11]

The case of Rahab appears in the book's first description of a battle in the mission of conquest. It is also the first instance of a failure in the campaign of total conquest; as such, it is extremely important for our understanding of the incomplete conquest (cf. Boling 1982:204–5). Polzin, who also sees the narratorial perspective of the book of Joshua as thoroughly ironic, suggests that this incident is symbolic:

> The complicated relationships in Deuteronomy 9:4–5 between God, Israel, and the other nations are once more affirmed in Joshua 2 with the spies taking the place of God, Rahab taking the place of Israel, and Israel taking the place of the other nations. Rahab's descendants will continue to dwell in the land not because of their own merit or integrity but because of the "wickedness" of Israel and the promise made to their ancestress by the Israelite spies (1980:90).

But if this first failure is purely a symbolic illustration of God's mercy toward Israel why, only three verses after mentioning this supposed act of symbolic mercy toward Israel, does

10 Cf. B. Uspensky (1973:126), who also says that it is primarily literary context that allows a reader to know when an authorial voice is ironic in tone.

11 All these questions depend, of course, on the common assumption that the Deuteronomistic narrative was written and should be read in the light of the book of Deuteronomy.

God's anger burn when a real Israelite, Achan, breaks the command banning collection of booty (7:1)? Where now is God's mercy, allowing Israel to inherit, even undeservedly, the land?[12] Why would the narrator symbolically represent God's mercy toward Israel in the Rahab episode, and then immediately contradict the symbolic instance with the actual case of Achan? Surely the infringement of the ban was more serious regarding the persons of Rahab and her household than it was in the case of individual theft of material objects.

A closer examination of Josh 2 reveals that there is much more than a symbolic meditation on the mercy of God towards Israel in this story. The failure to conquer Jericho totally—Rahab and her family are spared—is the result of lapses on the parts of both God and Joshua. As to motivations for these lapses the narrator maintains his characteristic reticence. But he has already revealed some of Joshua's doubts about God in the instance of the spies, who are not commissioned by God. And he will later (Judg 2:23) reveal that God intentionally undermined the totality of success in the conquest as a final trump to be played if Israel defected from its covenantal obligations, a betrayal about which God has already expressed suspicions (Deut 31:16–18).

Ironically, it is lapses in the role fulfilment of both God and Joshua that make room for Rahab to play her crucial role in the conquest of Jericho. Success here comes when both God and his servant Joshua fail their duties and an outsider comes to the rescue, affording the incomplete success that issues from the conquest of Jericho.

The reader comes to the tale of the Israelite encounter with Rahab in Josh 2 having read ch. 1. There is a striking discongruity between the two chapters. Sigmund Mowinckel's reaction is typical: "*Die Erzählung steht im krassesten Gegensatz zu den heiligen Legenden, die sie in Kap. 1 und in 3:1–15 umgeben*" (1964:13; cf. G.M. Tucker 1972:69). After Yahweh's ceremonious and detailed instructions to Joshua in ch. 1 the reader expects Joshua to act immediately in accordance with his

---

12 Nowhere is there any indication that "the ban" (*ḥerem*, Deut 7:25–6; 13:18) was of any greater importance than the command against fraternizing with the enemy. Cf. Boling (1982:220), "It is going too far to make the *ḥerem* into the central feature in holy war." Of course there is a way out of the contradiction in Polzin's reading, namely source analysis; the story of Achan is from a separate source or tradition. But Polzin would hardly take it.

orders. Such an expectation is grounded both on Joshua's prior performance (Num 14) and on the obvious fact that when God commands a prudent man obeys—to the letter! In addition, Yahweh's statements in ch. 1 suggest that the later battles of conquest will be won through guaranteed divine intervention on Israel's behalf.[13] As usual in subverting reader expectations, the contrast between the battle strategies of chs. 1–2 serves to focus reader attention on the specific issue at stake.

The narrator's omission of any explanation or discussion of the contrast between the commands of ch. 1 and Joshua's response in 2:1 creates suspense. A conflict is developing between Yahweh, famous for requiring strict obedience (e.g. Gen 22), and Joshua, who is being uncharacteristically naughty. What is missing from 2:1 is information about the reasons for Joshua's disobedience, and of course about Yahweh's unusual forbearance and how he will ultimately react. Joshua's incongruous response is a riddle that sparks reader interest and provokes a series of responses from the reader who attempts to understand Joshua's action and to predict its outcome (cf. Sternberg 1978:89). (Will Joshua be punished? Will the conquest fail as did the prior sortie contaminated by faithless spying (Num 13–14)? What has Yahweh done to provoke Joshua's uncertainty?)

The stage is set in ch. 1 for a total conquest of the land that God has promised. No sooner is the endeavour taken up than a problem arises: Joshua details two spies to reconnoitre the promised land. In ch. 1 God issued only two commands to Joshua: to rise and cross the Jordan (v. 2, *qûm ʿᵃbōr*) and to be strong and courageous (vv. 6, 7, 9 *ḥᵃzaq weʾᵉmāṣ*). Instead, Joshua responds by secretly sending two spies. The contrast could hardly be greater.[14]

The combined mention of Joshua and a spying mission recalls a prior incidence of the same combination (Num 13:16–

---

13 Cf. H. Gressmann (1914:130), who interprets the contrast in strategic action as result of the generic distinctiveness of ch. 2).

14 Cf. G.M. Tucker (1972:69, 72), who observes from a literary–historical perspective that ch. 1 should lead to a crossing of the Jordan and would more logically be followed by ch. 3:1ff. than ch. 2. G.J. Wenham (1971:141) says that the narrative emphasizes Joshua's obedience to the commands of ch. 1. He suggests that verbal repetition stresses the exact fidelity of Joshua in carrying out the commands. But his suggestions are undermined by ch. 2, in which the immediate response to the commands is presented with anything but word for word fidelity (cf. H.W. Hertzberg (1959:18)).

14:4).[15] The result of that mission was the Israelite people's failure of nerve. So the mission of conquest was aborted. When the same Joshua, previously a positive influence and model of obedience in the dark affair that arose out of an authorized spying mission, now initiates an unauthorized spying mission instead of responding positively to the commands issued in ch. 1, there is a strong, contextually induced presumption based on precedent that the mission may jeopardize the conquest. It is significant that the Israelite people are not implicated in any failings here regarding the spies, unlike the prior failure resulting from the spying mission in the book of Numbers. They are explicitly divorced from implication by the narrator, who reports that they exhorted Joshua to be "strong and courageous," (*ḥᵃzaq weʾᵉmāṣ*, 1:18), the same exhortation made by Yahweh himself three times previously (vv. 6, 7, 9). For the spies Joshua alone is responsible.[16]

The spying mission scuttles any chance of total conquest owing to the spies' contact with Rahab. For the favours that she does for them, the spies agree to grant her a sign of "faithfulness" (v. 12, *ʾᵉmet*) as a token of the covenant they have made with her and her family on behalf of Israel. The spies' action would ordinarily be unexceptionable. But these are no ordinary spies; they are representatives of Israel and are supposed to act in strict accord with the dictates of the Sinaitic covenant. In view of the legislation set down in Deut 7:2 prohibiting any covenants between Israel and the resident nations of the land, the spies' commitment to Rahab is wrong.[17] There is some mitigation for the spies' actions in the description of the circumstances under which they were asked to make the agreement with Rahab. The great length at which the narrator describes the extenuating circumstances (vv. 1–8) suggests that the reader is supposed to appreciate the dilemma that traps the spies.

---

15 B. Peckham (1984:428) provides a detailed listing of allusions to the books of Exodus and Deuteronomy in this episode.

16 Cf. McCarthy (1971:170). Against Wenham (1971:141), the "function of the spies"—in what context, one might ask—is not "to encourage Israel": that is after the fact. They are what they are—spies. As to their function, in the context of the narrative they instigate, via Joshua and Rahab, the illegal covenant with Rahab.

17 Against McCarthy (1971:174), who claims, "the only acceptable way to avoid the ban is to make a covenant with Israel. This can be done openly (Rahab) or by a trick (Gibeon) ..." There is no acceptable way to do so, given the explicit prohibition in Deuteronomy. Any exceptions are indications of a failure to uphold the covenantal standard on the parts of both Yahweh and Israel.

Blame for the unfortunate agreement with Rahab weighs, according to the narrative presentation, heavily on the decision to send a secret spying force into enemy territory.

Like the previous spying mission in Num 13, contact with the enemy before the conflict results in a situation that jeopardizes the success of the operation. And since it was Joshua who, on his own authority, issued the order for a spy force to be sent out, Joshua is responsible for this risk to the conquest. His failure to act in strict accord with the orders issued to him by God in ch. 1 leads to an intolerable pre-conflict interaction and an illegal relationship between Israel and the enemy. Though the narrator supplies a description of circumstances that mitigate the spies' action, there is no such supply for Joshua. His order for the secret mission is exposed in stark contrast to the standing orders of ch. 1.[18]

Note, however, that the narrator does not criticize Joshua's failure; he simply reports it. Yet here is a prime opportunity for the author to express his negative views of the fallible human participants in the covenant affair. Is this any way for a would-be theodicist to pursue his literary ends?

Rahab's decision to aid the Israelite spies is a remarkable display of foresight and knowledge of Israelite literature. As J.L. McKenzie's popular remark about Rahab's "confession" suggests—"Rahab is quoted as being rather well read in the Deuteronomic tradition of the exodus and the wilderness" (cited by Boling 1982:146)—the narrator's choice of wording for her confession shows a blatant disregard for verisimilitude. Given that the narrative otherwise exhibits an effort to preserve verisimilitude, an exhibition often naively assumed to show concern for accurate historiography, the exception of Rahab's confession demands closer examination.

The temporary dispensation of verisimilitude is like a signpost to the reader providing directions for the continuation of the reading journey. Like any signpost, the narrator's disregard for verisimilitude can be understood as an expression of its maker's intent to guide travellers—here readers—in the proper direction for the successful completion of their journey. To understand this narrative, the reading journey, one must read

18 Cf. Boling (1982:150), "there is a glaring internal contradiction between the warfare guide-lines in Deut 20:10–20 and this negotiated exception, which makes the Rahab story stick out like a sore thumb."

this sign closely and carefully.[19]

Rahab explains her friendly attitude toward the Israelite spies with reference to previous actions that God had performed on Israel's behalf. As a result of hearing about God's mighty deeds both Rahab's and the hearts of all the other inhabitants of the land, so she says, "melted" (*wayyimmas*) and they were left without courage (v. 11; cf. v. 9). Rahab makes reference to two specific events, the report of which has caused this universal demoralization among the inhabitants: the exodus from Egypt and the conquest of Sihon and Og (v. 10).

Dispelling the illusion of verisimilitude as he has, though characteristically not by direct address to the reader in his own narrating voice, the narrator shows a concern that the reader remember and understand something from these allusions to previous events. The reference to the exodus, Sihon and Og is matched by only one other reference in the book of Joshua. In 9:10 the Gibeonites also come to the Israelites asking for a covenant of peace, and—what a coincidence!—they too refer to what happened in Egypt and to Sihon and Og as the provocation for their request. This collocation of non–verisimilar allusions and covenant-seeking inhabitants who are granted illegal covenants as a result is striking and hardly accidental. The significance of the collocation appears in the common pattern between the incidences of allusion and the two separate allusions themselves.

What happened to Sihon (and Og) is related in Deut 2:30–33 (cf. 3:1–8). Moses explains that Sihon was defeated by the same mechanism used to defeat Pharaoh in the exodus from Egypt. To deliver Sihon into Israel's hands Yahweh hardened his spirit (*hiqšâ ʾet-rûḥî*) and strengthened his heart (*wᵉʾimmēṣ ʾet-lᵉbābô*). These kings are handed over to Israel in combat by ensuring that they are set up as adamant opponents, just as Pharaoh was (cf. Gunn 1982:72–96). This method quickly becomes Yahweh's favourite way of devastating human opponents: first they are set up and outfitted as mock rivals for a time and then they are destroyed. As in the case of Pharaoh and his armies in Exodus there is no question of any actual struggle between Yahweh and his human opponents (cf. Isa 10:15).

---

19 G.W. Coats (1985:51) provides the correct reader-response to the incongruity: "this speech reflects the interests of the redactor ...", though he does shift to a literary-historical hermeneutic and misses the point made in context; cf. Tucker 1972:78–9.

The strategy is clearly laid out by the narrator in Josh 11:20: "For it was from Yhwh to harden their hearts to meet Israel in battle to obliterate them so that there would be no mercy to them (*lᵉbiltî hᵉyôt-lāhem tᵉḥinnâ*), so that he could destroy them as Yhwh had commanded Moses." This is the same pattern described by the narrator of Deut 2:30 regarding the conflict with Sihon.[20] With hearts hardened by divine intervention, Israel's enemies are set up to go into a battle against Israel that they can never win, just as the Egyptian Pharaoh gets a hardening of his heart to set him up as the obstinate target of Yahweh's mighty acts in the exodus (Exod 7:3; 10:1–2; 14:4, 17–18; cf. Wenham 1971:146).

There is, however, a preliminary measure not mentioned in Josh 11:20. Even before the hardening of Sihon, the first victim to fall to the Israelite conquest, comes the first step in the psychological warfare against the inhabitants of the land. In Deut 2:25 Yahweh states that he is preparing for the mission of conquest by putting the "dread and fear" (*paḥdᵉkā wᵉyirʾātᵉkā*) of Israel on all people under the heavens so that they would be demoralized on Israel's account.

A significant presage of this battle plan is found in the poem that celebrates the paradigmatic victory over Pharaoh and his armies in Exod 15. Just as the Egyptians sank as a stone in the depths when faced by Yahweh's opposition (Exod 15:5), so the people who oppose Israel's entry into the land will be "still as stone" (v. 16) when they, in turn, face the terrific force of Yahweh's might (cf. vv. 6, 16). Hearing about how Egypt sank "like a stone," the inhabitants of Canaan become "still as stone." The causal concatenation between petrifications is highlighted by this parallelism.[21]

The parallelism of fates follows on the parallelism of methods used to defeat Egyptians and later opponents to the exodus and conquest; what happened to the Egyptians will also happen to the enemies of the conquest. The connection is detailed in Exod 15:14–16: the wars of conquest will be won because the nations have heard about the defeat of the Egyptians and are

---

20 The same pattern is also implied for the battle against Og as the vocabulary parallels between Deut 3:2–3 and 2:30–1 suggest. In addition Yahweh says in 3:2 that he has prepared the way for Israel to do to Og what it has already done to Sihon.

21 The connection between this passage and the obdurifications that are performed in the book of Joshua was already noted in the Mekilta (*T. Shirata* 9, 114).

demoralized: hearing, the people "tremble" (*yirgāzûn*); anguish grips them (*ḥîl ʾāḥaz*); the chiefs of Edom are terrified (*nibhᵃlû*); the leaders of Moab tremble uncontrollably (*yoʾḥᵃzēmô rāʿad*); the Canaanites "melt" (*nāmōgû*); terror and dread fall on them (*ʾêmātâ wāpaḥad*).[22]

The parallelism between the conquest of the inhabitants of the land and the Egyptians is, of course, made explicit by the symbolism of crossing the Jordan upon entry into the land (Josh 3–5).[23] The crossing of the Jordan is to the Canaanite inhabitants what the crossing of the Red Sea was to the Egyptians, only in a reverse and prophetic sequence. Instead of a culminating victory of Yahweh over Israel's enemies, the crossing of the Jordan is a victory proclamation that tells all involved that Yahweh is about to repeat the miraculous victory again. The pattern of relationship between the Jordan crossing and the crossing of the Red Sea is:

Despoiling the Egyptians (Exod 12:35–6)
Crossing of the Red Sea (Exod 14:29)
Crossing of the Jordan (Josh 3:14–7)
Dispossession of the Canaanites (Josh 5f.)

It should come as no surprise that the first Canaanite reaction that the narrator presents to the reader about the news of Israel's crossing of the Jordan is exactly the first stage in the psychological warfare previously employed against Pharaoh and the Egyptians (Josh 5:1; cf. below, next note).The sequence of the enterprise is therefore:

1. demoralization
2. obdurification
3. annihilation.[24]

---

22 Coats (1985:51) notes the parallels in psychological warfare tactics, but finds no significance in them.

23 Cf. C.A. Keller (1956:93), "... *so hat doch zweifellos die Erinnerung an das Geschehen vom Yam Suph Wesentliches zur Gestaltung der Jordanlegende beigetragen,*" and Cross (1973:104), who speaks of the "transparent symbolism" of the Jordan crossing.

24 The pattern has already appeared in the final conflict with Pharaoh and the Egyptians (1. Exod 11:6; 12:29–33; 2. Exod 14:3– 8; 3. Exod 14:24–30). Of course the most visible instance of this sequence of manipulations of Israel's enemies is the case of Pharaoh himself; having terrorized Pharaoh several times and obdurified him as many, Yahweh caps the repetitions of steps one and two with the third and conclusive step in the process:

Demoralization	*Obdurification*	*Annihilation*
8:8	8:15	

As the first enemy that Israel meets on its road to conquest, the conquest of Sihon is paradigmatic for later actions against enemies that oppose the progress of the conquest.[25] The same three stages should be repeated in each case if the mission is to succeed as the action against Sihon did. And the narratorial comment in Josh 11:20 suggests that this is exactly the way in which "the whole land" was taken (cf. 11:16, 19, 23). In ironic fact, of course, the narrator means to say exactly the opposite in the light of Rahab and the Gibeonites. This is how the whole land should have been taken, but was not.

The question raised by Rahab's request for covenantal relationship—"kind, faithful" treatment being a description of action dictated by covenantal terms[26]—is how could she do so if Yahweh had performed the requisite hardening of hearts? That Rahab should make reference to the textbook cases of Pharaoh, Sihon, and Og while making her plea is hardly fortuitous; the narrator could not have made the incongruity more obvious. Here is Rahab describing how the psychological warfare should operate in all cases (cf. McCarthy 1971:174) and yet existing as living proof of the failure to implement them completely. Yahweh's failure to harden Rahab's heart glares through her confession. Somehow she has been omitted, from the second stage of psychological preparation, which seems nevertheless to control the behaviour of her fellow Jerichonians (cf. Josh 2:2–3, 7, 22). So it is not only Joshua's failure to implement the commands of ch. 1 that creates a situation leading to a failure of total conquest at Jericho; Yahweh has a part in it too.[27] Rahab is

8:25	8:32	
9:27–8	9:34–5	
10:8	10:11	
10:16–7	10:20	
10:24	10:27	
12:31–2	14:5,8	14:27–8

25 Cf. Millard C. Lind (1980:50) who underlines the fact that it was Yahweh alone who defeated Egypt—apart from Israelite action. "The sea event has a causal effect upon relations with other Near Eastern peoples. The Egyptians went down "like a stone" ([Exod 15] v. 5); the nations whom Yahweh's people later contacted were "as still as a stone" ([Exod 15] v. 16). The effect of the exodus as a paradigm for Yahweh's saving action in Israel's difficult experiences is found within the poem itself."

26 Cf. Boling 1982:147. The formal covenantal structure of Rahab's request has been detailed by K.M. Campbell 1972:243–44.

27 Against McCarthy (1971:173), who says of the Rahab episode that "it includes a great confession of faith, and it shows Yahweh taking care of a singularly incompetent set of

characterized as a whore precisely because she is the door, left open by the divine whoremonger, through which the Israelites are led to stray, "a-whoring" after other gods.

It is interesting to see how the narrator arranges for the revelation of Yahweh's complicity in the failed conquest with respect to Rahab. He does not point out the problem with a bald, expositional assertion that Yahweh has failed to do his duty; his methods are far more subtle. Instead he uses dramatic irony by getting the very character whose request is a verbal testimony to Yahweh's failure to underline it. When Rahab alludes to the case of Sihon she instantaneously draws attention to the obvious difference between herself and Sihon, both inhabitants of the promised land yet different in their reception of Israel. Yahweh's failure to prepare Rahab is attested both by her request and by her seemingly innocent allusion to the prior cases of hardening of the heart as prime motivation for her request. This type of evaluation by implication is characteristic of biblical narrators. The bulk of evaluation, either of characters or events, is made to arise out of the story itself—from events, characters, actions etc.—rather than from the authoritative voice of the narrator. Especially in evaluating the divine character the biblical narrator is careful to divorce himself from the implications of his story.

Confirmation of Yahweh's confederate role in the establishment of the sinful covenant with Rahab is not long in coming. In the events that follow Yahweh shows by his actions, or rather his inaction, that he is somehow complicit in the wrongful arrangement made with Rahab. The pact made with Rahab is a direct contravention of the command in Deut 7:2. Consequently the endeavour against Jericho should fail according to the terms of the covenant governing success in warfare (cf. Deut 28:25 and the example in Josh 7:4–12). As the reader will see in the subsequent case of Achan's transgression of the terms of the covenant (Josh 7), Yahweh has not forgotten Israel's covenantal obligations and he is not slow to mete out severe punishment for lapses. The only explanation for Yahweh's failure to punish Israel for the pact with Rahab is that he himself wills its existence. The question of course—one not to

---

spies. One can rely on him." Both the confession and the failure to punish the spies for covenantal infringement show that Yahweh cannot be relied on. There are, in fact, unstated reasons for his unreliability, which will be revealed in Judg 2, but at this point those reasons are invisible.

be answered until the book of Judges—is why.

Instead of the expected descent of divine wrath on the Israelites the narrator describes how Yahweh joins in to defeat Jericho (6:2–5). Has Yahweh forgotten, is he so forgiving, or is there perhaps some other reason for his failure to punish Israel for this blatant sin against his commands? Though the reader will not be able to narrow the possibilities until he reads about what happens to Achan for an equally serious transgression, the implication, already supplied by Rahab's allusion to the case of Sihon, is that Yahweh fails to punish because, even though he may stoop to pimping on occasion, he is no hypocrite. Israel gets away with this transgression because Yahweh has neglected his own duty. No other explanation for the missing punishment is offered or implied in the narrative. But regarding the question of why Yahweh does not do his duty, even the case of Achan yields no insight.

During the battle Joshua reminds Israel of the standing orders for everything to be put under the ban (6:17, $w^{e}h\bar{a}y^{e}t\hat{a}$ *hāʿîr ḥerem hîʾ*). But in the very same breath he excludes Rahab and her house from the ban.[28] In spite of this blatantly conscious contravention of the command by Joshua himself, God himself provides a miraculous victory (v. 20). If Joshua has voiced his knowing agreement to the illegal agreement made with Rahab (v. 20), the miraculous victory is a resounding echo of Yahweh's approval of the proceedings (cf. Wenham 1971:142).

Yahweh's silence about Rahab's illegal survival is endowed with a loud voice in the narrative. His reticence on a matter of such obvious importance—the ban is mentioned no less than 11 times concerning the battle against Jericho (6:17, 18, 21; 7:1 (twice), 11, 12, 13 (twice), 15)—and his open approval of what is done are strong evidence of his complicity in the affair. The narrator repeatedly draws attention to the anomaly of Rahab's survival so that the reader cannot fail to notice it and the absence of divine censure (2:10–14,17–21; 6:17, 22–3, 25). But he goes even further in probing the issue in the subsequent narration of the sin of Achan (ch. 7). The collocation of these related incidents is not fortuitous. With Achan we have exactly the same contravention of the ban command as in the case of Ra-

---

28 Against Peckham (1984:429), "The fifth incident ... ensures that the ban is observed (6:17–19, 21, 24)."

hab.[29] Here Yahweh is not implicated in the commission of a sin as he was when he failed to harden the heart of Rahab. Now he is free to charge Israel with the sin and to withhold victory on that account (v. 5). The extensive discussion of the ban in ch. 7 and especially Yahweh's adamant refusal to ally himself with Israel so long as things under the ban remain in Israel's "midst" (*qrb*, v. 13) underline the seriousness of contravening this command (cf. Boling 1982:229).

The narrator's choice of words for Yahweh's threat of withdrawal in 7:12 create a vocabulary linkage—a *Leitwort*—back to the case of Rahab. In 6:25 the narrator says that Rahab has lived in Israel's "midst" (*qrb*) until this day. The duration of her sojourn amongst the Israelites, a seemingly innocuous anachronistic intrusion in the story, highlights the incongruity of her presence. She lives in Israel's "midst" as one illegally spared from the ban. But in the case of Achan's booty, also a thing under the ban yet existing in Israel's "midst" (v. 12), Yahweh threatens to withdraw further victory and explains past failure as the automatic consequence of the default on the ban. Either Yahweh reactions are capricious in response to the existence of things under the ban in Israel's "midst," or he does not complain about Rahab because his own hands are sullied in that case and he does not wish to air it.

The Case of the Gibeonites

The next item of interest regarding the subject of failed conquest is the covenant made with the Gibeonites in ch. 9. Once again the narrator presents a story about a treaty made by the Israelites with some of the inhabitants of the land. At issue, again, is the question of compliance with the "ban" command

29 Boling suggests that the story of Achan has been adapted to deal with the issue of the ban from an "old narrative core" in which Achan confessed only to having stolen from legitimate booty (1982:229). His suggestion, however, does not change the fact that in the existing narrative the ban is a central concern. In addition, Boling's literary–historical conclusion fails to consider the immediate environment of Achan's statement in 7:21, which does have an infra–narrative, story–world context.

The fact that Achan is in mortal danger when he admits to having stolen from the "booty" rather than from the things under the ban is most economically understood as Achan's attempt to evade the deadly consequence of his act. Before resorting to the context of literary history, it is methodologically sound to examine the existing narrative context as the frame in which various utterances and their nuances may be understood.

and the consequences of non-compliance.[30] In the case of the treaty with the Gibeonites, the illegal pact is the result of three things: 1. the deception of the Gibeonites; 2. Israel's failure to consult with Yahweh about the treaty; 3. Yahweh's failure to harden the hearts of the Gibeonites as he hardened the hearts of the remainder of the inhabitants (cf. 11:18–20).

The chain of causality between these three factors begins with Yahweh's failure to harden the Gibeonites' hearts. Once again the narrator endows his non-Israelite characters with knowledge of the book of Deuteronomy to have them make the crucial point from within the story. The Gibeonites explain their desire for a treaty with the Israelites on the same basis as Rahab: they have heard what Yahweh did in Egypt and what he did to Sihon and Og. As before, the characters' gifted understanding of Israel's sacred history makes for an allusion by tearing the veil of verisimilitude from the story.[31] And this break raises the question of why Yahweh has not done to the Gibeonites as he did to Egypt, Sihon, and Og. Had Yahweh done his duty, there would be no question of a treaty, as the example of the kings mentioned in 11:20 proves.

Second in causal order is the Gibeonite ruse. Thanks to their equally remarkable recollection of the book of Deuteronomy, here Deut 20:10–18, the Gibeonites pass themselves off as a group living outside the promised land and request the treaty relationship allowed such parties. The deception is such that if the Israelite leaders are taken in by it they will have done no conscious wrong in making a treaty with the Gibeonites. The parallel with the situation of the spies in ch. 2 is, as such parallels are wont to be in the Bible, no coincidence.

---

30 Though J. Dus (1960:372) notes an implicit awareness in the narrative of the unjust, anti–covenantal nature of the pact with Gibeon, he reifies this important perspectival signification into a hidden historical polemic by Ephraim against Benjamin. Moreover, he accepts Noth's suggestion that historically, assimilation of a Canaanite city was unexceptional, a simple fact if the manner of conquest (p. 371).

31 Scholarly readers have noted fictitious elements about the story of the Gibeonite covenant with Israel, but instead of taking the lack of verisimilitude as a sign post to the narrator's focus in this tale they have tracked such features as the spoor of unknown redactors who have left us a heritage of confused tradition (e.g. J.A. Soggin 1972:110–11 and others cited by him. Cf. J. Liver 1963:228). Why the Gibeonites should ask for a covenant is not the narrator's concern (against Soggin (1972:111), "If the Gibeonites claimed to come from a long way off (vv. 6b, 9, 22), why did they ask for a covenant? What use would it have been to them?") Such incongruities in the narrative should serve to point the reader away from what is obviously peripheral towards what is central, the making of the illegal covenant and the contributors thereto.

Third in order is Israel's "leaders" failure to consult Yahweh about the treaty.[32] There is, however, no specific injunction requiring Israel to seek Yahweh's advice in such a case (cf. Deut 20:10–15). The Israelite leaders, if they are duped, do whatever they do with clear deuteronomistic consciences.[33] It is also worth noting that the people are absolved of any complicity here. As in the case of Joshua's spies, the common populace is far removed by this narrator from even the hint of wrongdoing.

---

32 In Josh 9:14 MT reads, "So the men took their provisions," (*wayyiqḥû hā'ănāšîm miṣṣêdām),* whereas LXX has *hoi arxontes* which suggests an original *hannᵉśî'îm.* In favour of LXX are the following considerations:

1. MT's "the men" makes the subject of the verb ambiguous; which men is important since their action is important in paving the way to an agreement. Furthermore since there is a later division amongst the Israelites over the covenant and over the proceedings leading to it, and since the narrator does describe the rift in some detail, the ambiguous noun seems out of place.

2. In the surrounding context it is either Joshua and an unidentified man who deal with the Gibeonites (vv. 6, 8, 15, 22–3, 26–7) or the leaders (*hannᵉśî'îm*) who treat with the Gibeonites; the common Israelites play no part.

3. If it were simply "the men" who took the provisions from the Gibeonites, granting that "the men" refers to the Israelites and not Joshua and the unidentified man of vv. 6–7, and if this action is to be regarded as preliminary to formal ratification of a treaty (so most commentators), then the Israelites really have no call or grounds for the strong complaints they voice when the mistake is discovered. Either the congregation is hypocritical in vv. 18, 26, from which it seems that they were ready to properly exterminate the Gibeonites with whom they themselves had no pact, or it was the leaders who acted in v. 14.

4. The scribal error involved in transposing the letters of *hannᵉśî'îm* resulting in *hā'ănāšîm* is not implausible. Given the context in which *hannᵉśî'îm* appears in vv. 15, 18 (2X), 19, 21 (2X), all instances attributing responsibility for the covenant to the leaders, it seems most economical to accept LXX in v. 14 and to explain MT as a simple case of transposition.

5. The leaders strongly defensive stance in the face of criticism from the congregation (vv. 18–21) suggests that they accepted all responsibility for the covenant and that there were no grounds for placing any blame on the laity.

Boling (1982:265) rejects LXX because he believes that the narrator had "the men" here to show that fault for the covenant was shared. But what does one make, then, of the following context in which no one, the narrator included, disputes the congregation's self–righteous stance of innocence (cf. A. Malamat 1955:9)? Furthermore Boling states, "The LXX reading here mentioning "the leaders" instead of "the men" cannot be correct since this verse merely assigns fault, whereas "the leaders" are going to be the ones to salvage something out of the situation." Isn't it more likely that the leaders being the ones at fault are naturally also the ones that must do something to salvage the situation? The fact that the LXX reading of v. 14 identifies the leaders as the initiators of treaty proceedings is in no way contradictory to the subsequent context.

33 Against Wenham's (1971:142) reading and condemnation of the Israelites for supposedly having culpably omitted the query "and so afterwards regrets its action" (9:14). There is no regret in 9:14 nor at any point thereafter. For general discussion of the problem see B. Halpern 1975:310 n. 26.

The reader comes to the story of the Gibeonite treaty already educated by the Rahab story. Yahweh's failure in that incident is already known. The reader, thanks to the narrator's dispensation of some of his unconditioned knowledge about the true state of affairs in the Gibeonite ruse in 9:1–5, knows that the Gibeonites are living within the land and so should have been prepared psychologically by Yahweh. Their lack of preparation is underscored by the juxtaposition of descriptions in 9:1–2 (cf. 5:1), of the properly hardened, and in 9:3–5, of the anomalously unhardened. Such use of structure to make revealing comparisons between topics is a favourite device of biblical narrators (cf. J.P. Fokkelman 1975; 1981). So, when the reader hears of the Gibeonites' curiously soft–heartedness, there is virtual certainty that Yahweh is responsible, whatever his reasons.

Now the reader comes to the description of the leaders' fateful acceptance of the Gibeonites' provisions. V. 14 is structured as a grammatical chiasmus:

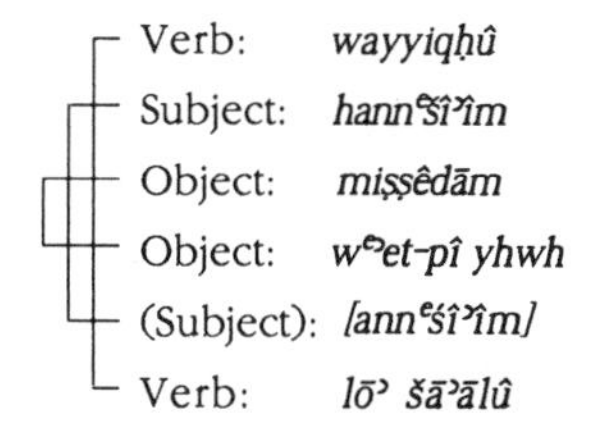

The chiastic narratorial description of the lack of communication with Yahweh juxtaposes two things at the centre of the chiasmus: the deceptive provisions and the counsel of Yahweh. A structural parallel is used to draw attention to two seemingly separate items whose close relationship is highlighted by this formal device. Standing opposite the deceptive provisions of the Gibeonites is the potentially revelatory counsel of Yahweh. What is the content of this potential revelation? It is not simply an exposition of the Gibeonite falsehood that lies hidden in the unbidden counsel of the Lord; there is also an explanation of how it is that the Gibeonites have come to the place of being able to pursue a course of deception instead of the headlong path to destruction taken by the rest of their fellow countrymen (9:1–2). Standing at the centre of the chiastic v. 14 are two deceptions: on an explicit level, the Gibeonites' stale provisions, and on a more secretive, subtle plane, Yahweh's failure to proclaim and explain his neglect of the psychological preparation due the Gibeonites.

The other parallelism created by the chiastic structure of v. 14 is between the verbs of each half. Just as the leaders accept the counterfeit provisions they also "accept" Yahweh's silence about the soft-heartedness of the Gibeonites. They accept Yahweh's silence by failing to question him about the Gibeonites' proposal. Such an inquiry could have received two explanations, at least from the perspective of the narrator and his reader. Yahweh could have alerted the leaders to the Gibeonite deception, a matter that would presumably be the object of the inquiry's interest in the first place. But it also could have led to disclosures, uncomfortable for Yahweh, about why it was that the Gibeonites should be coming forward in such a manner in the first place. Should the leaders have discovered that the Gibeonites were inhabitants of the land, the simple fact that they had come forward, unhardened as it were, with the proposition for peace would have indicated that Yahweh had not acted according to normal, covenantal expectation.

The focus of the chiastic structure in these verses is on deception and on Israel's leaders unwitting acceptance of deception. There is no evidence in the structure that the narrator has attempted to put the blame for this covenant on Israel's leaders, much less the Israelite people in general. Ultimately the narrative credits Yahweh with the lion's share of responsibility for the covenant with the Gibeonites. The Gibeonites could not have deceived and the leaders need not have asked, and Yahweh would not have had any secrets to keep if only he had hardened the Gibeonites along with the others who got theirs' in 9:1.

Later, in v. 24, the Gibeonites' statements show that though they have been demoralized, there has been no obdurification. As a result, the Gibeonites, like Rahab, dwell in Israel's "midst" (*qrb* 9:16; cf. 6:25): the second group of illegal aliens to receive unofficial divine sanction. Once again the *Leitwort* makes an elegant connection with no need for explicit narratorial exposition.

Like his description of the duration of Rahab's cohabitation with Israel, the narrator's description of the Gibeonites' stay extends "to this day" (*ʿad-hayyôm hazzeh* 9:27; cf. 6:25). In both descriptions the narrator draws attention to the abnormal, extended indwelling of these inhabitants of the land, who should have been exterminated under the ban. In both cases the continuation of normal covenantal relations between Yahweh and

Israel after these clear infractions of the covenanted requirement of the ban feature Yahweh's reluctance to veto the agreement and punish Israel for entering into it. Each time the unexpected divine condescension is the logical and structural counterpart to the unexpected failure to harden the hearts of Israel's opposition; both are actions expected of God but which he neglects to do. The connection is obvious and logical.

One common aspect has been overlookedin the comparison of Rahab and the Gibeonites: the parallel social contexts out of which each of these exceptional traitors come. Our interest, of course, is not any supposed historical social context, but the context created in the conventional story world reality of the narrative.

Reviewing the case of Rahab it is apparent that she stands alone among her peers in her reaction to the spies and the report of what had happened to Egypt, Sihon, and Og. As soon as the king of Jericho hears that there are Israelite spies in Jericho he issues an order for their arrest (2:2–3). If the reader accepts Rahab's word (2:9, 11) that all the inhabitants of the land melted at the report of what happened to previous resistors—a supposition supported by prior divine promises (Exod 23:27; Deut 2:25) and not contradicted by anything the narrator says or describes in the context of Rahab's statement—then it must be the case that the king of Jericho has later been hardened as would be expected according to the pattern of conquest previously described.

Rahab's uniqueness is further underlined with the characteristic device used in biblical narrative to focus reader attention, namely repetition. In the story of the spies the verb "to pursue" (*rdp*) together with the noun "pursuers" is repeated no less than seven times (vv. 5, 7 (2X), 16 (2X), 22 (2X)). By foregrounding the "pursuit" of the spies the narrator draws attention to the fact that the previously melted inhabitants have somehow gotten the courage to seek the curtailment of Israel's endeavours. In context, the most likely explanation for their change of heart (cf. v. 11) is, of course, that Yahweh has done to them what he did to Pharaoh, Sihon, and Og.

A similar situation exists in the case of the Gibeonites. Here the reader needs the intervening narration to perceive the pattern and the uniqueness of the Gibeonites' exceptional behaviour. In 5:1 the narrator describes the reaction of the Amorite and Canaanite kings to the report of how Yahweh "dried up the waters of the Jordan before the children of Israel." The reader cannot fail to recall the nearly identical formulation of 2:10:

2:10 *šāmaʿnû*
ʾet ʾăšer-hôbîš yhwh
ʾet-mê yam-sûp mippᵉnêkem

5:1 *kišmōaʿ kol-malkê hāʾĕmōrî ʾăšer bᵉʿēber hayyardēn*
ʾet ʾăšer-hôbîš yhwh
ʾet-mê-hayyardēn mipnê [bᵉnê-yiśrāʾēl]

The identity in vocabulary equates the two events, the crossings of the Red Sea and the Jordan, as motivators in this narrative for the later melting of the inhabitants. The reactions too are identical:

2:11 *wannišmaʿ wayyimmas lᵉbābēnû*
wᵉlōʾ-qāmâ ʿôd rûaḥ bᵉʾîš mippᵉnêkem

5:1 *wayyimmas lᵉbābām*
wᵉlōʾ-hāyâ bām ʿôd rûaḥ mippᵉnê bᵉnê-yiśrāʾēl

These kings, then, are set up just like the inhabitants that Rahab describes. The Gibeonites, as Hivites (9:7), are included among the hardened group (cf. 9:1), "... the Hivite, and the Jebusite ... "; their exceptional escape from the process of psychological manipulation comes only in the next step of the procedure.

The next step is described in 9:1. The literary device of resumptive repetition is used by the narrator to draw attention to the chain of psychological preparations.[34] 5:1 and 9:1 are tied by means of this device, which is used to show that the reactions described in each stand in direct temporal and causal concatenation:

5:1 *wayᵉhî kišmōaʿ kol-malkê hāʾĕmōrî*
ʾăšer bᵉʿēber hayyardēn

9:1 *wayᵉhî kišmōaʿ kol-hammlākîm*
ʾăšer beʿēber hayyardēn

After melting (5:1) comes, as ch. 2 has shown, the reaction,

---

[34] S. Talmon (1978:17) gives the following description of the technique. "By cutting the thread of a story at a convenient, or even not quite so convenient, juncture, then interweaving other matter of a different narrative character, and again resuming the first account by means of repeating the verse, phrase, or even the word, at which the cut-off had occurred, the author safeguards the linear continuity of the narration, and at the same time permits the listener or the reader to become aware of the synchroneity of the events related." Cf. Ramban's discussion of Exod 1:1 in his commentary on the Torah (1973:6).

which is best explained as a turnabout owing to hardening of the heart. Immediately following 5:1 in the temporal consecution of events in the story is 9:2: to paraphrase the effect, 'when all the kings heard how Yahweh dried the Jordan before the Israelites their hearts melted ... (when all the kings heard) they assembled with one accord to fight Joshua and the Israelites.' The kings of 9:1 are, like the king of Jericho, weirdly courageous after their demoralization; like Sihon, who came out to meet Israel in battle with all his people after his heart had been hardened, (Deut 2:32) all the kings come out to meet Israel in battle with one accord (9:1).

The exceptional nature of the Gibeonites' reaction is highlighted by the opening of the description of their response. It begins with the same phraseology as that used to describe the general reaction; "and the Gibeonites heard (*šmʿ*)" (cf. 5:1; 9:1). But their response is markedly different. Instead of marching out to meet Israel in battle, a battle that they could never win, the Gibeonites match the action of Joshua with their own crafty action; the parallel is highlighted by the vocabulary and the emphatic particle with the pronoun:

9:3 *šāmᵉʿû ʾēt ʾᵃšer ʿāśâ yᵉhôšuaʿ lîrîḥô wᵉlāʿāy*

9:4 *wayyaʿᵃśû gam-hēmmâ bᵉʿormâ*

The narrator has drawn attention to the Gibeonites' tit for tat with the emphatic restatement of the subject, "even they" (*gam-hēmmâ*). The emphasis draws even more attention to their unexpected response.

Again it is interesting to see how the narrator draws attention to the contrasting reactions of the general populace (as represented by their kings) and that of the Gibeonites. Avoiding any explicit statements about it, he uses structural and grammatical devices to focus attention on the crucial differences. With such a method of narratorial exposition it is impossible to recover the meaning of the narrative if one is not prepared to entertain implications that do not lie on the explicit plane of discourse in the narrative.

Given that the Gibeonite action parallels the action of the kings in 9:1—both are responses to "hearing" about the conquest—it is obvious from their response to the news that they have escaped the requisite hardening of heart. Their unique status of existing as eternally, covenantally bound servants of Israel (9:23) is ultimately due to Yahweh's unexplained failure to include them in the psychological manipulations accorded to the remainder of the resident population. Like the other exception, Rahab, the Gibeonites remain "to this day"—another *Leitwort* connection—illegal aliens dwelling in Israel's midst (9:27; 6:25). The repeated reference to the prolonged tenure of these profane intruders in Israel's sacred midst highlights and intensifies the wrongfulness of this situation.

Of the material devoted to describing the campaign of conquest in Josh 1–12, fully 47% is given to detailing the failures related to these two contraventions of the ban.[35] The relative balance between descriptions of success and these specific instances of failure indicates the latter's importance in the narrator's overall conception of the conquest: what he chooses to dwell on is what the reader should recognize as important in the narrative.

With this balance in mind, it seems to me impossible to turn again to the narrator's explicit summation of the campaign of chs. 1–12 and accept it at face value. There is definitely a tongue in that seemingly pious cheek. "So Joshua took the whole land, according to all that the Lord had spoken to Moses ..." (11:23 NASV). The land is not taken according to all that Yahweh spoke to Moses, at least not according to the book of Deuteronomy. And the blame for the failure to do so is laid primarily, *but only implicitly*, on Yahweh. Secondary responsibility goes to Joshua and to the leadership of Israel, who are also a divinely provided gift to Israel (e.g. Num 27:15–23).

The question of why Yahweh should fail to perform the operations necessary to the success of the conquest is not addressed by the narrator or the events of his story. Instead this question remains as an expositional gap in the narrative. The reader is left alone to raise and study possible explanations for Yahweh's anomalous behaviour. The effect of the gap on the reader's response to the narrator's ironic evaluations of the success of the conquest is to make them all the more provocative. The reader waits for some suggestion from the narrator, the source of authoritative explanations in the narrative, about Yahweh's motives regarding Rahab and the Gibeonites. What is given instead are the absurd statements that the conquest was a complete success. And what is more, the reader knows that both Yahweh and Joshua are to blame for the incompleteness.

---

35 The story of Achan's sin is counted as a contrastive element the Rahab account.

While reading the book of Joshua the reader never knows whether the narrator will ever clear up the mystery about Yahweh's motives. But it is clear from the cases of Rahab and the Gibeonites that the fulfilment of the promises to the patriarchs and the covenant relationship that depends on such a fulfilment get off to a bad start—at least from a human perspective[36]—in the book of Joshua.

To return to the beginning of our study—differences between the supposedly successful total conquest of the book of Joshua and the dismal success of the book of Judges—it seems that there has been a misunderstanding based on a confusion about the relationship between certain evaluations of the conquest made in the book of Joshua and the overall meaning, or "voice" with which the narrative speaks about the conquest. In the end Joshua's evaluations of the conquest are of a strictly localized validity. They cannot be accepted as a substitute for the narrative's own estimation of the conquest because they are subordinate, infra–narrative utterances. In his important discussion of character utterances M. Bakhtin (1984:186–7) says:

> Such speech has direct referential meaning, but it does not lie in the same plane with the author's speech; it observes, as it were, a certain distance and perspective. Such speech is meant to be understood not only from the point of view of its own referential object, but is itself, as characteristic, typical, colourful discourse, a referential object toward which something is directed.
>
> Whenever we have within the another's context the direct speech of, say, a certain character, we have within the limits of a single context two speech centres and two speech unities: the unity of the author's utterance and the unity of the character's utterance. But the second unity is not self-sufficient; it is subordinated to the first and incorporated into it as one of its components.

Bakhtin goes on to state that ultimate semantic authority, the "voice" of the narrative (Wayne Booth's implied author (1961)), resides with the author's voice, i.e. the narrator in the book of Joshua. As Bakhtin points out a major differences between poetry and artistic prose or narrative is that narrative employs many "discourses" (character perspectives and utterances) and holds them in creative tension within one overarching umbrella discourse. "For the prose artist the world is full of other peo-

---

36 As subsequent episodes in the Dtr narrative show and as the exodus story shows the divine accounting of the success or failure of his machinations in Israel's history are quite another matter.

ple's words, among which he must orient himself and whose speech characteristics he must be able to perceive with a very keen ear. He must introduce them into the plane of his own discourse, but in such a way that this plane is not destroyed" (1984:201). In the past scholarship has done exactly what Bakhtin says the prose artist must not do to succeed. Could this be why it has been seen as necessary to reorder, in terms of literary history, the literarily unsuccessful book of Joshua?

Things are less simple with the apparently confusing irony of the narrator's evaluations, which have led some readers to believe that the narrator wanted to portray a totally successful conquest. The reader has two primary options. If we accept the narrator's evaluations at face value, we have to scrap the narrative as a cohesive, coherent narrative description; it doesn't match the evaluation, which has been accepted as authoritative. The result: the narrative in the book of Joshua is a tangled patchwork of sources and traditions in irrevocable contradiction (Miller 1977:213, 215, 220–1, 230–6). The narrative is destroyed.

A simple reversal of our perception of where the ultimate semantic authority of the narrative must lie—that is in the narrative description of the facts, the realia of the story world—and the narrative rises phoenix-like from the rubble of historical-critical literary history. If we read the book of Joshua as a book and not as a jumbled collection of tales and traditions, then we must raise the narrator to the authoritative level that his narratorial situation alone grants him. And if we read the book of Joshua as a book, it is far from contradicting the opening passage of the book of Judges on the success of Israel's conquest.

CHAPTER 3

A NEW GENERATION IN ISRAEL

And also all that generation were gathered unto their fathers: and there arose another generation after them, which knew not the Lord, nor yet the works which he had done for Israel (Judges 2:10).

Conquest Gone Awry (Judg 1)

Through his opening sentence in the book of Judges the narrator directs the reader to the preceding book, the book of Joshua, as the interpretive context within which the events to follow may be understood. The imperfect *waw*-consecutive *wayy^e^hî* (cf. *GKC* §49b, n. 1) and the temporal specification, "after the death of Joshua," are literary connectors that link the events to follow with what has gone before in a cause and effect relationship. But while the connection does provide the reader with a well established context for interpretation, it also sets up a couple of obstacles that force the reader to struggle with the difficult and unorthodox view that the narrator is about to present.

First, the continuation of Judges 1:1 resurrects the scandalous dichotomy over the success and nature of the conquest. Despite the strong asseverations of Joshua and the narrator, nations did go unconquered between chs. 13 and 23. With the Israelites' question in Judg 1:1—"who will go up for us against the Canaanites?"—it seems that they remain so. This question underlines and supports the ironic view presented by the narrator in the book of Joshua, just as it undermines the wishful thinking of Joshua's fine rhetoric. Resounding from the interaction with both views from the book of Joshua, it resumes the focus on the strange lack of success and on the contentiousness of the theological difficulties thus created. Why did Joshua try to convince Israel that the conquest was a success when it was obvious, even to him, that it was not so (Josh 23:4)? Even more critical, why haven't all the promises been fulfilled and all the nations dispossessed? Why should the strongly ironic assertions of the narrator in, for example, Josh 21:43–5 be ironic at all? Such questions aim the reader at the central problem of the conquest: why has it not gone according to plan? What does the partial success mean? Why are the assertions of narrator and Joshua, which ring so true to the faith, so contradicted by the reality of events?

Sheep Without A Shepherd

A second difficulty posed by Judg 1:1 is related to the first; it appears when Judg 1:1 is compared with Josh 1:1, a comparison invited by a repeated formula and an identical situation in the office of Israel's human leadership. Both books open with the formulaic expression *wayy^{e}hî ʾaḥ^{a}rê môt* followed by the name of the deceased theocratic representative who will no longer guide Israel. Long before Moses died Yahweh took careful precautions to ensure a continuity of leadership (Num 27:15–23; Deut 31:3–8). There is a stark contrast between God's preparations for and swift response to the death of Moses and what he does, or rather does not do, in response to Joshua's death. Once again it is the introductory formula that draws the reader's attention to the similarity and difference of the two transitions:

Joshua 1:1	*Judges 1:1*
The problem stated:	
way^{e}hî ʾaḥ^{a}rê môt mōšeh	*way^{e}hî ʾaḥ^{a}rê môt y^{e}hôšuaʿ*
Respondent:	
yhwh	*b^{e}nê yiśrāʾēl*
Solution:	
qûm ʿ^{a}bōr ʾet-hayyardēn ʾel-hā-ʾāreṣ ʾ^{a}šer ʾānōkî nōtēn lāhem	*wayyiš^{ʾa}lû b^{e}nê yiśrāʾēl byhwh lēʾmōr mî yaʿ^{a}leh-lānû ʾel-hakk^{e}naʿ^{a}nî*

In Josh 1:1, Yahweh took immediate action to ensure the continuity of leadership so vital to the covenantal relationship. In Judg 1:1, on the other hand, it is Israel that must leap into the breach created by Joshua's death and Yahweh's strange inaction and silence. Yahweh's solution to the death of Moses (Josh 1:1) is framed by two imperatives, ***qûm*** ***ᶜᵃbōr***, which direct Joshua to lead Israel into the land Yahweh (note the emphatic "I,"*ʾānōkî*) is giving to Israel. The Israelites have only to cross over, following their God-given leader, and receive that which is given. In Judg 1:1, however, Yahweh's failure to provide a solution to Joshua's death forces the Israelites to ask for one.

The question is, why did Yahweh not arrange for a successor? As Moses had pointed out long before, the Israelites without a God-given leader were sheep without a shepherd (Num 27:17); that was why God pre-ordained Joshua even before Moses' death (Num 27:18–23).

The connection between these two difficulties in Judg 1:1 is revealed in Israel's question to God. They need a leader, which God has neglected to provide, to fight the Canaanites whose presence in the land raises doubts about the truth of assertions such as those made in Josh 21:43–45. For Israel, in the story, the answers are not obvious and in fact it seems that they never get them. For the reader, outside that story world and those events, the narrator will eventually provide an answer to these two expositional gaps, which block any facile interpretation of Judg 1. But the narrator withholds any such explanation until ch. 2.

A primary reason for withholding such expositional information in narrative literature is to increase reader interest and so, to increase reader involvement, familiarity and comprehension of the perspective presented by the narrator. By holding back his disclosure of the reasons for these two anomalies and first describing the consequences thereof, the narrator pricks the reader's curiosity and involves the reader in the quest for the rationale of these events. The suspense about the meaning of the problems outlined in Judg 1 leads the reader to entertain various hypotheses and expectations. The reader gets caught up in the story and, more important, in the authoritative interpretation that the narrator finally doles out. The expositional gap created by withholding the explanations serves two purposes: it serves as a goad to the reader's curiosity, prodding him on to receive the message (cf. M. Sternberg 1978:45–55) and it involves the reader in active interaction with the text so that the meaning or message has a greater impact on the reader. Given the controversial nature of the narrator's view, already visible in the ironies of the book of Joshua, it is essential that the reader by brought "on board" by whatever literary means are at the author"s disposal. Teasing suspense followed by an all-encompassing revelation are not the least important tools for such ideological persuasion.

To study this narrator's expositional strategy one must not anticipate him too much: one must follow the course of reading that he has laid out for his reader. The narrative in Judg 1 paints a picture of a growing crisis in the affairs of a leaderless Israel. The conquest of the land resumes with God's reaffirmation of his intent to give the land over to Israel (v. 2). The process of conquering continues much the same course that it took in the book of Joshua until v. 19, in which the narrator notes that the tribe of Judah could not dispossess (*yrš*) the valley dwellers because they had iron chariots.[1] The narrator's explanation of Judah's inability would be plausible if it stood by itself, but coming just after the observation that "Yahweh was with Judah" it raises a critical theological question by answering a trivial, logistic one.

An underlying assumption of Israelite theology and military strategy was that if Yahweh was with Israel in the battles of conquest then no one, no matter what their military advantage, could stand against them. Joshua says as much in response to the tribe of Joseph when they had doubts about their chances against the very same iron chariots of the Canaanites (Josh 17:16–18; cf. 23:9–10). The narrator phrases the mitigating circumstance in Judg 1:19 as an allusion to the previous concerns of expressed by the tribe of Joseph to highlight, once again, the contrast between the high-minded ideology expressed by Joshua and the reality of the situation as Israel finds it. Yes, Joshua should be right in theory; but no, in practice, he is wrong. The reader can only draw one conclusion from Judg 1:19; Yahweh did not support the campaign. Having pin-pointed a major difficulty, once again by subtle implication, here through the technique of literary allusion, the narrator leaves

---

1 In v. 19 there are two occurrences of the verb *yrš*, the first an active 3rd m.s. form, and the second an infinitive construct in a *kî* clause: *kî lōʾ lᵉhôrîš*. It is generally agreed that context and grammar require the governing verb *ykl* before the infinitive construct here (e.g. Moore 1895:38; Boling 1975:58, a reading witnessed by three versions and two manuscripts (cf., however, Driver 1892: §204).

the question—why has God done so?—unanswered. The reader is left with a question but no answer. This process will be repeated several times more, preparing the reader to accept the reasonable, if shocking, solution that will finally be proffered, but not until the end of ch. 2.

The narrator does not dwell overmuch on this first intimation of problems in the post-Joshuan conquest. Having planted his seeds of orthodox consternation, he goes on to trace the development of other problems as they unfold in the campaigns of the other tribes. First, and in an illuminative contrast to all the others, is the case of Caleb who is given a territory and successfully dispossesses (*yrš*) the inhabitants. The narrator carefully points out that Caleb's success fulfils the promise made by God in Num 14:24. Subsequent to Caleb's success, however, the record of failure to dispossess the inhabitants grows longer and longer, verse by verse. Though Judg 1:1–20, 25 depict a series of twelve instances of conquest after Joshua's death, these successes are outweighed by twenty separate instances of failure to dispossess (*yrš*) the inhabitants in vv. 19, 21, 27–36.

Two features of the decline are repeatedly brought to the reader's attention. First, the verb *yrš*, "to dispossess," appears no less than nine times in the space of fourteen verses (vv. 19–33). Each time, the verb is negated and one of the Israelite tribes is subject. The highlighted reiteration is the narrator's way of showing the importance of this verb without resorting to explicit commentary.[2]

To understand the significance of Israel's nine-fold failure to dispossess the inhabitants one must turn to the book of Deuteronomy, the interpretive key to the book of Judges and all deuteronomistic narrative. The word *yrš* appears frequently in Deuteronomy; "possession" of the land is interchangeable with "dispossession" of the inhabitants of the land and both depend upon Israel's obedience to the commands of Yahweh.

> All the commandments that I am commanding you today you shall be careful to do, that you may live and multiply, and go in and possess (*yrš*) the land which the Lord swore to give to your

---

2 Cf. M. Buber (1964:1097), "*Das ist nicht beiläufige Wiederholung, sondern die aus zahlreichen Stellen zu belegende phonetisch–rhythmische oder paronomastische Method der Bibel, ein Wort oder eine Wortfolge von einer besondern Wichtigkeit—sei es einer nur innerhalb dieses Textes, sei es einer über ihn hinaus—dem Hörer oder Leser einzuprägen.*"

forefathers (Deut 8:1, *NASV*).[3]

God gives the land to Israel and it possesses if it has kept the commandments.[4] Possessing the land is the culminating act of obedience to the commands of Yahweh. The opportunity to "possess" depends upon prior obedience to the commands, but the possessing is itself another act of obedience, also governed by commands.[5]

The evidence of Deuteronomy sheds a new light on Israel's behaviour after Judah's inexplicable inability to dispossess the inhabitants. Unlike Judah, who was ***unable*** to dispossess (*lōʾ yākᵉlû lᵉhôrîš*) the inhabitants, all subsequent failures are presented in the form of negated ***Hiphʿil*** verbs. In each case, Israel is responsible for not dispossessing the inhabitants.[6] Not once, however, does the narrator condemn Israel for any wrongdoing. Instead he simply presents the evidence which speaks for itself, just as in v. 19 he presents, without comment, an apparent instance of Yahweh's failure to hand the charioteers over to Judah. Throughout the narrator avoids simplistic momentary evaluations, steering instead, towards a comprehensive overview within which wrong-doing is apparent but understandable because we are given enough information and an objective stance from which to view it. The goal seems not to blame, a trivial and obvious game in any analysis of divine-human relations in the Bible, but to comprehend.

---

3 Cf. Deut 4:1, 5, 14, 22; 5:31–3; 6:1, 11, 17–18; 7:1–5; 8:1, 11; 11:2–8, 22–3, 29, 31–2; 12:1; 15:4; 16:20; 27:21; 30:18; also, immediately prior to Judge 1, in Josh 23:5–13 Joshua makes it clear that for Israel to continue possessing the land it must remain faithful to the terms and conditions of the covenant.

4 Deut 2:31; 3:12, 18, 20; 11:31; 12:29; 17:14; 19:1; 26:1; 30:5; 31:3; cf. Josh 1:11, 15; 18:3.

5 The parallel statements in Deut 31:3, 5 reveal the two–fold nature of "dispossession" as both blessing and duty:

Verse 3	Verse 5
1. Preparatory act of God:	
hûʾ-yašmîd ʾet-haggôyim hāʾēleh millᵉpāneyka	*ûnᵉtānām yhwh lipnêkem*
2. Israel's part:	
wîrištām	*waʿᵃśîtem lāhem kᵉkol-hammiṣwâ ʾᵃšer ṣiwwîtî ʾetkem*

6 Halpern (1988:135) agrees—"the failure was willful"—but misses the subsequent mitigation produced by the narrator himself (2:6–10).

The narrator does, nevertheless, reinforce a presumption of some wrong-doing on Israel's part by adding descriptions of eleven instances of Israelite fraternization with the enemy (vv. 7, 16, 21, 25–6, 27–30, 32, 33, 35) to the nine cases of failed dispossession. Once again the narrator depends on the reader's familiarity with Deuteronomy, which contains a strict command against consorting with the enemy during and after the conquest (7:2; cf. Exod 23:32). Linked as they are with the nine failures to dispossess the inhabitants, these frequent transgressions of the law lead the reader to the belief that following Joshua's death, for some unstated reason, Israel became increasingly disobedient to the prohibition against fraternization. There is some suggestion that the failure to dispossess and the fraternization may be a reaction to Yahweh's failure to give the charioteers of v. 19 over to Judah, but the narrator leaves it to the reader to make that causal connection; it is only a plausible hypothesis called forth by the lack of narratorial exposition. As with the explanation of Yahweh's aberrancy in v. 19, the reader is kept hanging until ch. 2 before he is given the narrator's authoritative exposition on Israel's reasons for transgressing these commandments. In the mean time, should the reader decide to act as judge and jury in condemnation of Israel's defection, the final reckoning provided by the narrator near the end of ch. 2 will only be more effective as a vehicle for convicting the self-righteous reader for judgement where understanding and compassion were (finally) elicited.

What the narrator has done in Judg 1 is to raise several questions about the post-Joshuan conquest without giving any explicit answers. He supplies the reader with descriptions of character action but withholds the evaluations that would allow the reader to draw any certain conclusions about the overall meaning of this narrative. It seems to be another story about how Israelite sin wrecks God's plans for his people, but then there is the muted suggestion that Yahweh, too, may have failed to fulfil his duties in v. 19. And why did he not ordain a successor to Joshua? Why are there any inhabitants remaining in the land for Israel to fraternize with at all? Didn't Yahweh promise Joshua complete success (Josh 1:3–5)? Didn't Joshua have complete success (Josh 21:43–45; 23:1)?

Judges 2

Yahweh's View (Judg 2:1–5)

The silence from within the narrative about these vexing issues is first broken *from within the story world* by a messenger from Yahweh (Judg 2:1). God is granted the first word on what has gone wrong in Judg 1. Although the messenger's words are directed to the Israelites in the story, the reader is also led, initially, to accept them as a valid assessment of the problem in Judg 1. Two things encourage the reader to adopt Yahweh's explanation. As a source of information Yahweh seems a priori to be the most reliable character in biblical narrative; he is, after all, God. Second there are no immediate contradictions from the narrator, who portrays Yahweh's message to Israel without any immediate comment on its soundness.

Yahweh's assessment of the situation in ch. 1 has two parts. First he mentions his act of benefaction on Israel's behalf; because Yahweh brought Israel up out of Egypt, Israel was obliged to obey the duties it accepted when it made a covenant with its benefactor (2:1–2). Yahweh points out that not only has he brought Israel out of Egypt, he has also brought the nation to the land that he had promised to the patriarchs. Having recalled his magnanimity to Israel's attention, Yahweh proceeds to contrast the nation's ungrateful response. The order of his itemized appraisal alludes to the formal features of the covenant; it shows that he regards Israel's actions in ch. 1 as a clear-cut case of covenantal misfeasance:

v. 1 the historical "prologue" establishing Israel's indebtedness.
v. 2a the stipulations, which Israel was supposed to obey as a proper response.
v. 2b Israel's transgression and disobedience.
v. 3 the lawful punishment invoked (cf. Num 33:55).[7]

From the narrator's description of the many instances of fraternization in ch. 1 it seems that Yahweh's denouncement is appropriate. Though the narrator has not described any

---

7 Allusions to the formal structure of the treaty format are frequent in the O.T. The example in Judg 2:1–3 shows how an author could summarize, or omit elements, or simply allude to the basis for the covenant in order to make his point, and yet still assume that his covenantal reference would be understood. Cf. McCarthy 1978:291.

specific instances of treaty making between Israel and the inhabitants or any cases of Israelite apostasy, the fact that Israel did not "dispossess" the inhabitants and sometimes made forced labourers of them shows that they have broken the spirit of the command that Yahweh cites, if not the letter (cf. Deut 7:2). The punishment for disobedience is the withdrawal of divine support in the conquest; because Israel refused its tasks of "dispossession" (*yrš*) and dissociation, Yahweh says he declines his—"I will not drive them out (*grš*) before you."[8]

Taken at face value Yahweh's appraisal of Israel's action seems accurate and his response appropriate. They had had ample warning; the withdrawal of divine support and the consequent assurance of an incomplete conquest are Israel's sole responsibility. Yahweh had done his part in the exodus and in the conquest thus far; Israel alone is to blame for the failure. The terms of the covenant and justice itself demand the punishment that Yahweh sets. The only thing that stops the reader from swallowing Yahweh's line is the implication, back in 1:19, that Yahweh may himself have had a contributory role to play in Israel's defection. Nevertheless the combination of the narrator's silence on that point, the compatibility of Yahweh's analysis and Israel's behaviour, and the well-established presumption in biblical literature that problems in the covenantal relationship are generally Israel's doing all dispose the reader to accept Yahweh's diagnosis of the past and to put the blame on Israel for the darkening of its future hopes. Such disposal is, however, a trap that will be sprung to catch the unwary reader in the grips of his own orthodox, ill-considered prejudices.

In response to Yahweh's announcement Israel weeps and offers sacrifice to Yahweh as a visible sign of contrition. Obviously the nation accepts the validity of Yahweh's claim and hopes to soften the judgement through its display. The narrator's description of the people's response goes further to strengthen the reader's belief that Israel is responsible for this catastrophe—if Israel accepts its own guilt, why should the reader question it? But the description of a weeping, sacrificing

8 The suitability of the requital appears in the light of two occurrences of the verb *grš* in the book of Exodus. In both Exod 23:30 and 34:11 Yahweh promises to "drive out" (*grš*) the inhabitants followed by a reminder that Israel must make no covenant with the inhabitants and must destroy their religious facilities.

Israel also establishes that the people, confronted by the covenantal reality of their behaviour, are contrite—they weep—and desire reconciliation—they sacrifice. The importance of their acts of contrition in the story of the post-Joshuan conquest only surfaces much later when the narrator begins his own analysis of the events following Joshua's death.

A More Complex Vision (Judg 2:6–23)

Scholarly readers have generally understood Judg 2:6–23 as a prolegomena to issues and questions that arise in subsequent episodes (up to ch. 17) of the book of Judges. The abstracted description of cycles of sin followed by punishment, repentance, and forgiveness has been read as an authoritative interpretation of the period of the Judges. The explanation: Israel sinned, was deservedly punished and then graciously pardoned by Yahweh, a chain of events that goes through a monotonous series of repetitions.[9] The declining course that Israelite history and fortunes take is determined and powered by Israelite sin. The divine response is seen and supposedly presented as the just response called forth by the terms of the covenantal framework within which all behaviour must be judged. The gracious pardon that completes each phase does not materially change the deteriorating course; the former only allows the latter to continue in the same direction. That God's grace does not call forth a directional change in Israel's history shows that the nation's sin is the mainspring powering the movement.

A question raised by this accepted reading of the deuteronomistic narrative is the motivation for Israel's sudden and decisive turn towards evil. If we accept the statement in Judg 2:7 about Israel's unsullied fidelity to Yahweh during the lifetime of Joshua and for an indeterminate period thereafter, why do the people suddenly decide to behave in a contrary way?

Israel's conversion to the life of an outlaw is not simply fickle; the rest of the book describes a strong tendency for Israel to act in contravention of the covenantal agreement whenever one of Yahweh's agents is not exerting a contrary

---

9 E.g. Moore (1895:62–3), who cites Vatke's *Biblische Theologie* (1835), and Boling (1975:75–6), who echoes Moore's reiteration of Vatke's assessment.

influence. Left to its own devices Israel seems to ignore the restrictions that the covenant imposed. If the nation's behaviour were arbitrary and unwitting, statistical probability would lead us to expect an even division between actions falling inside and outside the covenantally allowable limits. Furthermore the transition from generation to generation should result, even by chance alone, in some generations that are faithful to Yahweh and some that are not; the transition in Judg 2:10 would be evidence enough for that. Could such a united will to sin, a whole nation through numerous generations, be the result of chance or arbitrary choice? Or taking a different perspective, would these post-Joshuan generations continue to take the punishment and abuse of being handed over to their enemies just to carry on the tradition begun by the new generation of Judg 2:10? Such behaviour goes beyond any notion of inherited sin; it would be, rather, inherited stupidity.

On the accepted reading of the deuteronomistic aetiology of the nation's downfall, then, the deuteronomist has offered only a simplistic explanation. If he was indeed trying to write history, his "historical" answer to the question, "Why did the nation fall?", falls a little short of the mark. Even judged by the more flexible standards of verisimilitude the deuteronomist's generations of uniformly sinful Israelites are unbelievable characters whose years of begging for punishment make even the labels "stupid" or "idiotic" a strain on credulity. For historians, believers, or ordinary readers of biblical narrative, this reading of the narrative makes the deuteronomistic explanation of Israel's downfall hard to accept.[10]

If, on the other hand, one returns to Judg 2:6–23 without preconceptions about what the deuteronomistic narrative is all about and considers this piece of narratorial exposition in relation to the preceding context of Judg 1 and the book of Joshua—and this is the natural way to read, that is, in the order that the work is presented to the reader—a very different understanding of Judges 2 emerges.

---

10 Cf. G.E. Wright (with R.G. Boling) 1982:52–5. Wright nevertheless offers a historicist's apology for the deuteronomist's supposed views.

Seeing Is Believing(Judg 2:6–10)

Judg 2:6 is another example of resumptive repetition.[11] With this literary convention the narrator indicates that he is breaking off the temporal consecution to return to a prior moment, already described once in Josh 24:28–31. In Judg 2:6 the narrator does not return to the moment when Joshua dismissed the people to relate a series of actions and events that simply parallel those of Judg 1; rather, he turns back the clock to describe actions, circumstances, and facts that have a direct bearing on the understanding and evaluation of Israel's deeds in Judg 1.[12]

The narrator even hints right at the beginning that this literary backtracking will deal with the problem of Israel's failure to "possess" (*yrš*) the land. Comparing the repetition in Judg 2:6 with the original (Josh 24:28), a significant modification appears. In the Judges passage the narrator adds, "And the children of Israel went ... to possess (*lārešet*) the land." Given the repeated emphasis on the verb *yrš* in Judg 1 and the fact that this addition stands out from the otherwise verbatim repetition, the reader can scarcely miss the narrator's hint that what follows contains important information on the failed conquest.

The hint at an explanation of the failure to "dispossess" (*yrš*) the inhabitants of the land is also the beginning of the explanation itself. Here, in v. 6, we see Israel actively going out (*wayyēlᵉkû*) to take possession of the land when Joshua dismisses them. Obviously there is a drastic change between Israel's attitude at the time of their commission (Judg 2:6 = Josh 24:28) and the final result in Judg 1:21–36. Judg 1 records the consequences (cf. Webb 1987:107), Judg 2:1–3 records the

---

11 Cf. Polzin (1980:151), "temporal shift"; B. Webb (1987:106), "flashback." Resumptive repetition is described by H.M. Wiener 1929; cf. K. Kuhl 1952:1–11; S. Talmon 1978:12–25; B.O. Long 1987:385–99. See above, "These Nations That Remain," n. 32.

The narrator indicates that he is returning to a previous point in narrative time by repeating, more or less verbatim, a sentence or a number of sentences from his prior narration. In Judg 2:6–9 he repeats Josh 24:28–31. The order of the repetition is slightly changed as are some words, but there is no doubt that the narrator is resuming his narration at that point in narrative time (cf. R. Polzin (1980:151)). What follows the repeated items is information about events, actions, and states of affairs that are temporally parallel to those described after Josh 24:31; that is, Judg 2:10–22 parallels Josh 24:31 – Judg 1.

12 Cf. Webb (1987:106), "... the focus is shifted by the speech from the strategic [the concern of ch. 1] to the religious implications of this."

divine reaction, and Judg 2:6–23 is the narrator's analytical review.

The narrator continues his description of Israel's fidelity to its God in v. 7. He has altered the order in which these observations occur in Joshua 24 so that the reiteration here begins with two statements about Israel's fidelity (vv. 6–7). The re-ordering emphasizes Israel's faithfulness to Yahweh while Joshua was yet alive. Verse 7 diverges in two places from the text of Josh 24:31: instead of, "and Israel served Yahweh," we read, "And the people served Yahweh"; instead of the elders "who knew the whole work of Yahweh," we read about the elders "who saw the whole great work of Yahweh." It is difficult to interpret the first variation—it may indicate an effort to emphasize the collective unity of obedience—but the implication of the second is clear. Israel continued to serve Yahweh so long as someone who had actually *seen* "all the great work" that Yahweh had done for Israel. There can be no doubt that the great work referred to here is the complex of acts that Yahweh performed on Israel's behalf as he led them out of the land of bondage to the promised land (cf. Moore 1895:65; Boling 1975:71). As Israel recognized, it was because of these acts of benefaction, which Yahweh did "before our very eyes" (*waʾᵃšer ʿāśâ leʿênênû*) that Israel owed covenantal allegiance to Yahweh (Josh 24:17). The people's sense of obligation was the direct product of their own unmediated personal experience.

The problem with this covenant based on divine works is intimated by Moses in Deut 11. Moses enjoins Israel to obey the commands, pointing out that his audience was witness to the very deeds that require Israel's obedience as a response (*kî ʿênêkem hārōʾōt ʾet-kol-maʿᵃśēh*, 11:7). In contrast to those who have seen the "great work" of Yahweh and so must obey, Moses sets their sons who have neither known (*lōʾ yādeʿû*) nor seen (*lōʾ rāʾû*) the instruction (*mûsar*) of Yahweh, that is the lesson of obedience to be learned from the exodus (11:2, cf. Deut 31:13).[13]

The implication of the contrast, which hinges on whether or not one has seen (*rʾh*) the exodus, is that those who have not

---

13 In Deut 11:2 the word *mûsar* is defined by the following series of parallel objective and subordinate relative clauses that are governed by the same verbs, *rʾh* and *ydʿ*, that govern *mûsar*. The "instruction of the Lord," therefore, is the exodus that he performed for Israel's benefit. The event teaches those who experienced the event to be obedient to their benefactor.

seen cannot be expected to obey the covenant. They have not got the first-hand experiential basis that, together with the "great work," constrains Israelites to be faithful to the covenant. Though Moses' concern is rhetorical in Deut 11, so that he does not go into these problematic implications, the problem is there and it surfaces after Joshua's death, as the narrator shows in Judg 2:6–11.[14]

Having assured his reader that Israel was loyal to Yahweh during the lifetime of Joshua and during the lifetime of any others who had witnessed the exodus,[15] the narrator is free to introduce his analysis of the problem posed by the death of the witnesses without worrying that the reader's prejudice will prevent him from understanding the objective explanation. Contrary to the universal human tendency to blame humanity's problems in its relationship with God on humanity's perversity, and contrary to the derivative biblical tendency to blame Israel for all the ills of the theocracy, this narrator has a neutral, historiographic explanation.[16]

---

14 In Deut 29, another chapter devoted to Moses' efforts to promote obedience to the covenant, Moses begins and ends his speech with reference to the compulsive nature of witnessing the events.

> And he said to them, "*You* have seen (*ʾattem rᵉʾîtem*) everything that Yhwh did before your eyes (*lᵉʿênêkem*) in the land of Egypt … the great trials that your eyes saw (*ʾᵃšer rāʾû ʿêneykā*), the signs and those great miracles" (Deut 29:1–2).
>
> "The hidden things belong to Yhwh, our God, but the things revealed (*hanniglōt*) are ours and our sons forever, to do all the words of this law" (Deut 29:28).

Here Moses notes the essential psychological precondition for covenantal obedience even as he tries to extend it "forever" to subsequent, non–witnessing generations as well. Heavy emphasis falls on the sense obligation produced by the exodus experience. Those who lived through it could never forget their obligation, at least in theory. As Yahweh's preacher, however, Moses tries also to involve subsequent generations in the obligation, even though they could never be a real party to it.

15 According to Num 14:29, survivors of the wilderness period who had witnessed the exodus would have been limited to Joshua, Caleb, and anyone under the age of 20 years at the time the punishment was announced to the generation of grumblers. The point of the Numbers' story is to highlight another of these discontinuities (cf. D.T. Olson 1985), the difficulties of which attracted a variety of responses in Israelite thought and religion. But the continuity of those who have witnessed the exodus events is not broken until the event described in Judg 2:10.

16 By historiographic I do not mean that the explanation is historical and even less that it is intended to be so, though it might be both things. I only mean to point out that this explanation of a covenantal crisis is unusual in tracing the problem to a chain of events and a set of circumstances that are beyond the control of all the characters. Halpern's reading of authorial intent—"to construe history" (1988:138)—is plausible but beyond verification. One could as easily believe that the author uses verisimilitude and objectivity as a cloak for self-conscious partisan views. After all, even an overt statement of historiographic intent such as the opening of the gospel of Luke can be read with

Following his relocation of the material in v. 7 the narrator returns, in v. 8, to follow the order of narration in Josh 24. Joshua dies and is buried in his territorial inheritance. Verses 8–9 are word for word repetitions of Josh 24:29–30, so that the new material in v. 10 stands out as an additional piece of information. In v. 10 the narrator describes the generation gap that contributes to the breakdown of the relationship between Yahweh and Israel. The narrator focuses attention on one specific feature of the break in the continuity of generations, namely the new generation's ignorance of Yahweh and "the work" (*hammaᶜᵃśeh*) for which Israel owed its obedience to Yahweh.[17]

Like the sons of Moses' audience in Deut 11:2, the new generation was not yet born when Yahweh laid the foundation for the covenant. Without the guidance of Joshua and his generation, who had actually experience "the work" that compelled obedience to the covenantal obligations, Israel was in Moses' words, "sheep without a shepherd" (Num 27:17). And though the narrator does not offer any explicit accusations, and so avoids any pious reader's charge of blasphemy, it is quite apparent from the conspicuous absence of a replacement for Joshua (cf. Judg 1:1) that if anyone is to be held responsible for the waywardness of the ignorant new generation, it must be Yahweh. He alone might have bridged the gap between those who saw the exodus and those who did not.[18] In fact, not even

suspicion (see, for example, the discussion in J.A. Fitzmyer (1981:14–18). Either way, reading authorial motivations from a text is a tricky business; wagering either way, in a case such as the book of Judges, is pointless since we haven't the means to call the bet.

17 Boling (1975:72) suggests that the verb *ydᶜ*, "to know," means "to acknowledge," referring to an article by H. Huffmon (*BASOR* 181 (1966) 31–37) and to Josh 24:31 in support. Josh 24:31 is itself ambiguous with regard to the meaning of *ydᶜ*, but it becomes unequivocal in the light of Deut 11:2. There the verb *ydᶜ* is hendiadically linked with *rʾh*, both verbs taking the exodus events as object (vv. 2–6; see also n. 15). The sons of Deut 11:2 are not presented as individuals refusing to acknowledge the exodus events. Rather they, in contrast to the preceding generation (v. 7), simply have not had the opportunity to know or see "the instruction of the Lord." The parallel with the new generation of Judg 2:10 is unmistakeable and the ambiguity of Josh 24:31 is resolved. Those elders have known the exodus event and consequently, they are obedient to Yahweh (cf. Judg 2:7, which parallels Josh 24:31 but replaces *ydᶜ* with *rʾh*; and Moore (1895:67)).

18 In fact it was Yahweh's decision to punish the complaining generation of exodus–experienced Israelites that created the slender connection in the form of Joshua and Caleb, the sole adult survivors of the exodus to enter the land (Deut 1:35–9; cf. Num 14:23–4, 29–31; cf. above n. 13). Yahweh was well aware of the limited experience of the generation that he was installing to replace the exodus–experienced generation. When Yahweh made his decision, the generation to go in and "possess" (*yrš*) the land knew

God is blamed for this tragedy because even his divine resources are not enough to resolve the difficulty, which is human mortality. After Joshua and his generation, there simply were no experienced Israelites to choose as a bridge: all were dead. That is the essential fact indicated by the narrator in Judg 2:10. Consequently the blame for the post-Joshuan failure falls neither on man or God. The narrator points no accusing finger; he simply states the "historical" facts which speak for themselves. There is no blame for mortality, at least not in this narrative. Israel and God and their covenantal relationship fall to the mercies of death itself.

The excusable ignorance of the new generation is paralleled by that of the sons in Deut 11:2. There is yet another parallel by which the narrator supplies the reader with covert commentary about this new generation of Israelites. As many commentators have noted, the description of Israel in v. 10 is very close to that of the new Pharaoh in Exod 1:8.[19] The similarity of circumstances attending the rise of the new generation and the new Pharaoh are also highlighted by a phraseological parallel between v. 10 and Exod 1:6:

Judg 2:8, 10	*Exod 1:6, 8*
The passing of the old generation:	
wayyāmot yᵉhôšuaʿ wᵉgam kol-haddôr hahûʾ neʾespû ʾel-ᵃbôtāyw	*wayyāmot yôsēp wᵉkol-ʾeḥāyw wᵉkol haddôr hahûʾ*
The rise of the new:	
wayyāqom dôr ʾaḥēr ʾaḥᵃrêhem ʾᵃšer lōʾ-yādᵉʿû ʾet-yhwh wᵉgam ʾet-hammaʿᵃśeh ʾᵃšer ʿāśâ lᵉyiśrāʾēl	*wayyāqom melek-ḥādāš ʿal-miṣrāyim ʾăser lōʾ-yādaʿ ʾet-yôsēp*

The primary implication of these remarkable linkages is that the succeeding generation of Israel has become like the new

---

neither good nor evil (Deut 1:39), let alone the exodus events. So though it was the constant grumbling of the Israelites that provoked Yahweh to limit the numbers of exodus-experienced Israelites to get into the land, it was his action that shaved the connecting link between generations to a dangerously thin strand.

19 E.g. Moore (1895:67). Th. C. Vriezen (1967:334–44) did a detailed form-critical study of the parallel.

Pharaoh, both arising in an identical manner after the passing of a former generation of Israelites. Because he did not know Yahweh (*lōʾ yādaʿtî ʾet-yhwh*, Exod 5:2), Pharaoh refused to obey Yahweh (Exod 5:2). Similarly the new Israelites, not knowing Yahweh, do evil in his sight and forsake him (Judg 2:11–12). Only when the Pharaoh had witnessed Yahweh's miracles did he finally capitulate (Exod 12:32). The new generation of Israelites in v. 10 stands in the same place where the new Pharaoh stood before he received the "instruction of the lord" (*mūsar yhwh*), the miraculous plagues on his country. Having become like that Pharaoh through no fault of its own, the new generation has brought the covenant relationship full circle. If Yahweh wishes to continue his affiliation with this nation he will have to re-educate them in much the same manner that he educated their forefathers in the exodus from Egypt. The narrator's allusive equation points the way to the only solution to the problem of the generation gap: a new exodus. Paradoxically, Israel must take the roles of both the Pharaoh and Israel in this new course of instruction. That paradox takes form in Judg 2:14–22.

Apostasy in God's Eyes (Judg 2:11–12)

The narrator's retrospective analysis does not end with the climactic statement in v. 10; having explained why the post-Joshuan Israelites neglected their duties in ch. 1, he adds a further description of their transgression that sheds light on Yahweh's own response in 2:1–3. In addition to their failures of ch. 1 the Israelites had apostatized. There are two features of this revelation that warrant comment. First the narrator does present an evaluation of the Israelite apostasy—it is "the evil" (*hāraʿ*)—but he immediately ascribes that judgement to a character in the story—"in the sight of Yahweh." In view of his fictional role as the strict historical objectivist, analyzing and describing the course of Israel's history, especially in this section of resumed repetition, the narrator's self-dissociation from the moral evaluation of Israel's conduct is not surprising.

The second point of interest in vv. 11–12 is the connection of the apostasy with the patriarchs (and the promises made to them) and the exodus, as though the apostasy were a direct repudiation of those vital elements of Israelite identity. Yet for the narrator and his reader the apostasy, in the face of the patriarchal legacy and the exodus as it were, is far from flagrant ingratitude. The mitigation is manifest in v. 10. Rather, it is Yahweh who finds the deed "evil" and a source of vexation (*wayyakʿisû*, v. 12). And so the narrator's additional explanation within the confines of the resumption in vv. 6–12 also explains Yahweh's response in 2:1–3; vv. 11–12 are temporally prior, in terms of story time, to 2:1–3 and they reveal the hitherto unrevealed source of Yahweh's discontent at that point. The causal and temporal connection is underlined when we read vv. 11–12 prior to vv. 1–3, which is the temporally correct consecution. The topical points of contact are as follows:

- apostasy
- God of fathers forsaken
- exodus deliverer forsaken
- (Yahweh provoked) (vv. 11–12)
- exodus recollected as reminder of obligation
- fulfilled promise to fathers recollected
- commandment against apostasy recollected
- (punishment) (vv. 1–3)

The introverted parallelism of the issues supports the narrator's paralleling of 1:1–2:3 and 2:4–12 by means of the device of resumptive repetition. It also clarifies why Israel became increasingly wayward after the Joshuan generation's death and why Yahweh accused Israel of fraternization and apostasy, a sin that the reader had not seen portrayed until the resumptive explanation in 2:11–12.

An important feature of this exposition is the narrator's steadfast abstention from evaluation of either God's or Israel's behaviour. Instead of saying Israel did a wicked thing by fraternizing and apostatizing the narrator explains that the nation did not know Yahweh or the exodus. And when Yahweh punishes this ignorant generation, which could not justly be held responsible for its sin, the narrator shows how Yahweh's unfairness is the product of his own ignorance, willful or otherwise, of the new generation's ignorance about himself and the exodus. Though the exodus is a counterweight in this causal engine—not knowing it, Israel sins, and demanding recognition of it, Yahweh punishes—the crankshaft upon which the pistons of sin and punishment turn is the lack of continuity in the Mosaic office of mediator. And while the reader might have blamed Yahweh for failing to provide a successor to Joshua back when he read 1:1, the fact of the matter is that there simply were no candidates for the job.

Nobody who had witnessed the exodus remained to tell of it. Both man and God face the same problem; it is a simple fact of the limiting conditions within which the covenantal relationship operates. There is, therefore, no condemnation for the characters in this narrative.

Apostasy Recompensed (Judg 2:13–14)

The narrator signals the close of his resumptive analysis by opening a new section with yet another resumptive repetition. By repeating, more or less verbatim, in vv. 13–14a what he said in vv. 11–12 the narrator indicates that he is taking up his narration at the point where he left off, namely Israel's apostasy (v. 11 = v. 13) and Yahweh's consequent anger (v. 12b = the response in vv. 1–3 = v. 14). As with his first employment of this literary device, the narrator uses the resumption to move the tale forward by adding new pieces of information. In v. 13 the reader is told that the Ashtaroth were also among the recipients of Israel's apostatic attentions.

In v. 13 the narrative is branched out into yet another temporal parallelism. In vv. 11–12 the narrator outlined the next generation's behaviour following the death of Joshua and his exodus experienced peers. Now in vv. 13–14 the narrator parallels Yahweh's meticulously measured punitive response. Once again the device of resumptive repetition alerts the reader to the parallelism:

v. 11b	*wayyaʿabdû*	*ʾet-habbᵉʿālîm*
v. 12	*wayyaʿazbû*	*ʾet-yhwh*
v. 13a	*wayyaʿazbû*	*ʾet-yhwh*
v. 13b	*wayyaʿabdû*	*labbaʿal wᵉlāʿaštārôt*

The introverted parallelism of the resumption would disturb no reader familiar with this convention (cf. Webb 1987:109). it is used here, perhaps, because neither time elapses nor event intervenes between the two sections; there is no narrative interlude to distract the reader from understanding and appreciating the device. Yahweh's response matches Israel's apostasy blow for blow:

Israel	*Yahweh*
1. Forsakes the God of their fathers, who led them out of Egypt to follow gods of the people round about them (*s^e bîbôtêhem*, v. 12).	1. Gives Israel over to their plunderers; sells them to their enemies round about (*missābîb*, v. 14).
2. Bow themselves down to the gods of these surrounding peoples (v. 12).	2. (Sells Israel) so that they can no longer stand before their enemies (v. 14).

He may not know everything he is supposed to know or act on everything that he does know, but Yahweh cannot be faulted for his sense of justice.[20]

The Cycle Begins: (Judg 2:15–19)

The narrator extends this particular vision of Israel and Yahweh's post-Joshuan interaction on into the indefinite future—which is, nevertheless, past for the narrator and his reader—with a description of the cycle that this engine of sin and punishment goes through. In vv. 15–19 we see how the Israelite generation become like Pharaoh is alternately beaten and then enticed to acknowledge Yahweh as its sovereign. First the covenantal blessing of not having an enemy capable of standing before Israel (cf. Deut 7:24; 11:25) is reversed; Israel stands beyond the pale of covenantal blessing and its enemies enjoy the role Israel formerly held (cf. Josh 1:5; 10:8; 23:9). Then, having devastated the wayward generation, Yahweh attempts to win its allegiance by raising up judges to deliver Israel from its plunderers. The plan is modeled on the once successful pattern of the exodus from Egypt, as is made clear by the common vocabulary shared by v. 18 and Exod 2:24, 3:9, and 6:5.

But the plan is not successful. Even though there is a divinely appointed judge to lead Israel, the post-Joshuan

20 Though Webb (1987:110) sees the balanced approach, as replicated in the literary structure of the passage, he wrongly intimates that this reflects the narrator's alignment with Yahweh's perspective—"Considerable pains are taken here to depict Yahweh's angry response as controlled *and fully justified*" (my emphasis). The narrator retains his usual semblance of objectivity; Yahweh's response, however measured, is his and his alone.

generation continues to behave as it did before the new judge was appointed (v. 17, cf. v. 12). The narrator reminds the reader of the reason for this apparent pigheadedness on Israel's part in v. 19, which parallels v. 17. Though he says, in v. 17, that Israel would not listen to the judges, in v. 19 the narrator states that after the death of the judge Israel would return to its apostasy. The parallel with the response to Joshua's death reminds the reader that the whole cycle was brought on by the death of the last leader-witness to the exodus event. Dead (v. 10) or alive (v. 17) there is nobody who can make Israel return to its loyalty to Yahweh after the death of Joshua. And there is no new exodus-like experience that can convince Israel that it owes allegiance to Yahweh. What vv. 14–19 depict is the problem that Yahweh will face for the duration of Israelite history as he tries to regain Israel's allegiance again and again. Without an experiential knowledge of Yahweh through the exodus event, or at least the leadership of such an experienced person, Israel exhibits no sense of obligation to Yahweh and he can do nothing to force it. The predicament of Judges 2 looks forward in anticipation of the new exodus promised by Isaiah and Ezekiel.

God Only Knows (Judg 2:20–22)

Finally the narrator returns to that point in story time from which he developed his overview in vv. 14–19. Once more the device of resumptive repetition is brought into play with the first sentence of v. 20 repeating, verbatim, the first sentence of v. 14. In vv. 20–22 the reader is granted a privileged access to a divine monologue. Speaking to no one but himself,[21] Yahweh reveals his most personal, unguarded thoughts on the subject of Israel's apostasy. Since the monologue occurs at the same point in story time as v. 14, which occurs at just after v. 13, and since v. 13 occurs at the same time as vv. 11–12a, which occur just before Yahweh makes his public announcement in vv. 1–3, this monologue must occur, in story time, almost simultaneously with the public version that the messenger proclaims. These linkages by means of resumed repetitions are confirmed by the

---

21 Cf. Webb (1987:113), "Yahweh no longer speaks *to* the Israelites ... but *about* them. ... Perhaps it [the divine monologue] is meant for the ears of the heavenly court ..." Whatever the merit of the hypothesis of a divine court—none plays a role in this narrative—Webb's response registers the oddity of this fascinating revelation into an unguarded moment in the divine mind.

parallelism of subject matter and language between the monologue and the proclamation.

In private Yahweh's views have a slightly different emphasis, from those he makes known to Israel:

Monologue	*Proclamation*
v. 20 This nation has transgressed my covenant which I commanded their fathers ...	v. 1 ... and brought you to the land that promised to your fathers and I said will never break my covenant with you.
v. 20 They do not hearken to my voice.	v. 2 But you do not hearken to my voice. (Preceded by a reminder of the prohibitions against fraternization and the injun–ction to destroy foreign cults.)
v. 21 So I will no longer dispossess any man before them from the nations that Joshua left when he died.	v. 3 So I will not drive them out before you and they will be waylayers to you and their gods will be snares for you.

The primary difference appears in the first part. In public, to the people, Yahweh emphasizes how he has fulfilled his obligations and how he planned to continue to do so; but to himself what is foremost is Israel's transgression of injunctions laid upon the fathers. Both monologue and proclamation reveal Yahweh's belief that his past acts of benefaction on Israel's behalf, especially the exodus upon which the covenant was based, still oblige Israel to obey his commands. In the proclamation he presents a reasoned defence of his view; in the monologue he simply states his personal reaction—'Israel is reneging on the debt it owes me.' As the reader reads Yahweh's monologue, hearing the argument for the second time, but now knowing that the exodus can no longer support Yahweh's clam, the pathos in his personal appraisal emerges. At the same time, the reader is reminded of the basic problem that plagues the subsequent course of Israelite history. Yahweh (and his associates) demands obedience because of the exodus but the post-Joshuan generations "do not know Yahweh or the work that he did for Israel" (v. 10).

There is little difference between monologue and proclamation in the second part: in public Yahweh reminds Israel of the commands that they have broken; for himself, of course, he needs no reminder.

The primary difference in the third part is what Yahweh says about the people who are not evacuated to make room for Israel. To Israel, God points out that these foreign peoples will be a source of irritation and confusion. The proclamation concentrates on the future consequences of the partial conquest. In private, however, Yahweh characterizes these remaining peoples with regards to the past; they are "the nations that Joshua left."

This characterization might seem matter of fact and uninteresting—the presence of unconquered inhabitants in the land after Joshua's death is a common feature of chs. 1 and 2. But when we remember that the presence of the inhabitants after Joshua's death is a problem in Judg 1, Yahweh's private characterization begins to shed a revealing light on his own part in the failed conquest and on his part in the failure of the covenantal relationship. Here, at last, the narrator reveals to his reader, via an uninvited audition into Yahweh's most private musings, the logic of the the partial conquest.

Yahweh's punishment on the renegade Israelites is to refuse to drive out any more of the original inhabitants. But how is this possible if, as he maintains, Yahweh has thus far fulfilled his own covenantal obligation, which included his duty to displace these people (e.g. Exod 33:2; 34:11; Deut 4:38; 6:19)? The answer that Yahweh wills to believe is that Joshua left those nations. Consequently the availability of the remaining nations as a punishment is due to Joshua's failure to remove them; Yahweh is merely taking advantage of an unforseen but, for his purposes, propitious state of affairs. The monologue also makes known Yahweh's purpose for leaving the nations in the land; they are to be a test for Israel, which has demonstrated its potential for treachery (1; 2:11–13), to see if Israel will reform (v. 22).

Yahweh, so it seems, wishes to believe that the continuing presence of the former inhabitants in the promised land is solely due to Joshua's leaving them and Israel's sin. As far as he is concerned, his hands are clean. But are they? From the narrator's comment in v. 23, the answer would seem to be no, they are not.

Full Disclosure (Judg 2:23)

In the first sentence of v. 23 the narrator points to the ironic result of Yahweh's decision. The result of the conquest, supposedly achieved near the end of Joshua's lifetime was for Israel to have rest (*nûaḥ*) from its enemies (e.g. Deut 3:20; 12:10; 15:19; Josh 1:13; 21:44; 22:4; 23:1). But now, in Judg 2:23, the narrator states that Yahweh gave the same "rest" (*wayyannaḥ*) to the remaining nations, who are not quickly expelled. instead they are to remain to afflict the generation that has become like the Pharaoh of Exodus. Now Yahweh too joins Israel in taking on a role and attitude diametrically opposed to the role each played in the exodus and Sinai narrative.

In the second sentence of v. 23 the narrator privileges the reader with a fascinating revelation about the real reason for the continued presence of the original inhabitants in the promised land: they are there because Yahweh did not give them into Joshua's hand. The narrator's explanation is in stark and measured contrast to Yahweh's own explanation in v. 21. Yahweh says, "I will no longer drive out anyone"; the narrator says, "Yahweh gave them rest." Yahweh says, "Joshua left them when he died"; the narrator says, "he did not give them into Joshua's hand." The revelation shows a world upside-down: the nations in Israel's place, Israel in theirs, and a God who seems more human than divine.

The obvious question of why Yahweh did not allow Joshua to complete the conquest—a question that nags the reader through the book of Joshua and into the book of Judges—is finally addressed by the narratorial exposition in v. 23. Coming just after Yahweh's monologue, in which his plans to use the nations as a test are exposed, the exposition reveals motive; means and opportunity are obviously available to the divine character.[22] But this explanation of the incomplete conquest

---

[22] Halpern (1988:134) also sees the nations that remain as the focal point of the narrator's explanation for the course Israel's history takes, but he does not study the narrative carefully enough to discern the subtle exposition provided by the carefully structured parallels and voicing. Halpern also sees the nations that are left as a means to "keep Israel honest" and give them knowledge of Yahweh's power through warfare (1988:135). Such may, in fact, have been one of Yahweh's underlying motivations. But there was only one exodus and it alone, as all of the references back to it as key covenantal motivator show, could elicit obedience. When Israel finally perceived that

requires that Yahweh knew aforehand that Israel would break his commands and refuse to walk in the way of Yahweh, as their fathers hand.

While it is almost certain that Yahweh did not know, either before or after Joshua's death, why Israel broke fealty, it is certain that he did know that Israel would abandon him once the promised land was reached. The so-called Song of Moses (Deut 32) is preceded by an introduction in which Yahweh reveals his foreknowledge and presents the song as a testimony against Israel (Deut 31:16–21). The narrator's exposition in Judg 2:23, carefully postponed just after the monologue in vv. 21–22, suggests that Yahweh withheld complete success because he held back one final trump card with which to force Israel's hand at obedience.

Ironically it is the continued presence of the foreign nations in the land that creates the opportunity for the new generation to fraternize and apostasize. Here too, Yahweh is credited with some responsibility for the breakdown in Judg 1. The test of the continuing presence of the foreign nations has been in place and operating during the entire conquest. Failure came to Israel only when the exodus connection was broken.

The narratorial explanation in v. 23 reaches all the way back into the book of Joshua to explain the anomaly of the partial conquest. The questions of why the nations persisted in the land even after the death of Joshua (cf. Josh 1), of why the narrator is so sarcastic in the latter part of the book of Joshua, and of why Joshua is forced into self-contradiction in his retirement speech are all answered here in Judg 2:23.[23]

Though the revelation might seem, in itself, to be a strong condemnation of Yahweh, the absence of any explicit narratorial evaluation is characteristic of this narrator. He does not tell us that Yahweh was ultimately responsible for leading Israel into temptation by not letting Joshua clear the foreign nations out, just as he did not criticize Yahweh for leaving Israel without a leader after Joshua's death. Conversely, neither does he excuse Yahweh, saying that the maintenance of the foreign

---

the exodus event could no longer serve such a role it turned toward the notion of a new exodus on the same grand experiential scale.

23 Polzin's reading of Judg 2:23 (1980:147), that it refers "to the previous generation's inability under Joshua to drive out the nations," contradicts the plain meaning of the sentence, in which Yahweh is the subject of the two verbs, the grammatical subject of which allows the foreign nations to stay.

nations was a necessary evil forced on Yahweh because of the hereditary decadence of his human covenantal partners. The reader is free to draw such deductions; in fact the silence on these critical theological matters from within the narrative begs such conceptual exploration from the reader. What it does not permit, is any dogmatic blaming or exoneration; the truth of the matter, now that the narrator has revealed it, are much too complex for that.

In sum, Judg 1–2 is an intricate analysis of a crucial transition in the Israel's political history. The author employs a scrupulously objective narrator who does not blame either Israel or God for the failure in the conquest and the covenant.[24] Instead he shows how both Israel and Yahweh contributed to the breakdown.

Ultimately the fate of covenant and conquest is determined more by circumstances beyond the characters' control than by anything that they do. God's failure to provide a replacement for Joshua is a result of the simple fact that none is available. Israel's post-Joshuan sin is the result of its ignorance about Yahweh and the exodus. God's decision to leave some inhabitants unconquered is the product of his foreknowledge that Israel would go astray and the obvious need to have a means of coercing the wayward nation.

Instead of a simplistic aetiology of Israel's catastrophic history this narrator presents a subtle historiographical review that reveals some of the problems that attend the covenant of God and Israel. No solutions to the problems are offered explicitly or even implied by the thematic lines of the story. Understanding and insight, not evaluation or exhortation, are the destinations to which the reader is brought by this narrator; his story offers theology, not theodicy.

---

24 I do not mean to suggest that either the narrator or the narrative, nor especially the author was truly objective. The appearance of objectivity is manipulated as a literary device by which the author presents his interpretation, which may well be thoroughly partisan.

CHAPTER 4

A KING IN WHOM THERE IS NO PROFIT

But do not turn aside after vanity, which cannot profit or deliver, for such things are vain (1 Samuel 12:21).

1 Samuel 12 is a chapter in the deuteronomistic narrative devoted entirely to a report of a high-powered speech and demonstration that Samuel gives to Israel. Samuel, despite his undisguised opposition to the idea (1 Sam 8:6, 10–18, 22;[1] 10:17–19a), has just installed Saul as Israel's new king. Samuel has two primary rhetorical aims for his speech: exoneration, first for himself and his family (vv. 1–5) and (only) then for God (vv. 6–12), and castigation, a barrage of it loosed on his Israelite audience for daring to ask for a king. Though the monarchy is now a matter of fact and its existence cannot be undone—God, after all, designed and approved it—Samuel aims to reduce its importance in the eyes of the people and to re-assert their dependence on Yahweh's and his own good auspices. His initial concern over the request for a king (8:6) revealed his own personal reaction; as God correctly pointed out, the request was not simply an attempt to replace the office of the judge with the office of a king, but that is what Samuel took it for.[2] His speech in ch. 12 shows that Samuel is still bothered by the implications for his own employment, though now he is also aware of the anti-theocratic aim.

---

1 Samuel is so opposed to the idea that he even goes so far as to disobey Yahweh's direct order to install a king in ch. 8 (Eslinger 1985:269–73).

2 "Samuel's personal dislike for the request receives additional emphasis in the narrator's description of what specifically bothered Samuel about it: 'The matter displeased Samuel because (*ka'ăšer*) they said, "Give us a king to judge us".' Point-

In his foundational study, Martin Noth suggested that 1 Sam 12 is a systematic deuteronomistic editorial outline of prospects for the new monarchy set against the historical background of Israel's relationship with Yahweh (1967:5, 10, 47). This view has met with broad agreement (e.g. Boecker 1969:63f; Miller 1974:161; Fritz 1976:360; Mettinger 1976:82; Veijola 1977:83; Mayes 1978:10 n. 40). In this conventional view, 1 Sam 12 is one of those places where, "Dtr brings forward the leading personages with a speech, long or short, which looks forward and backward in an attempt to interpret the course of events, and draws the relevant practical conclusions about what people should do" (Noth 1981:5).

From a literary point of view there is an obvious weakness in such a view of Samuel's speech in its complete neglect of the narrative's ontology and voice structure. The all-important matter of the narrator's stance toward the character utterances that he reports is not examined; it is, rather, assumed that the author/narrator must agree with Samuel's sentiments else he would not report them. There is, in such a view, no theoretical foundation for distinguishing between the views of characters with whom the narrator disagrees and those with whom he does agree. The unexpressed basis for such distinctions is a simple, "seat of the pants" belief about what the author/narrator would have believed and so about what he would and would not have found himself in agreement with.[3] Obviously such assumptions will prejudice the reading of the narrative precisely in the direction of the underlying assumptions about what the narrator ought to have believed. Little wonder, then, that the majority of readings of the deuteronomistic narratives find in it a conventional Judeo-Christian theology, an ideology whose assumptions form the common framework of biblical studies past and present. What else could the pious authors and redactors of the Bible have believed?[4]

---

edly left out is the crucial information about the covenantal implication of the request (*kekol-haggôyim*) in order to show that Samuel's interest is, at this point, focused on the personal import of the request .... Samuel is concerned *only* with the administrative switch from judge to king" (Eslinger 1985:260).

3 Cf. G.E. Gerbrandt (1986:40) on the predeterminative role that assumptions about Dtr's political attitudes have played in portraits of the narrative and its politics.

4 The commentary of R.W. Klein (1983) is the most recent example of such a response. His straightforward acceptance of Samuel's rhetoric, including the factual errors that Samuel makes—the late dating of the request for a king to the Ammonite crisis—lead him to the assertion that ch. 12 was written by a different person than ch. 11 (p.

Given the narratorial situation from which the narrator describes Samuel's speech—it is the situation of an external, unconditioned narrator—a safer assumption, with regard to the voice and views of the author (redactor, editor), would be that there will be a marked difference between the views of a character within the story world and those of the narrator (the voice of the author and supposed deuteronomistic editor) outside it. The narrative's ontology puts them worlds apart with an incredible discrepancy in the degree of involvement in the events of concern and an even larger disparity between their comprehension of those same events. This is an assumption that should have been built up and established by observation of the narratorial situation that prevails in 1 Samuel up to this point and which continues on through the rest of the book and the entire narrative. It is, in fact, the narrative situation that has been used from the book of Deuteronomy on. It is an assumption that should be all that much more common and reliable when the character utterance in question comes from a character who evaluates persons or events in which he is deeply involved, as Samuel is here.

What is it about Samuel's speech that has led scholarly readers to hear in it the voice of the author? Given the common perception that the deuteronomistic narrative is an assessment of Israel's history for purposes of writing a theodicy, one would expect a large quantity of narratorial exposition—evaluative discourse from the narrator/editor— or an especially striking character in it. If the narrative had such an evaluative perspective one would expect to hear frequently from the narrator who wants to interpret and evaluate the events and characters he describes. But on the relative scales of evaluative prominence, the sheer quantity of evaluative language, 1 Sam 12 does not score that high. Hannah's prayer, in 1 Sam 2, is far more prominent. Yet scholarly readers have only seen the former, and not the latter, as an outlet of narratorial exposition. So it cannot be for sheer mass of evaluative language that 1 Sam 12 is identified as a critical passage for comprehending the narrative's evaluative stance. Quantity of evaluation, though important, is alone not enough to get scholars to characterize an inset

---

113). Any reader operating under such an assumption cannot see that Samuel's rhetoric leaves the facts behind, a price that Samuel's tendentious revisionism must and can well afford to pay—he has plenty of backing from his thundering God (vv. 17–19)—to rewrite the history of the monarchic affair.

evaluative discourse as narratorial exposition. Evaluative discourse in the deuteronomistic narrative must, it seems, also have a certain quality, assumed theological propensity, or tone to be labeled as redactional exposition from the deuteronomist(s).

One such quality, shared in some measure by several of the speeches that Noth and others have identified as key orations through which the author/editor is supposed to speak, is the retrospective or prospective character of the evaluation.[5] A prominent character will evaluate events and characters, among whom Israel is usually included, with a view to summarizing the consequences of past actions and the projections for the future. Samuel's speech in 1 Sam 12 is exemplary in this respect. His broad review of Israel's covenantal history with God (vv. 7–12) is designed to prove that the request for a king was unwarranted and indefensible in terms of covenantal categories. God had, according to Samuel, done everything that he had promised and more than everything that could be expected of him. Israel's request for a king to replace the divine monarch was (v. 12) characteristic of its history of wanton covenantal behaviour (vv. 8–9). Perhaps more than anything else in the speech it has been this sweeping historical review that has led scholarly readers to the belief that here the historically oriented editor(s) of the narrative speak in their own native tongue. History, so the assumption goes, is written by history writers.

Another quality of Samuel's speech that has supported biblical scholars' beliefs about the telling characteristics of the first, is the pious remonstrative theological tone of this speech. Many scholarly readers share the fundamental assumption that the deuteronomistic narrative was written to explain Israel's fate by impugning Israel for covenantal infidelity. It would be difficult for the such readers not to believe that the author speaks through, or at least supports Samuel's speech when its tone so obviously supports such a view. By way of contrast, Hannah's song, though loaded with strong evaluative piety, lacks the parenetic tone and the historical sweep that readers have identified as the supposed hallmarks of this (these) author(s) / redactor(s).

---

5 Weinfeld (1972:12) has noted that the orations frequently occur on the occasion of a change in leadership, at the end of "an historical period." The situation explains the retrospective and prospective character of the oration.

If Samuel's speech and its theological sentiments are not those of the narrator one would expect that there would be some indication of the discrepancy in the narrative context. Given that the rhetorical floor is, more or less, monopolized by Samuel in ch. 12, one would look to the immediate context of the chapter, especially its preceding context which is so important to Samuel's remarks in ch. 12, for evidence of the narrator's agreement or difference from Samuel's view. In any piece of narrative it is the description of events, the overall narrative description, that most accurately reflects the opinions of its creator and it is against this backdrop of authorial perspective that character evaluations must be measured (cf. "These Nation That Remain", n. 3). It is especially important to look at how any given character evaluation fits in, in agreement or otherwise, with the author's explicitly established voice in the narrative, the voice of the narrator. If Samuel's views are not identical with those of the narrator, as the ontology of the narrative in which the speech is set would lead us to believe, then there is every reason to reject the view that this supposed key speech reflects the views of the narrator and his narrative as a whole.

Verse 1

Samuel's opening remarks imply, for the benefit of his Israelite audience in the story world, that the constitutionally limited monarchy of Saul is "everything they asked for" (*lᵉkōl ʾᵃšer-ʾᵃmartem*). They also remind the reader of Samuel's initial worries that the people were rejecting him (8:6), fears that were only allayed when Yahweh told him to "listen to the people, to *everything* they say" (*lᵉkol-ʾᵃšer-yōʾmᵉrû ʾēleykā*, 8:7). Samuel's implication is a blatant effort to gloss over the difference between the monarchy that is Saul's and the one that the people originally asked for.[6] The people, or at least some of them, have already shown that they know they have not gotten what they asked for (10:26–27; Eslinger 1985:355–8).

For the reader, to whom the narrator has granted the privileged insight into Samuel's heart (8:6) and the privileged audition of the conversation between Samuel and God on the matter of the request (8:7–9, 22), Samuel's quotation of Yahweh's words betray a shallow effort at self-reassurance in the face of

6 On the difference between these two kinds of monarchy see M. Buber (1956:128).

the now firmly established monarchy, which at first seemed to him to be a threat to his own office. His quotation of Yahweh seems a reminder that the request for a king was a direct threat against Yahweh's position, not his own. Later in his speech Samuel's rhetoric will reveal how much Samuel's own position with respect to the monarchy is a still major concern to him. He will go to great lengths to ensure that his preeminence is understood and accepted by the people (vv. 16–25).

Supplementing such self-assurance is Samuel's obvious effort to assert continuing authority over Israel after the acceptance of King Saul. The first thing Samuel does after the renewal is to claim credit for the creation of the monarchy—"I made a king over you." As Dhorme observes, he seems to quote Yahweh (8:22) here, but makes one small alteration (1910:100). Yahweh said, "Make a king *for* them (*lāhem*)," but Samuel says "I made a king *over* you (*ᶜalêkem*)." The emphasis, from Samuel's point of view, falls on Israel's subordination to the king and on the authority of Samuel who places the king over them. Samuel's character and personal involvement are revealed both by what he says and by what he changes when he quotes Yahweh (cf. Alter 1981:70, 97). Both quotations—from 8:7 and 22—betray his on-going apprehension about the security of his position as theocratic mediator, a reasonable anxiety in view of the *de facto* status of the new monarchy.

Verse 2

Marking the change of topic with the introductory particle ***wᵉᶜattâ***, Samuel switches to another concern, separate from the particulars of the monarchic installation (cf. Veijola 1977:92f; Vannoy 1978:11 n. 5). He points out, using the demonstrative particle "***hinnēh***" (cf. Labuschagne 1973:74), that the path to monarchy has been followed to its conclusion: "And now, take note. The king walks before you. As for me, I am old and grey. My sons are with you and I have walked before you from my youth up to this very day." He states the result of the request for a king, touching only lightly, and noncommittally at that, on the request's immediate catalyst, the state of affairs in his own family .

The presentational order of Samuel's recollections actually reverses the historical order—history being determined, under the conventions within which this narrative operates, by the prior reportage of the external unconditioned narrator—of the events he describes. Hidden between the king who now walks before the people and Samuel who has walked before them, in Samuel's version, is his own painful recollection of the request for a king.[7] The emphatic juxtaposition of himself and the king as the past and present "walkers" (cf. Langlamet 1978:289 n.12; Vannoy 1978:11; McCarter 1980:212f) reveals Samuel's continuing anxiety that the king might yet replace him, or somehow encroach on his monopoly of walking before the people.

Samuel presents the historical recapitulation in v. 2 as a matter-of-fact reiteration of events, especially those concerning his sons.[8] From the reader's perspective, the combination of Samuel's concern over his own post-monarchic status (cf. vv. 1, 3–5) and the soft-selling tone in the representation of the sons in v. 2 comes across as the biased opinion of a father trying to maintain family honour in the community (cf. Gunn 1981:64). Closer examination from this angle uncovers Samuel's defensive tactics.

Samuel's reference to his sons is surrounded by two self-references, both begun with the words "as for me" (*waʾănî*), both serving as contrasts between himself and the new king. He sandwiches his sons between two protective self-references: his own honour is beyond reproach, or so he thinks, and should cover the petty misdoings of his sons. Samuel's structural rhetoric, in which he cloaks the misdeeds of his sons, aims to suggest that it was his own behaviour that sparked the explanation for the request. What were his failings? He is old and grey from a lifetime of serving ("walking before") the people! The old prophet's insinuation is that the request for a king is grudging and thankless. He sees everything in the light of his long career, which he believes is uncompromised (cf. vv. 3–5).

Samuel's sons, moreover, are yet "with the people," a phrase with which he proposes a camaraderie between sons and people, unseemly to all that have witnessed the doings of ch. 8. The sons are even yoked with the people's new king by means of parallel introductions with the particle ***hinnēh***; they are included along with the king, joint heirs to his heritage and gifts to the Is-

---

7 Cf. (Gunn 1980:64), "Again we are given a hint of Samuel's sense of personal rejection ..."

8 Weiser is an example of a reader taken in by Samuel's rhetoric. He goes so far as to suggest that the author of 12:2 seems neither to presuppose nor even to be aware of the sins of the sons as they are described in 8:3, mistaking Samuel's disingenuity for literary disparity (1962:80; cf. Veijola 1977:95; Crüsemann 1978:61f).

raelites. Samuel's sons are the chink in his armour. He tries to hide their failings behind his own merits, dwelling on the latter at the cost of a gnawing silence on the former. More than such seemingly matter-of-fact reference to his crooked sons this master rhetorician will not make. It is more than enough to have exposed even this small patch of flesh (cf. Gunn 1981:64).

For the reader, who has seen the request for a king develop precisely for reasons of Samuel's sons' behaviour and the manner in which that seems to portend another disaster for Israel (cf. 1 Sam 4; Eslinger 1985:254–5), Samuel's rhetoric is false and empty. For the Israelites in the story world, one would think it could hardly be otherwise, though Samuel leaves them no breach into which they might interject an objection.

Verse 3

Once more Samuel redirects his audience's attention to himself, again with the third repetition of the demonstrative particle, "*hinnî*." Having glossed the real source of provocation for the people's request for a king, Samuel continues his revisionist's recollection of the conditions surrounding the inauguration of the monarchy—a recollection having little in common with the reality of conditions authoritatively described in 8:1–3. In v. 3, he lays the groundwork for an presentation of his own perspective as Israel's incumbent theocratic mediator. The people have had their say about him and his sons; their request has been partially granted. Now he sets about the task of re-framing the entire sequence from his own "orthodox" perspective.

The people are called to testify against Samuel if he has has committed any of the crimes that he lists. As part of his rhetorical strategy, Samuel includes "the anointed" as one of the unquestionable judges of his own blameless career. This accomplishes two things, both important for Samuel's immediate purposes.[9]

---

9 Samuel's specification that testimony be made before Yahweh's anointed as well as before Yahweh has sometimes been considered a secondary expansion, largely on the basis of grammatical considerations in v. 5 (e.g. Veijola 1977:94; Crüsemann 1978:63). B. Birch (1967:67) and McCarter (1980:213) also regard the positive sounding reference to the king as Yahweh's "anointed" as incongruent with the remainder of the speech, which is uniformly critical of the monarchy (McCarter; cf. Veijola 1977:94) and in which this title is not used (Birch; McCarter).

The title is, however, a functional element in Samuel's rhetoric. As for the supposed anti-monarchic stance of the speech, Samuel is not so much critical of the new monar-

First, Samuel implies that the law and legal practises of Israel still remain a theocratic province, even when it is the theocratic mediator that is being tried. Though they now have a king (requested, we are reminded by v. 2, on account of corrupt judges [cf. 8:3–5]) he is by definition "*Yahweh's* anointed" and not an alternative or separate authority (cf. Gutbrod 1956:87). The new king has not altered the judicial hierarchy in Israel, even though it had been expected that a king would do so by judging Israel "like all the nations" (8:5). The "anointed" stands with Yahweh.

Second, Samuel puts himself on trial with the confident expectation of being cleared. He risks little, given the contrived charges he offers against himself. Samuel recruits the new king, his supposed replacement, as a witness to the fact that such replacement was uncalled for. The king is made to witness to his own redundancy in Israel's legal system and testimony to Samuel's own virtue is wrung from both the new king and the hapless people who dared try to replace him.

The injustices that Samuel denies stand in obvious contrast to the provocative misdeeds of Samuel's sons (Boecker 1969:70; Crüsemann 1978:64f; Vannoy 1978:12 n.12a) but more particularly to the manner of the king in 8:11–8 (Budde 1902:78; Schulz 1919:168; Boecker 1969:70; Veijola 1977:95; Crüsemann 1978:64f; Vannoy 1978:16). Unlike the hypothetical acquisitive king that he had warned about in 8:11–8, Samuel claims that he has taken (*lqḥ*) no livestock and has wronged or abused no one. And unlike his sons, Samuel has taken no bribes.[10] Samuel sets up the questions, all relating to the abuse of power by a mediator, an abuse of which he knows himself innocent. No one every questioned his integrity, that was not the issue. But the real issue in the request for a king is not what Samuel wants to make an issue of here. Should his audience admit his innocence, his rhetorical ploy will trap them in the implication that nothing was

---

chy, which is recognized as God–given (v. 13), as he is of the reasons and attitudes displayed by Israel in its bid for political change (cf. McCarthy 1974:102).

10 The contrasts between Samuel and his sons do not consist of the verbal linkages so often used when contrasts and comparisons are made in biblical narrative (cf. Crüsemann 1978:64f). This vagueness is purposeful; Samuel is trying to prove that the request for a king was unwarranted. He does so, in part, by pointing to his own uprightness in the office of judge while avoiding any reference to the wrongdoing of his sons. Samuel is significantly more specific in his allusions to 8:11–18; he does not take (*lqḥ*) livestock, but the king does (8:16f; cf. Boecker 1969:70; Vannoy 1978:16).

wrong in the pre-monarchic offices of theocratic mediation. Samuel is careful to avoid mentioning any of the specific misdeeds of his sons, neither does he ask his audience about their opinion of his sons' performance in office.

Verse 4

The people answer with a complete acquittal for Samuel on all charges. They may not agree with his representations of the sources of their discontent, but that is not the question that Samuel poses to them. They are caught in his rhetoric.[11] Needless to say, the fact that they are rhetorically coerced into accepting Samuel's revisionism does not mean that the narrator (author/redactor) favours Samuel's position and so shows their capitulation. Far from it. His presentation of the scene, though very restrained in terms of explicit evaluation of any character, highlights the forced, bombastic nature of Samuel's effort.

Verse 5

Samuel capitalizes on his exoneration by reversing the roles of Yahweh and his anointed. Instead of witnessing claims of injustice against Samuel, they now stand as witnesses against the people (*bākem*) that Samuel's hands are clean (*lōʾ mᵉṣāʾtem bᵉyādî mᵉʾûmâ*). Though the aim of this public exoneration is not immediately apparent, the fact that Samuel enlists the support of Yahweh and his anointed is reason enough to suspect some further action or claim (cf. Weiser 1962:84). Since it is Samuel's activities as theocratic mediator that are cleared of suspicion, it is a good bet that any further claims will have direct bearing on the question of his partial or complete replacement by the new king (cf. Keil & Delitzsch 1880:116).

The final sentence in v. 5 is problematic on account of the unidentified subject of the verb "*wayyōʾmer*." Who says "witness"? A common solution to the problem is to follow versional readings in which the verb is plural (e.g. Smith 1899:84f; Stoebe 1973:232). The people, who express their assent to Samuel's legal claim with the single word "witness," are thus

---

11 Cf. Gunn (1981:64), "The people without further ado bear witness loyally to Samuel's personal integrity—and thereby appear to put themselves in the wrong. If they have nothing against Samuel why then should they have demanded a king? The prophet now moves easily into a broader attack."

subject of the verb. Whether one follows the plural of the versions or simply understands Israel as a unit to be subject of the singular (so Keil & Delitzsch 1880:116; cf. Vannoy 1978:18 n. 23), the context seems to demand that the subject be the people, who agree to Samuel's claim: in v. 3, Samuel calls for testimony against himself; in v. 4, the people reply (3rd pl. of *ʾmr* without specified subject), clearing him; in v. 5a, Samuel replies (3rd sing. of *ʾmr* without specified subject) with a citation of witnesses; in v. 5b, the people reply (3rd sing. of *ʾmr* without specified subject) in agreement; and, finally, in v. 6, Samuel replies (3rd sing. of *ʾmr* with specified subject, necessary for clarity on account of the singular in v. 5b) with a comment on the people's agreement. Both the alternating dialogue and the explicit subject of v. 6 suggest that the unidentified subject of v. 5b is the people. The fact that Samuel is specified as the new subject of *ʾmr* in v. 6 also suggests that the verb in v. 5b should be left in the singular: if it were plural, there would be no need to re-identify Samuel as the respondent, since he is the subject of all third person singular utterances in ch. 12 up to v. 5b.[12]

Verse 6

Inextricably linked to the difficulties in v. 5 is Samuel's description of Yahweh in v. 6.[13] Attempts to regularize the syntax of the verb have either followed 𝔊 and inserted *ʿēd* before *yhwh* (e.g. Thenius 1864:47), or inserted the pronoun *hûʾ* between the words *yhwh* and *ʾăšer* (e.g. Ehrlich 1910:207). The syntactic difficulty of v. 6 can also be alleviated (as Keil & Delitzsch suggest [1880:116]) without alteration on the basis of versions by careful attention to context.

Identifying Samuel's as the speaker in v. 6 clarifies any confusion produced by the last sentence in v. 5. His answer in-

12 McCarter offers the interesting suggestion that the last sentence in v. 5 and the first in v. 6 are conflate variants, "And he said 'Witness.' And Samuel said to the people, 'Witness,' ..." (restoring a second *ʿd* after *hʿm* with 𝔊) (1980:210). He opts for a conglomerate reading using elements from both variants—"'Yahweh is witness,' he said ..." (1980:208, 210), a solution that removes the difficulty by creating a new version. The new version also creates a new problem for the reader, who must now supply the connection between Samuel's discourse on Yahweh's past history and the preceding dialogue. If the reader follows MT, the connection is supplied by the logic of the alternating dialogue between Samuel and the people.

13 Cf. Buber (1956:157f) who eliminates both vv. 5 and 6 as, respectively, insertion and gloss on insertion.

trudes on the people's response (*wayyōʾmer ʿēd*, v. 5), so that his first word, *yhwh*, follows immediately after the word *ʿēd* voiced by the people in v. 5. Samuel interrupts, in v. 6, to give an impromptu definition of who it is that is called and accepted as witness to Samuel's integrity.[14] As Ehrlich noted against a correction on the basis of 𝔊, nothing has dropped out of MT before the word *yhwh* (1910:207). "He (they) said, "Witness," and Samuel said to the people, "(Is) Yahweh ...". " Samuel's response, in v. 6 functions, in part, as a concluding answer to vv. 1–5.[15]

Samuel reminds the people that the witness to his integrity as mediator is Yahweh. More specifically he points out that his divine witness is the same Yahweh who "made" Moses and Aaron and brought the fathers from the land of Egypt—biographical information important to Yahweh's status as witness.[16] What were Moses and Aaron? The answer, provided by the allusion in the second biographical detail, is that they were Israel's theocratic mediators throughout the fundamental event of the exodus. The syntax of v. 6 sets the act of making of Moses and Aaron as a parallel to the act of bringing of the fathers up from the land of Egypt:

yhwh ʾᵃšer ʿāśâ ʾet-mōšeh wᵉʾet-ʾahᵃrōn
waʾᵃšer heʿᵉlâ ʾet-ʾᵃbōtêkem mēʾereṣ miṣrāyim

The witness to Samuel's integrity is Yahweh, creator of the offices of theocratic representatives in the exodus and "maker" of Moses and Aaron, the archetypal mediators. Samuel's credentials as an upright mediator are, in this rhetorical light, immaculate: testified to by the people, and witnessed by

---

14 In contrast to Keil and Delitzsch, who suggest only that "the context itself is sufficient to show that the expression "is witness" is understood" (1880:116), I would maintain that Samuel's interruption incorporates the last word of v. 5, '*ʿed*,' into his own sentence, and hence that nothing needs to be presumed. In other words,Samuel interrupts to finish that last sentence of v. 5 with his own conclusion, thus shaping the people's admission to suit his own purposes before they have a chance to change the direction in which he wishes to go.

15 Against Smith (1899:85); Ehrlich (1910:207); Birch (1976:65); Veijola (1977:94f); Vannoy (1978:21-3); McCarter (1980:214), who all read v. 6 exclusively as an introduction to vv. 7–12.

16 Some, on the other hand, have regarded this information, especially the peculiar note that Yahweh "established" [*ʿāśâ*] Moses and Aaron as justifiable grounds for excising at least v. 6b as a secondary intrusion; e.g. Buber 1956:157f; Noth 1967:59 n.3; Boecker 1969:71; Stoebe 1973:237; Veijola 1977:94; McCarthy 1978:207, "a gloss as in v. 8?"). Keil & Delitzsch suggest that the expression "he made Moses and Aaron," means "to make a person what he is to be" (1880:116; cf. Driver 1913:92).

Yahweh. Vannoy notes that the verb *ʿśh* in the phrase, "who made (*ʿśh*) ...," are intended to bring out a particular emphasis (1978:23 nn. 39f). He observes that the same verb is used in v. 7 with reference to the *ṣidqôt yhwh*, "Yahweh's acts of justification."[17] *ʿśh* also occurs in 11:13 with Yahweh as subject: "Yahweh has made deliverance" (*ʿāśâ-yhwh tᵉšûʿâ*). Placing all three occurrences together, it seems that Samuel, following Saul's use of *ʿśh* in 11:13, places Moses and Aaron in the same category as "deliverance" and "acts of justification." All are things "made" (*ʿśh*) by Yahweh for Israel's benefit when in need. The witness to Samuel's integrity as mediator is none other than the God who first created that position for Israel's benefit.

The political evolution mapped out by Samuel highlights the common ingratiousness that pollutes the atmosphere of this king's succession to a position previously occupied by the theocratic mediator alone. The people have moved to replace the covenantal mediator, whose office is ranked alongside Yahweh's deliverance and saving deeds, with a king. Moreover, they have done so while openly admitting Samuel's rectitude. This grave injustice amounts to a rejection of Yahweh's unwarranted graciousness. If Samuel's audience accepts his claims, and it seems bound to do so by its testimony to his integrity,[18]

---

17 According to W. Eichrodt, the *ṣidqôt yhwh* are Yahweh's military victories on Israel's behalf, which, as proofs of Yahweh's righteousness, suggests why they are labeled *ṣdq* (1961 vol. 1:242).

Zimmerli touches on a more appropriate understanding of Yahweh's *ṣdq* with respect to Yahweh's relationship with Israel. "When the Old Testament speaks of "Yahweh's righteousness" it means rather the social bond existing between him and his people and Yahweh's actions based on this bond" (1978:142). With respect to Yahweh's *ṣidqôt* in Judg 5:11 and 1 Sam 12:7, both in a context of recitations of Yahweh's military acts on Israel's behalf, it would appear that these acts are called *ṣidqôt* because they justify Yahweh's covenantal claim on Israel. Yahweh's *ṣidqôt* are those actions that justify (or make right, and hence "righteous") Yahweh's status as Israel's political leader, the divine king. "Yahweh is acclaimed as king in the light of the victories [*ṣidqôt yhwh*] which he and his armies have wrought ..." (P.D. Miller 1973:84).

18 Of course I speak of Samuel's rhetoric and presentation, not the narrator's. Even the audience within the story world would only be compelled to admit Samuel's argument if they allowed Samuel's suggestion that the request for a king was partly or wholly entailed by his own performance as mediator. That the narrator does not share Samuel's perspective is evident from his authoritative presentation of the problem in 8:1–3. The fact that Samuel's audience seems to accept his views is explained by the combination of Samuel's overbearing rhetoric—they can hardly get in a word edgewise (v. 5)—and their characteristic docility. Samuel's rhetoric not withstanding, their admission of his innocence does not, according to the preceding events described by the narrator, extend to cover the sins of his sons.

the request for the monarchy appears unbelievably wanton. The reasons for the pains that Samuel takes to persuade Israel that the request was not legitimate, even though the monarchy is already in place, are only revealed later in his oration.

Just because v. 6 functions as a conclusion for vv. 1–5 does not mean that it does not also serve as an introduction to vv. 7ff. Verse 6 introduces the topics of the archetypal mediators Moses and Aaron and the exodus event with which these figures are associated.[19] Samuel's brief recollection of the origins of his office in v. 6 is a turning point at which he shifts from the vindication of his own performance in office to a historical retrospect covering the entire line of theocratic mediators. Having obtained a public acknowledgement of his personal integrity in office, he moves on to defend the office itself. He begins already in v. 6 with his recollection of the exodus, Israel's birth story as a nation, and the provision of mediators whose important role was known by all Israelites (cf. Vannoy 1978:21). These memories are aimed at reminding Samuel's audience of a time and place when the mediator was of irreplaceable benefit to Israel, as Yahweh worked through Moses and Aaron to bring Israel up out of Egypt.

Verse 7

Samuel marks a shift to a new topic in Israel's political affairs beginning, once again, with the introductory expression *w*^{e}*ᶜattâ*, "so now," so employed at three places in his presentation (vv. 2, 7, 16; cf. Muilenburg 1959:361–63; 1968:171 n. 2; Veijola 1977:92f; Vannoy 1977:11 n. 5, 24f). He proposes to review Yahweh's past performance.

Like the preceding section introduced by *w*^{e}*ᶜattâ* (vv. 2–5 [6]), vv. 7–12 stand in relationship to v. 1, which gives the basic

19 Boecker argues that the references to Moses and Aaron in v. 6 (and v. 8) are conspicuous and without contextual mooring (1969:71; cf. Veijola 1977:85). But Samuel has already shown great concern for the office of mediator in vv. 1–5 and v. 6 also bears on that topic. Samuel continues in the same vein as he traces both the benefits and the lineage of mediators from the paradigmatic Moses and Aaron down to himself (vv. 6–11). To deny the rhetorical logic of the connection between Moses and Aaron and Samuel's remarks on Yahweh and his beneficial mediators one must ignore the syntactic parallels between the descriptions of Moses and Aaron (v. 8) and the other judges (vv. 10–12). Both form and content speak against the elimination of Moses and Aaron from Samuel's speech.

datum to which all of Samuel's reviews are related. In summary form the relationship is:

v. 1 Samuel said, "I have listened to everything you said and set a king over you ...

vv. 2–5 (6) "And now," as for Samuel's conduct.

vv. (6) 7–12 "And now," as for Yahweh's conduct.

In contrast to his own case, where he called on the people to testify against him before Yahweh and his anointed (v. 3), Samuel expresses his desire to dispute with Israel, before Yahweh, all the acts of justification that Yahweh has done for them and their fathers. The pious prophet takes up the sword as defender of the faith.[20]

Samuel is bold about his bias concerning Yahweh's irreproachability: he does not broach even the possibility, let alone the prior actuality (Eslinger 1985:161–87), that Yahweh has ever acted in a way detrimental to Israel's well-being. As in Samuel's non-committal reference to his sons' performance in v. 2, the obvious catalyst for the people's request for a king (8:1–3), Samuel carefully skirts the real reasons for Israel's request for a king. It was not for Yahweh's performance of any such acts of deliverance as Samuel presents here that Israel requested a king to replace him. Rather it was, as the narrator clearly shows in the preceding context, on account of Yahweh's failure to perform these same covenantally assured acts (cf. ch. 4; Eslinger 1985:161–86). But Samuel's rhetorical purpose is formal vindication for himself and for Yahweh, not an impartial review of faults. Viewed in such a light, his rhetorical revisionism is, so long as he is able to sustain it, effective. But the reader must be careful, or so it seems given the reading history of this chapter, not to be taken unawares.

Verse 7 begins a section in ch. 12 that seems to have been modeled on the literary forms of covenant documents (e.g. Muilenburg 1959:360–5; Baltzer 1964:73–6; Stoebe 1973:237; Birch 1976:68–70; McCarthy 1978:213–21; Vannoy 1978; McCarter 1980:220f). Samuel's use of this literary genre is not slavish; he bends it to suit his immediate purpose.[21] Samuel

---

20 Presentations of the two sides to the insoluble grammatical dispute over v. 7 may be found in Driver 1913:92f (favouring 𝔊) and Vannoy 1978:24-6 (favouring MT). Cf. König 1897:267 §288k.

21 Cf. B. Birch (1976:68), "We do not have a covenant or a treaty document but a speech by Samuel that shows the influence of the covenant form." Caution in the matter of perceiving formal literary patterns need not be taken to the extreme of denying

draws attention to the seriousness and the covenantal dimensions of the business at hand with a formal call to assembly (*w*[e]*ʿattâ hityaṣṣ*[e]*bû*), an expression that Muilenburg identified as a common feature of covenantal formulations (1959:361, 363, cf. Baltzer 1964:74 n. 1; McCarthy 1978:207; Vannoy 1978:24f). Samuel had last called such a formal assembly in 10:19 (also *w*[e]*ʿattâ hityaṣṣ*[e]*bû*) when he installed Saul under the guise of a replacement for Yahweh. The re-assembly in 12:7 recalls the assembly of 10:19 and its mood. At both gatherings Yahweh's history of beneficent acts on Israel's behalf is invoked as a demonstration of the senselessness of the request for a human king (cf. Boecker 1969:74).

Verse 8

Samuel begins his recitation, naturally enough, with the exodus. In Samuel's version it is Israel, represented here by Jacob, that gets itself into trouble in Egypt. Yahweh has no involvement in the migration to Egypt, only in the positive events leading out of it (contrast Gen 15:13). Because Samuel wants to focus on the series of interactions between Yahweh and Israel he dispenses with the Egyptian oppression and moves directly from Israel's entrance into Egypt to Israel's cry to Yahweh for

---

such affiliations unless exact replication of all elements is present. Veijola, for example, denies the validity of reading ch. 12 in the light of covenantal forms, "because here it is neither a matter of a "covenant" nor a monarchic constitution" (1977:95 n.79). McCarthy rightly stresses the covenantal aspects of Samuel's presentation, even though there is no strict adherence to any idealized covenant form (1978:218).

Cf. A. Fowler (1982:38), "The literary genre, moreover, is a type of a special sort. When we assign a work to a generic type, we do not suppose that all its characteristic traits need be shared by every other embodiment of the type. In particular, new works in the genre may contribute additional characteristics. In this way a literary genre changes with time, so that its boundaries cannot be defined by any single set of characteristics such as would determine a class. The matter of change we shall return to later. Here the notion of type is introduced to emphasize that genres have to do with identifying and communicating rather than with defining and classifying. We identify the genre to interpret the exemplar."

One might add that the story as developed up to this point requires neither a new covenant nor a covenant renewal. The fact that the people have accepted Saul and renewed the kingdom by making Saul king before Yahweh (11:14f) is a sufficient expression of their willingness to remain under and within the theocracy. Covenantal relationship at the end of ch. 11—Yahweh having given a conditional monarchy and the people having accepted it—is restored and in no need of repair. If Samuel presents his argument in ch. 12 in covenantal terms, we must read this in terms of his own peculiar rhetorical purpose, which is to re-define the whole escapade from the theocratic perspective.

help.[22] Yahweh's immediate response to the fathers' cries for help is to send Moses and Aaron, his mediators, to their aid. It is Moses and Aaron—not Yahweh—who bring (*wayyōṣîʾû*) the fathers out of Egypt and settle them (*wayyōšibûm*) in the land of Israel (literally "this place").

In this paradigmatic instance Yahweh accomplishes his justifying acts through the agency of his mediators; the only verb of which Yahweh is subject is *wayyišlaḥ*, "he sent Moses and Aaron."[23] The mediator, suggests Samuel, is essential to success, working more even than Yahweh. Samuel, never one to be too subtle, brings the implications of the paradigm up to date with his description of the place where the fathers of his audience were settled: it is "this place" (*bammāqôm hazzeh*), the very place where he and the people stand and ponder the apparent replacement of the last mediator by a king.[24] By invoking Yahweh, maker of Moses and Aaron, as witness to his integrity as mediator, and reminding his audience that it was Yahweh who sent Moses and Aaron as mediators of the paradigmatic exodus, Samuel manages to suggest that by replacing him the people are

---

22 The omission of the oppression is more elegantly (and agnostically) explained as a rhetorical feature than as a textual error (against Driver 1913:93) or an alternate tradition about the exodus.

23 Several scholars have objected to the plural verbs in v. 8 and have accordingly followed 𝔊 in which the verbs 'brought out' (𝔊A, Targum, Vulgate) and 'settled' (𝔊BL, Syriac, Vulgate) are singular, with Yahweh understood as subject (e.g. Stoebe 1973:233 and scholars cited by him; McCarter 1980:210). As Driver puts it, the plural verb 'they settled' "expresses just what Moses and Aaron did not do" (1913:93).

Underlying the text–critical judgement is an exegetical presupposition that Samuel's presentation of the exodus and settlement stories should agree, or be made to agree with the presentations in the Pentateuch and Joshua. It is equally possible, however, that the plurals of 𝔊 are the product of the same harmonistic presuppositions that lead modern scholars to prefer the versional readings.

The alternative path is to consider the singular verbs as meaningful, important and integral to the context of Samuel's rehearsal of Yahweh's "acts of justification."

Ehrlich recognizes the validity of the plurals in MT, but short–circuits the interpretation of the verb numbers by shifting to tradition history. "The received text is probably correct here, but it presupposed an older tradition that did not have Joshua as Moses' successor" (1910:207).

24 Veijola's use of the words *bammaqôm hazzeh* to draw redactional conclusions about ch. 12 suffers from inattention to the contextual utility of Samuel's choice of words. The expression might, indeed, be "one of the inconspicuous dtr terms that allow dtr rhetoric its timeliness and broad interpretational application because of the minimal concreteness of their content" (Veijola 1977:86). Before we resort to such second order explanations and their great complexity it is required of all readers, historical–critical not excluded, to explore the possibility of a local literary context in which the discourse makes some sense.

disrupting Yahweh's self-justifying mechanism of salvation and deliverance. If the divinely appointed mediators Moses and Aaron brought "your fathers" to "this place," why replace their successor to whose untarnished record you have just testified before Yahweh?

Verse 9

Yahweh arranges for his people to be brought out of Egypt. Israel expresses its gratitude by forgetting him! In Samuel's historical concatenation Israel is allowed only an unequivocal thanklessness in response to Yahweh's beneficence. To "forget" Yahweh is to destroy the relationship between Israel and Yahweh (McCarthy 1978:219f). This aspect of Israel's forgetfulness is highlighted by Samuel, who says, "They forgot Yahweh, their God ...." Samuel draws the contrast between Yahweh and Israel with bold strokes that pay for an unambiguously dark view of Israel with the coin of obvious inaccuracy, especially in the light of recent events. Yahweh seeks to build a relationship between himself and Israel and is, therefore, good; Israel's forgetfulness is destructive of Yahweh's efforts and Israel is, therefore, bad. The problem, of course, is that it had been Yahweh who had appeared to forget Israel for a time, not Israel (Buber 1956:118; Eslinger 1985:230–1). And Israel's request for a king was not forgetfulness, but remembrance of Yahweh's previous actions (Eslinger 1985:256–8).

Yahweh's response to Israel's forgetfulness is to "sell out" (*wayyimkōr* ... *bᵉyad*) Israel to its enemies in warfare—an action that is presented as a direct reflection of Israel's own forgetfulness. They forget him so he abandons them on the battlefield. Like Israel's first misfortunes in Egypt, these difficulties are brought on by the people themselves. Though Yahweh is now inextricably linked to all of Israel's experiences, Samuel claims that adversity within the period of covenantal relationship was the just and necessary result of Israel's own failings. This is theodicy pure and simple. Its power lies in its elegant, one-to-one historiography and in its ability to draw on the strong resource of universal guilt feelings that run so strong and deep in the collective consciousness of the Israelite religious tradition.

The theodicy is important to Samuel's presentation; through it he attempts to establish a historical precedent for an alternate interpretation of Israel's disastrous defeat at the hands of the Philistines. If Israel's military failings were previously caused by Israel's own misbehaviour, why should the recent case have been different? The brief list of enemies to whom Israel is sold out does not correspond to the fuller enumeration given in the book of Judges. As in v. 8, Samuel takes liberties with tradition as with history to create his own biased version of where Israel has come from and where it is going to.[25] Here an abbreviated allusion to the tales from the period of judges suffices. Samuel mentions only three representative examples, paradigmatic characterizations of the entire period of the judges, an unmitigated round of Israelite forgetfulness met by Yahweh's own gracious remedial mediators. Samuel does reverse his tendency towards abbreviation though, extending the abbreviated list with the addition of the Philistines. The implication of this reversed rhetorical strategem is that even the defeat of ch. 4 should be understood as an example of this paradigmatic cycle. Of course that is exactly the opposite interpretation of that made by Israel in ch. 4 (Eslinger 1985:164–7).

Verse 10

Not surprisingly, given that we know that Yahweh has delivered Israel to its enemies, Samuel portrays a helpless Israel after the battle (*wayyillāḥᵃmû bām wayyizᶜᵃqû ʾel-yhwh*, vv. 9f). The people are in the same straits in which their fathers found themselves in Egypt; like their fathers, their only recourse is to "cry to Yahweh" (vv. 8, 10). Suffering alone turns Israel towards Yahweh. With admissions of sin and apostasy the people promise renewed service to Yahweh if he will deliver them from their enemies. Samuel draws on the traditional language and theological historiography first presented by Moses in the book of Deuteronomy (cf. Birch 1976:70f; McCarthy 1978:208f; Vannoy 1978:33–7; McCarter 1980:214), a traditional outlook that the narrator has already done much to undercut in the books of Joshua and Judges (cf. preceding chapters; Polzin 1980:208). The cycle in v. 10 is predicate to the allusion to previous cycles in v. 9 and is, therefore, presented as a summary of the pre-

---

25 Though McCarthy sees the sequence of names as an example of the conservation of a tradition by the deuteronomist(s) that did not agree with his (their) own portrayal in Judges (1978:208f; cf. Stoebe 1973:237f), it is not difficult to forego such conjecture, so long as readers are prepared to offer Samuel a little rhetorical freedom: "The list of oppressors here, 'Sisera, the Philistines, the king of Moab', does not pretend to follow the order of the Book of Judges" (Smith 1899:86; cf. Vannoy 1978:36f; McCarter 1980:215).

monarchic history of covenantal relations between Israel and Yahweh. That this cycle is supposed to depict the characteristic shape of relations is confirmed in v. 11; here Samuel describes a succession of emissaries sent by Yahweh to rescue Israel again and again from the paradigmatic destitution he describes in v. 10. In the pre-monarchic period Samuel characterizes Israel as ever the back-slider, Yahweh, ever the forgiving and faithful benefactor (cf. Vannoy 1978:36f).

Verse 11

As in the exodus (v. 8), Yahweh sent various individuals throughout the entire pre-monarchic period to rescue Israel. The names of these emissaries, like the names of the adversaries in v. 9, are allusive metonyms. The names Jerubbaal and Samuel establish the chronological limits for the period in which these emissaries functioned. The middle names, Bedan and Jepthah, represent those mediators sent during this period to deliver Israel from its enemies.[26] Samuel ventures even further, adding his own name to the list of Yahweh's agents. This move, though obviously discordant with the book of Judges, is in keeping with Samuel's rhetorical intent. He exculpates Yahweh of any failings that could justify the request for a king and extols the human emissaries who are Yahweh's agents. By including him-

---

26 "... the fact remains that Dtr. wishes to remind us of all the "saviour" figures of the "Judges" period" (Noth 1981:51 [=1967:59]).

The widely accepted emendation that reads Barak (following 𝔊) rather than the obscure Bedan (e.g. Driver 1913:93) receives support from the widespread use of allusion in the immediate context. If Samuel's aim is to convey a general impression of the entire period, the introduction of an almost unknown character among the allusions would be a poor rhetorical strategy.

Zakovitch's suggestion (1972:124f) would alleviate this difficulty. He suggests that Bedan, identified as a Gileadite in 1 Chron 7:17 is actually another name for Jepthah, also a Gileadite (Judg 11:1). The existence of two names for the same man is paralleled by the case of Gideon-Jerubbaal. Originally the list in 1 Sam 12:11 contained only the names Jerubbaal, Bedan and Samuel. A copyist or redactor who knew that Jepthah = Bedan inserted the name Jepthah after Bedan to explain the relatively obscure Bedan. Finally a later copyist, not knowing that Jepthah was intended as a gloss on Bedan, added the words *w*^{e}*ʾet* before Jepthah (1972:125).

Whether one follows 𝔊 (Barak) or Zakovitch, the result is much the same: Samuel alludes to the period of the judges. If, on the other hand, one follows MT, one must assume that Bedan was a judge, whose memory has been lost, of whom Samuel could assume his audience's knowledge.

Finally it is just possible that Samuel, in the heat of the moment, might make a rhetorical blunder by introducing a character that did not fit his overall rhetorical purpose.

self amongst the latter he suggests that Yahweh had provided for national defense and leadership up to and including his own time.[27]

Samuel's self-inclusion numbers his own actions on Israel's behalf among Yahweh's acts of justification. As Keil and Delitzsch observe, he could justify such apparent self-aggrandizement by his role in the events of ch. 7 (1880:118). By tracing the continuing acts of justification through emissaries up to the contemporary moment, he places any defection from this divinely implemented system in the same class with all other such defections (Smith 1899:86).

Verse 11 is the capstone of Samuel's historical argument against the validity of the request for a king. He has established a set of causal principles running beneath Israel's history and has traced their operation into the contemporary situation. Since the people have already exonerated his performance as mediator, they are sitting ducks for the volley he now fires at them. In their quest to replace Yahweh or Samuel, the people have in fact rejected Yahweh's justifying acts, a sin even worse than their predecessors' continual forgetfulness.

The final sentences of v. 11 stand together in a relationship of cause and effect. Together they offer a picture of Israel's security under Yahweh's protection. Samuel signifies this security with the word ***beṭaḥ***, "security," which evokes a sense of the complete peace of mind Israel gained by Yahweh's victories over their enemies. Because ***beṭaḥ*** is only positively toned as a description of human behaviour when Yahweh is its object or inspiration, Samuel must say that Yahweh (the implicit subject), rather than the emissaries, "delivered" the people (*wayyaṣṣēl ʾetkem*).[28] Since he has already established his claim for the im-

27 "... in order to make his case relevant to the current situation, and the request for a king" (Vannoy 1978:37; cf. Hertzberg 1964:99).

28 "In passages where derivatives of the root ***bṭḥ*** are used to describe relationships between human beings, frequently they describe security that is taken for granted, but which also turns out to be disappointed, i.e. a credulous, frivolous, or even arrogant unconcern and security ... Frequently ***bṭḥ*** is used to describe a person who thinks he is secure, but is deceived because the object on which his feeling of security is based is unreliable. When we take all the passages in which ***bṭḥ*** is used in this sense, we get a picture of everything to which the heart of man clings and on which he believes he can build his life, but which will end in failure" (Jepsen.1977:90).

portance of the emissaries in the larger framework of the continuing acts of justification Samuel shifts his focus, from the beneficial acts and actors to the resulting peace of mind given to Israel. Samuel ensures that no one will misunderstand the ambiguous word *bṭḥ* by making it clear that any feeling of security was a response to an act of God.

As Smith notes, the picture of peaceful external relations in v. 11 is similar to the situation with which ch. 7 concludes (1899:86; cf. Schulz 1919:170). Samuel paints this pastoral backdrop in anticipation of his next point: the senseless, unwarranted nature of the request for a king. His description of Israel's security relies on the thought and language of such passages as Deut 12:10, 25:19, and Josh 23:1, a portrait of Israel's past that the narrator has already gone far to undermine (cf. above, "These Nations That Remain"). The attainment of such a state of peaceful security, courtesy of Yahweh, was the goal of Israelite existence; according to Samuel's review, therefore, there was nothing more to be achieved and nothing more that Israel could have wished for.[29] Such peace established, Israel ought to act in accordance with the wishes of Yahweh, who has fulfilled his covenantal commitment by giving them this secure refuge.

Both Samuel's audience and the reader know, however, that his recollection of the past is, mildly put, selective. He has avoided any reference to the disastrous events of chs. 2–6 and it was for those events, not the pastoral pastimes of Samuel's reminiscences, that Israel rebelled against God and Samuel. But no one in Samuel's audience objects to Samuel's contrived fiction. This silence from within the story world goads the reader to voice the necessary objections to Samuel's "official version." The narrator's own expositional silence on Samuel's offensive rhetoric only increases the reader's provocation. Far from

---

"In contrast to this clear linguistic usage of *bṭḥ* there is another that is even clearer. The community of Yahweh can know for sure that it can rely on him" (Jepsen 1977:92).

"Thus the feeling of being secure in God is the only certain support for human life. When Israel lives securely, it is a result of divine guidance: 1 S. 12:11; 1 K 5:5 (4:25); Ps. 78:53" (Jepsen 1977:93).

29 According to Deut 12:9 this security is part of the "rest and inheritance" given by Yahweh to Israel. Only when these are actualized is Israel allowed to establish the place of sacrificial worship that Yahweh will choose (vv. 8–11). So also in Josh 23, the supposed achievement of this security is presented as cause for a moment of recollection and re–commitment to maintain the achievement.

speaking through the voice of Samuel here, the narrator and the narrative present that voice in its most offensive, jarring dissonance. It disagrees with the reality of events that has already been presented in the narrative. Its strident pieties move the reader to reject such officious platitudes, here and anywhere else such similar sentiments might find expression in the narrative. The speech, then, does not express the narrator's opinions, but it is given full, unhindered expression to spur the reader to his own seemingly unabetted reaction against the fraud that seems to go unrequitted on both the levels of the story world and the narrative. Samuel's speech may not express the narrator's view, but it serves it well.

Verse 12

Nowhere is the discrepancy between Samuel's presentation and what actually happened (according to the narrator) more obvious than in v. 12.[30] Samuel's blatant attempt to rewrite history, the reality of which has already been presented by the authoritative voice of the external narrator, is an error that works to characterize Samuel. His view is the product of his own involvement, of his bias for Yahweh and against the monarchy, of his fear of losing his cherished status (Eslinger 1985:259–62; 1 Sam 12:1–5).[31]

According to Samuel the request for a king was simply another in the series of Israelite defections from loyalty to Yahweh. When the people saw Nahash the Ammonite advancing against them they said, "No, but a king shall be king over us"—yet Yahweh was their king. Having just rehearsed the usual course of action when faced with an external threat—to cry to Yahweh (v. 10)—Samuel obviously regards Israel's "no" as a rejection of the theocratic framework for national defense, a framework that he claims to have defended. In place of the cry to Yahweh for help, Samuel says, Israel uttered its unutterable "no—but a king shall be king over us" (Boecker 1969:76; Veijola 1977:96f). The request for a king, which Samuel quotes from the stronger, reactionary formulation of 8:19 rather than the true

---

30 Cf. D. Jobling (1985:65), "this claim flies in the face of ch. 8."

31 Vannoy is a reader who comes close to this conclusion: "Samuel's statement in 1 Samuel 12:12 is thus compatible with chapters 8, 10, and 11, but more important is that *it reveals his own analysis* of the motivation behind the initial request of the elders for a king" (my emphasis, 1978:39).

initial request of 8:5, is a rejection of Yahweh, comprehensible only as the fruit of ingrained stubbornness and stupidity, the heritage of their fathers' sins (vv. 9f).[32]

For the reader, Samuel's recollection of the request offers nothing other than an insight into his character: here is a loyal Yahwist refusing to admit the validity of Israel's reasons for that request. Whether or not a reader entertains the historical possibility that the Ammonite threat lay behind the request in ch. 8 (Vannoy 1978:38f)—an impossibility if we accept the authoritative historiographic description presented by the narrator, with those of ch. 11 following the events of ch. 8—Samuel has omitted its real justification: Yahweh's past behaviour (chs. 4–6) and the immediate danger threatened by the behaviour of Samuel's wayward sons. By avoiding the real reasons and occasion for the request, Samuel exposes his own sensitivity to it (cf. 8:6f). The discrepancy between the request as described in ch. 8 and ch. 12 is a relatively simple matter of a disparity between the way it was, and the way a deeply involved character would like everyone to believe it was.

In spite of the reader's awareness that Samuel is hopelessly biased here (and elsewhere, e.g. 10:17–24), the failing is partially mitigated. Samuel's evasion is the defense of an old man who has spent all his life as a servant of God and people. Both his pride in a lifetime of flawless service and even his continued existence in the office of mediator were jeopardized by the request. Yet he himself had done nothing to deserve dismissal. The narrator does not chastise Samuel for his bias; he simply exposes it so that the reader may see what effect this particular leader's own involvement has on the direction that Israel's history takes. Comprehension, not vilification: that is the goal of this narrator and the view presented in this narrative.

Having proven, at least to his own satisfaction, the vanity of Israel's request for a king, Samuel turns to its present result: Is-

---

32 Against the counter–proposals of Stoebe (1973:238) and McCarthy (1978:214), who suggest that the request is not viewed negatively in v. 12, one must affirm with Veijola (1977:97 n.85) that the context speaks against such a view. The request displaces the cry to Yahweh in a situation of need, and the people are subsequently forced to admit that their request was sinful (v. 19). The thunderstorm is staged by Samuel so that Yahweh has a chance to show his displeasure at the request (***rā̆ʾatkem rabbâ*** ... ***bᵉʿênê yhwh lišʾôl lāḵem melek***, v. 17). The monarchy in the form created by Yahweh, where Saul is Yahweh's anointed designate, is not regarded as sinful by Yahweh and Samuel, but the request for a king in place of Yahweh is.

rael's new king. He introduces the king first as "the king whom you have chosen," an expression that Samuel last used in 8:18, his attempt to dissuade the people. There is no suggestion in this allusion that they might have obtained the despot against which Samuel sought to advise them. Instead the allusion emphasizes that the people have gotten what they wanted. Samuel's second characterization of the king continues in the same vein. The king is as the one "whom you requested," implying, with this play on the name ***šāʿûl*** and the verb ***šᵉʾeltem*** that King Saul is in fact a king such as they had asked for (cf. 10:22). Samuel wants Israel to be happy with its new monarchy, however far the actuality is from the original vision of a non-theocratic state.

Samuel shifts, next, from congratulating Israel on its accomplishment—hollow salutations in the light of his view of the monarchy's origin—to the task of dictating correct behaviour for the future. He signals this shift with another introductory use of the particle ***hinnēh*** (cf. Boecker 1969:77). "So now, Yahweh has installed a king over you."

The combination of the verb ***ntn*** with the preposition *ʿl*, "over," stresses the hierarchy of the new arrangement: Yahweh is over the king, by virtue of being the one to install him, and the king is over "you" by virtue of the manner of installation (*ʿl*) (cf. McCarthy 1978:214; Weiser 1962:86). Samuel's emphasis has shifted from the people's will regarding the king, to Yahweh's. The presentation begins to take on a positive, hortatory tone with the statement that Yahweh installed the king. Yahweh's action seems in fact and in Samuel's view to have converted the people's idea of monarchy into something palatable to the theocratic regime.[33] As the request for a king was linked to the long history of Israelite defections, so Yahweh's response is the most recent in a series of gracious responses. Israel's defection is forgiven and arrangements are made for the continuation of relations between Yahweh and Israel.

---

33 "[Verse] 13 marks the climax of the formulation and it reverses the history of sin. The king is no longer the sign of a great infidelity; he is Yahweh's gift" (McCarthy 1974:102; cf. Muilenburg 1959:363; Boecker 1969:77; Birch 1976:69).

Verse 14

Samuel proceeds to lay down the conditions under which the new political organization will function. McCarthy notes that the conditional protases of vv. 14–15 are typically deuteronomistic in concern and formulation, excepting the use of "rebel" for a future possibility (1978:209f). As with Moses and Joshua before, the narrator allows this important character to give vent to an ideology and its vocabulary with which he is not in obvious agreement. Samuel lays down the deuteronomic law in a context that shows he has no moral right to do so, just as Joshua before him vaunted a fraudulent claim, framed in deuteronomistic language, to the completion of the conquest that was belied by the narrator's own description of those same events.[34] With these conditions Samuel aims to show that Israel remains firmly bound by the same covenantal stipulations as before. The monarchy has changed little if anything. In spite of the fact that they now have a king, Yahweh continues to be the only one to whom Israel owes its loyalty (cf. Vannoy 1978:44). Should the people and their king agree to the terms that Samuel presents in v. 14 they will also implicitly agree to his tendentious view of the past. So Samuel offers Israel a form of truce, wherein the would-be secular kingdom is allowed (forced?) to return to the protection offered by the theocracy under Yahweh. If Israel and its king will obey, they will be, once more, "after Yahweh."[35]

What Samuel offers is a renewal of the very theocratic state that Israel had tried to throw off in its bid for monarchy (Eslinger 1985:254–9). From Israel's perspective there is no great gain, but perhaps a truce when the potential adversary is the powerful Yahweh and his contentious servant is enough.

---

[34] Solomon, too, will be given the floor to voice the deuteronomic phrasings and he too will have his rhetoric undercut by the surrounding narrative context. See below, "King Solomon's Prayers."

[35] Boecker has shown that the expression ***hāyâ ʾaḥar,*** "to be behind," is a suitable apodosis in v. 14 (1969:77–82). By fulfilling all the conditions mentioned by Samuel, the people and their king will be true followers of Yahweh. As the phrase reveals in other contexts (2 Sam 2:10; 15:13; 1 Kgs 12:20; 16:21), to be a true follower of Yahweh means to recognize him as king. "***hāyâ ʾaḥar,*** to be after or behind a person, is good Hebrew and is frequently met with, particularly in the sense of attaching one's self to the king, or holding to him" (Keil & Delitzsch 1880:119; cf. Boecker 1969:80; McCarthy 1978:215f; Vannoy 1978:42f).

Samuel's revisionism may be incorrect, but it conveys a certain impression of a will to power that Israel cannot afford to ignore in either the servant or his master. The promised reward of the truce is, in any case, not so important as winning Israel's assent to Samuel's creative rewriting of the past.

Verse 15

In a further step to strengthen the theocratic position, Samuel characterizes the alternative to accepting his terms as disobedience to Yahweh, and rebellion against his commands. The consequence of such lawlessness would be disastrous for Israel: "The hand of Yahweh will be against you and against your fathers to destroy you." If Israel and its king are not willing to be subject to Yahweh and reap the benefits of being his followers, then they will be treated as an enemy. The same "hand of Yahweh" that the reader has seen in devastating action against the Philistine enemy (1 Sam 4) will turn against monarchic Israel. The choice Samuel offers is clear-cut: Israel and their king can either be for Yahweh or against him.[36] The results of each option are two sides of the same coin: obedience allows unification with Yahweh and disobedience turns him into their enemy (Boecker 1969:82; McCarthy 1978:210). Israel hardly has a choice: Samuel's fraudulent view of the past will become, in the story world, the official view of the future. If theodicy wins out in the story world, it loses in the view presented by the narrator. Theodicy is a view that is characterized as expeditious propaganda, far from the reality of the events that the narrator has described and Israel experienced.

Considered from the larger perspective of Israel's past relationship with Yahweh, the new conditions laid down by Samuel, paralleling as they do the blessing and curse portions of the covenant, indicate that the monarchy has changed nothing essential in Israel's political structure. Everything still depends on Yahweh's expressed desires for Israelite behaviour and on Israel's conformity with those stipulations. The king, originally

---

36 Many scholars have argued that vv. 14f constitute a representation of the covenant blessing and curse, indicating that Israel is being offered a fresh beginning in its relationship with Yahweh (Muilenburg 1959:363; Weiser 1962:86f; Boecker 1969:81f; Veijola 1977:87f; Vannoy 1978:46f).

requested as an instrument of political change, is publicly subsumed within the old order.[37]

Verse 16

Verse 16 marks a new stage in the proceedings: *gam-ʾattâ* links the verse back to the prior use of *ʾattâ* in v. 7. The emphatic particle *gam* renews Samuel's formal call to assembly (*hityaṣṣᵉbû*).[38] Samuel's emphasis, in his redoubled call to assemble, lies not so much on the physical detail as on the psychological attitudes and religious meaning of the act of assembly.[39] The people are called to assemble and witness "this tremendous deed" which Yahweh is about to do before their very eyes. Samuel (and God) want a duly impressed and submissive Israel to issue from the occasion.

Vannoy has observed that there is a close phraseological resemblance between Samuel's introduction of this phenomenon and Moses' introduction to Yahweh's deliverance at the Reed Sea (1978:47f). Samuel sets himself up as a Moses figure, leading Israel to a new or renewed experience of relationship with Yahweh. The formation of the relationship in Exodus and the reformation in vv. 16–25 are catalyzed by the experience of Yahweh's miraculous deeds. In the exodus experience the miracle of the Red Sea was enough to make the Israelites fear Yahweh and believe in Yahweh and in Moses (*wayyîrʾû hāʿām ʾet-yhwh wayyaʾᵃmînû bayhwh ûbᵉmōšeh ʿabdô*, Exod 14:31). Likewise, the thunderstorm is aimed to convince the people, whose quest for a king has already been compared to Israel's apostasy dur-

---

37 It is important to note, with regard to the suggestion of a supposed anti-monarchistic dtr redactor speaking through Samuel in ch. 12, that at this crucial juncture where the conditions for Israel's survival under the monarchy are established, no special emphasis is placed on the behaviour of the king as opposed to the people. People and king stand together under the call to obedience. Considered together with the fact that what Samuel criticizes in ch. 12 is not the monarchy, but *the request for a king in place of Yahweh*, ch. 12 can no longer be marshaled in support of the literary-historical claim that the deuteronomist, supposed to speak through Samuel in ch. 12, saw the monarchy as Israel's downfall (so Noth 1967:54f).

38 Cf. Ehrlich (1910:208) against Buber (1956:158), who says "the *gam-ʾattâ* of v. 16 is completely meaningless."

39 Both Muilenburg (1959:359, 363) and Harrelson (cited by Vannoy 1978:47 n.106) suggest that the verb *htyṣb* is used in such contexts as a formal expression.

ing and since the exodus (1 Sam 8:8; 12:8–12; cf. 10:18f),[40] that their request for a king was sinful.

The plan does, in fact, meet with success: Israel does fear Yahweh and Samuel (*wayyîrâʾ kol-hāʿām m^{e}ʾōd ʾet-yhwh w^{e}ʾet-š^{e}mûʾēl*, v. 18).[41] The opening phrases show Samuel operating in the role of mediator; once more in a position of dominance, he exhibits an attitude of assurance. Though he began his remarks with intimations that he would step down from his post in deference to the new king and perhaps to the younger generation (v. 2), Samuel's demonstration of power, both Yahweh's and his, puts him right back in the position he last held in ch. 7.

Structural Excursus

Both Buber (1956:158) and Seebass (1965:294f.) have seen the parallels between 12:16–25 and ch. 7 (cf. Press 1938:211f; Hertzberg 1964:100). Seebass even argues that this section in ch. 12 is modeled on ch. 7 (1965:294f; cf. Birch 1976:70, criticizing Seebass' proposal). The parallelism is not accidental, nor is it evidence of a vapid redactor forced to repeat himself for lack of traditional material or a fertile imagination.

The demonstration in ch. 12 is an affair staged for Israel's benefit, no less a part of the effort to convict Israel than Samuel's own walloping rhetoric. The primary difference between the demonstration of power and the preceding historical revisionism is that Yahweh is complicit in the demonstration, with an appropriate escalation in the force of the argument. The parallel between vv. 16–25 and ch. 7, the second to last such demonstration of divine might in the arena of Israel's experience, aims to cultivate a similar response in Israel. The parallel is intentional, a part of Samuel's and God's effort to re-enlist Is-

---

40 Cf. Speiser (1971:283), who also notes that Yahweh and Samuel see the request for a king as comparable to Israel's previous expressions of desire to return to a lifestyle such as they had when they were slaves in Egypt. "Thus 'the manner of the king' as it is stigmatized in I Sam 8.11-8, could just as aptly have been labeled in that context 'the Egyptian manner'."

41 Buber's impression that "the combination of Yahweh and Samuel in v. 18b seems almost a travesty in comparison to Exod 14:31" (1956:159) is a good example of a reader response to the self–aggrandizing tendency in Samuel's rhetoric. Samuel seeks to secure the position of mediator, first held by Moses, for himself (cf. vv. 6–11). The parallel with Moses in the exodus is, therefore, an important recollection of the fundamental role that Samuel plays here: he achieves his goal.

rael as an obedient partner in the theocratic covenant that they believe defines Israel's essence.

Chapter 7	*Chapter 12*
Israel is exhorted to put away foreign gods and Ashtaroth, to direct its heart to Yahweh, and to serve him only; then he will deliver it from the Philistines (v. 3)	Israel is promised that if they will fear Yahweh and serve him, heed his voice and not rebel against his command, then Israel and its king will be behind Yahweh and by implication Yahweh will be before them (v. 14).
Samuel directs Israel to assemble (*qbṣ*) at Mizpah, where he will pray to Yahweh for them (v. 5).	Samuel says to assemble (*htyṣb*) to see the tremendous deed that Yahweh is about to perform for them. Though it is now harvest time, Samuel will call to Yahweh and he will send thunder and rain so that Israel will recognize and see the great evil that they have done in Yahweh's eyes, by asking for a king (vv. 16f).
Israel gathers at Mizpah. They draw and pour out water before Yahweh, they fast on that day (*bayyôm hahûʾ*) and confess their sin against Yahweh (v. 6).	Samuel calls to Yahweh and he sends thunder and rain on that day (*bayyôm hahûʾ*) (v. 18).
Hearing that the Israelites have assembled at Mizpah, the Philistine leaders go up to Israel. Israel hears about it and fears (*wayyirʾû*) the Philistines (v. 7).	As a result of Samuel's call and Yahweh's response, the people greatly fear (*wayyîraʾ*) Yahweh and Samuel (v. 18).

The Israelites tell (*wayyōʾmᵉrû ʾel- šᵉmûʾēl*) Samuel "Do not refuse to cry for us to Yahweh, our God (*ʾᵉlōhênû*), that he may deliver us from the Philistines" (v. 8).	The people tell Samuel (*wayyōʾmᵉrû ʾel- šᵉmûʾēl*) "Pray on your servants' behalf to Yahweh, your God (*ʾᵉlōhêkā*), that we might not be killed because we have added to all our sins the evil of asking for a king" (v. 19).
Samuel takes a suckling lamb and offers it as an offering to Yahweh. Samuel cries to Yahweh on Israel's behalf, and Yahweh answers him. When the Philistines close for the attack, Yahweh thunders against them with a great voice. The Philistines are duly confused and then routed before Israel (vv. 9–10).	Samuel tells the people not to be afraid. Though they have done this evil, they should not turn away from Yahweh; they should serve him with all their heart. They should not turn aside after vain things, which are profitless and unable to rescue because they are vain. Yahweh will not abandon his people on account of his reputation ("great name") for it was Yahweh's pleasure to make them into a people for himself (vv. 20–22).
Yahweh has shown willingness to be reunited with Israel, and continues to demonstrate it by giving by giving Israel victory over some neighbours and peace with others. Samuel is established as judge over Israel for the rest of his days (vv. 12–17).	Yahweh will not abandon his people and Samuel promises that he shall not sin against Yahweh by ceasing to offer intercessory prayer on Israel's behalf (cf. 7:8); he will teach Israel to walk the straight and narrow (v. 23). In vv. 24f he sets to that task.

In both cases the proceedings conclude with Yahweh sitting in firm possession and leadership over a penitent Israel guided by his watchful servant (Israel's intercessor) Samuel. The second demonstration is modeled on the first with the aim of getting a similar result. The hope is fulfilled. The reader, of course, sees Samuel's demonstration of Yahweh's power neither from the position of the Israelites, who are frightened into confessions of sin, nor from Samuel's (and probably Yahweh's) point of view, from which the demonstration evokes a proper and needful response from Israel. Instead the reader is the aloof onlooker, viewing things from the distance created by the narrator's external perspective. This distanced viewpoint is undisturbed by the immediate turbulence of the thunderstorm and its mortifying implications. Israel experiences the rhetoric of the event and is subdued by it; the reader's experience and comprehension is a far different affair. From his distant, untroubled vantage the reader is privileged to be able to reflect on this particular instance of revelation in history. The resulting reflections are far from the comforting theodicy that most scholarly readers have found in their redactional readings of this chapter.

Verse 17

Samuel sets up a demonstration to prove two points. The show takes the form of a miraculous phenomenon, a freak thunderstorm in the dry season.[42] Samuel tells his audience that this weird event, which is at his call, is supposed to show them how poorly Yahweh viewed their request.[43] A second purpose of the demonstration, unmentioned by Samuel but obvious to both his audience and the reader, is to prove the strength of Samuel's ties with Yahweh and their agreement concerning the monarchy (cf. McCarter 1980:216). If Samuel's relationship with Yahweh were weak, or if Yahweh did not regard the request as evil, he would not answer the prophet. Samuel's confident flair is intended to make the demonstration all the more convincing. He is so sure of himself and of Yahweh's opinions that he willingly stakes his reputation on the success of the demonstration.

---

42 Cf. G. A. Smith (in a chapter appropriately titled "The climate and fertility of the land, with their effects on its religion"): "In May showers are very rare, and from then till October, not only is there no rain, but a cloud seldom passes over the sky, and a thunderstorm is a miracle" (1900:65)

Ehrlich suggests a third implication of the out–of–season shower. With it, Yahweh shows "that he finds his people's wish for a king [equally] untimely" (1910:209).

43 In view of the widespread belief that ch. 12 is critical of the monarchy, it is worth pointing out that Samuel only says that the show of force is supposed to convince the people of the evil of *their request* (*liš*ʾ*ôl lākem melek*). The thunderstorm is not a criticism of the monarchy of Saul, an institution created and implemented by Yahweh himself.

The parallel between v. 17 and 7:5 also bears the trademark of this coercive setup. Back in 7:5, Samuel had gathered a scattered Israel, which, at that point, was experiencing a loss of faith in Yahweh on account of his aloofness. Samuel promised to pray for them with the unstated goal of bringing them back together with Yahweh. Now in v. 17, Samuel has called another assembly in which he will effect another communication between Yahweh and Israel.

This time, though, it is a message from Yahweh to the people who have cast a vote of non-confidence against him and Samuel. Beside the difference in the direction of the communication—now from Yahweh to Israel—there is also a difference in tone. When Israel feels rejected by Yahweh it seeks reunification through intercessory prayer (at Samuel's suggestion): when Yahweh feels rejected by Israel he uses the heavy-handed route of miraculous thunder and rain. Yahweh's position—he is God—allows him to express his displeasure but it also smells of coercion, especially against the backdrop of Israel's passive submission through Samuel's intercession.

This contrast between the communicative styles of the two parties seeking reconciliation is partly explained by the fact that here reconciliation over the matter of kingship has already taken place (ch. 11). Yahweh has already acceded to Israel's demand by allowing a conditional monarchy. So the demonstration of v. 17 is not so much reconciliation as it is a restoration of what Yahweh (and Samuel) see as a respectful distance in the existing relationship. Israel has questioned Yahweh and experienced some success in its petition. The demonstration will put Israel back in its proper place through a show of divine force.

The actions in 12:17 and 7:5 are similar assemblies for the purpose of a divine-human interchange through the agency of Samuel. The action in v. 17 differs because it is an effort at restoring proper relationship; 7:5 is only a request for renewed relationship. The difference is caused by the intervening request for a king which, though granted, is impudent, improper and in need of redress. At least that is what Yahweh and Samuel believe.

For the reader the parallel shows only how Israel must submit to the perceptions of Yahweh and his mediator, even when those perceptions refuse to admit the reality that undercuts them. Israel begs for renewed relationship in ch. 7, even though it was not at fault in the rupture. Yahweh gets away with gracious condescension. Yahweh forces a confession in ch. 12, even though the request for a king was a restrained response to the behaviour of Yahweh and his priestly mediators. Israel is forced into humble submission.

Verse 18

Having presented Samuel's description of what he was about, the narrator describes the undertaking itself. Samuel's actions correspond word for word with what he said he would do, as do Yahweh's supporting actions.

The thunderstorm serves both as a theophany and a sign (cf. Vannoy 1978:50f; McCarter 1980:216).[44] The people fear Yahweh and Samuel, a twofold result corresponding to these two sides of the demonstration. On the one side, Birch observes that thunder (*qôl*) is common to theophanies (1976:70). Both the people's fear of Yahweh (v. 18) and their fear that they might die if Samuel did not pray for them suggest a response to a theophany (cf. Birch 1976:70). "God, who had been shoved aside as a shadowy unreality by Israel with its insistent demand for a king, plainly reveals himself as the living one, who is quite able to annihilate his creature" (Gutbrod 1956:90f). The manifestation of divine power as a displeased reaction to their request seems to the people to threaten their very existence (v. 19; cf. McCarthy 1978:217; Vannoy 1978:50f).

On the other hand, the demonstration also serves to legitimate Samuel by showing the people that they need his services as mediator to pray on their behalf.[45] The storm proves that Yahweh's real power and real domination over Israel con-

---

44 The significance of Yahweh's response is disputed;, some view the thunder (and rain) as an echo of theophany, especially the Sinai theophany (Weiser 1962:87); others argue that the out-of-season storm is a visible manifestation of Yahweh's power, a sign in response to Samuel's call and so an authentification of Samuel as mediator (Boecker 1969:85; Stoebe 1973:238f; Veijola 1977:98).

45 McCarter confuses the issue. "The point of the narrator is clear: a prophet is the proper and divinely sanctioned channel between man and God, and in this respect the request for a king is a great evil" (1980:216). Nobody has suggested that the king might replace the prophet as channel. The king was intended to replace both prophet and God as Israel's political leader. He obviates this sort of communication with God in times of need. What the demonstration does show with reference to McCarter's concerns, is that even though Israel now has a king it is still in need of Samuel's intercession precisely because it has made the request and so displeased Yahweh. King or no king, the people cannot escape Yahweh. They need a Samuel to pray for them.

tinues (cf. Boecker 1969:85). On account of his intimacy with this powerful God and their shared antipathy towards the request for a king, Samuel is a man to be feared alongside God. Think what he could call down upon them if they angered him by not heeding Yahweh's "voice" (*qôl*, v. 14 = *qôlôt* v. 18 "thunder") or rebelling against Yahweh's "mouth" (v. 14, Samuel?)!

Verse 19

There is only one way to soothe Yahweh's ill feelings over the request: Israel adopts the attitude of humble, repentant submission. In the first words allowed them since Samuel began his presentation all the people tell Samuel: "Pray on behalf of your servants to Yahweh your God." The people acknowledge their need of Samuel's service as intercessor; he and God have won their suit. The people speak of Yahweh as Samuel's God (*ʾᵉlōheykā*), recognizing that their request has alienated God from themselves (cf. Vannoy 1978:52). They express the hope that Samuel's prayers will prevent their death, a punishment that they seem to see lurking in the thunderstorm. Finally they confess that over and above all their sins, they have gone and added to the evil by asking for a king for themselves.

The demonstration is a complete success (Veijola 1977:98f). The people have been frightened into a recognition of their need of Samuel and a confession of their sin in asking for a king (cf. Vannoy 1978:52). The relative positions of Israel, Samuel, and Yahweh are restored to the divinely approved order sketched by Samuel. No longer looking to a human king as a possible source of relief the Israelites return entirely to theocratic dependence.

A parallel with 7:8 provides an interesting contrast that highlights their weakened position. In 7:8 the people ask Samuel to cry to Yahweh "our God"; in v. 19 they ask Samuel to pray to Yahweh "your God." Having spurned Yahweh by asking for a king, the people no longer believe that they have the unquestioned right to call Yahweh "our God" (Vannoy 1978:52). The last state is worse than the first and they are as much under the theocratic thumb as they hoped to be free of it.

The reader's perception of the thunderstorm is an entirely different matter, privileged as it is by an accurate and unintimidated recollection of the narrative past. Israel's humble confession is not the utterance of deep reflection and consequent repentance. It is a forced confession, extorted under duress, in fear for life itself (cf. Gunn 1981:65). The people beg for Samuel's intercession and confess in order to avoid sudden death (*wᵉʾal-nāmût*). The reader, however, faces no such threat and is consequently free to share in the unabashed narratorial perspective from which the strong-arm tactics of the theocrats can be seen for what they are. Far from speaking through Samuel, the narrator decries Samuel's theory of Israelite history and the means he (and his accessory, God) choose to advance it.

Verse 20

Once again Samuel holds his position as sole recognized authority, mediator between Israel and Yahweh (Weiser 1962:87). "Samuel leaps into the breach before the forlorn people together with its king" (Gutbrod 1956:91).

The people have asked for Samuel's prayers and, if he is favourably disposed towards them, we expect him to pray for them. The people in v. 19 believe that they are in a life or death situation and beg Samuel to intercede that they might live. But Samuel proceeds, first, to retrain the penitents' perception of their request and the meaning of their new political existence as a monarchy under theocracy. He capitalizes on their helplessness to give another repetitious (cf. vv. 14f) lecture on the reformed behaviour required of them. The fact that Samuel pursues this didactic course here shows that he knows another side of the demonstration. From his point of view, the thunderstorm is a capital opportunity to inculcate a lesson: he has a captivated audience, ready to swallow anything simply to stay alive.

Samuel's first words to the fearful Israelites are a clear exhibition of his own interests and concerns; "Fear not! *You*[46] have done all this evil, but do not turn aside from after Yahweh and serve Yahweh with all your hearts." He plays on his audience's moment of terror to re-define the legitimate request from the covenantal perspective as though it were a simple act of unprovoked disobedience and faithlessness.

---

46 "You" (*ʾattem*) is positioned emphatically (Driver 1913:95) as a further means of drawing Israel's attention to its culpability.

Verse 21

Though v. 21 is frequently discarded as a late gloss on account of the supposed anachronism of the word *tōhû* ("empty," e.g. Budde 1902:81; Buber 1956:159; Stoebe 1973:239; cf:, however, Deut 32:10) and the ease with which the verse may be omitted without disturbing the sense of the context (Budde 1902:81; Boecker 1969:86), it is not entirely inappropriate. As Boecker observes, v. 21 is connected to v. 20 by the repetition of the verb *tāsûrû*, which is given an expanded interpretation in v. 21 (1969:68; cf. Seebass 1965:295 n.21). Repetitious, yes, but it is part of Samuel's expansionistic rhetoric. The repeated exhortation taken from v. 20 is "Do not turn aside." Following the exhortation is a *kî* clause explaining why one should not turn (cf. Muilenburg 1961:157). "Do not turn aside, for (*kî*) [it is] after vanities which can neither benefit nor deliver because they are vain."

The word *tōhû*, though usually understood as a reference to false gods on the basis of Deutero-Isaiah (e.g. Keil & Delitzsch 1880:121; Hertzberg 1964:100), has a more specific reference in this context. In v. 20, Samuel balances the evil that has been done—the request for a king—against the exhortation not to turn aside any more from after Yahweh. By a series of associations Samuel equates the anti-covenantal request for a king like the nations with defection (*swr*) from Yahweh: 1. the request for a king was evil (v. 17); 2. the evil (the request) done is not a cause for fear so long as Israel no longer turns aside, as it did in the request, from after Yahweh (v. 20); 3. one should not turn aside because the things so pursued are worthless (v. 21). In v. 21, Samuel provides even more detail. Israel should not engage in such defections. Why? Because all such things are worthless. They are profitless (*lōʾ yôʿîlû*) and unable to deliver (*lōʾ yaṣṣîlû*). In contrast to these worthless things—such as the kingship the people had requested—are Yahweh's actions. He brought Israel up (*heʿᵉlêtî*, 10:18) from Egypt, and he delivered (*wāʾaṣṣîl*, 10:18; cf. 12:11) Israel from all its enemies. No one but Yahweh, says Samuel, is of any use to Israel as a source of security: in comparison, everything else is *hattōhû*, "worthlessness."

Verse 22

Israel is not to turn aside because Yahweh will not forsake his people. He has a reputation to maintain. It is staked on Israel's fortunes because he made them into his people, and so they need never fear for their political existence. So long as Yahweh's "great name" means anything to him, Israel's continued survival as his people is guaranteed. Samuel does not paint a pretty picture of divine solicitude for the cares of his people. He is more interested in ensuring, by whatever means, that Israel does not repeat its anti-covenantal efforts.

From any perspective educated by preceding events, Samuel's assurances are less than assuring. Only seven chapters before, Yahweh took action to protect his reputation, but that action was of no benefit to Israel. Both before and after the Philistines were forced to confess to the greatness of the mighty exodus God, Israel was subjected to unwarranted abuse at the hands of Yahweh. So the reader, and Israel too if it were in any position to be able to listen critically, hears a hollow ring to Samuel's assurances in v. 22.

Samuel's tendentious interpretation of the past and his dubious reassurances about the future hardly bear the promise of a firm foundation for the political organization that is being reaffirmed. Once again the narrator allows Samuel to hoist himself in the eyes of anyone who has ears to hear, and certainly the reader has been given such ears by the narrative distance and privileged information supplied by the narrator. The inadequate half-measure of a theocratically designated king has only smoothed over the problem raised by the request. Samuel's reassessment of the request only buries the seeds of legitimate discontent under the facade of covenant renewal, and it is Israel that has to do all of the recanting.

The language and ideas of v. 22 draw upon Israel's covenant ideology (Weiser 1962:87; McCarthy 1974:102; Veijola 1977:90). In view of the context some scholars have suggested that v. 22 renews the covenant between Israel and Yahweh (Boecker 1969:87; McCarthy 1973:412; 1978:217). Certainly Samuel does seem to hold out such a prospect to his newly converted audience. But does v. 22 really re-establish the covenant? What v. 22 does, in fact, is to point back to the realities that have always governed Israel's covenantal existence: Israel's election serves

Yahweh's purposes, one of which is the maintenance of his great name (cf. Muilenburg 1959:364; Payne 1972:324).[47]

Verse 23

Samuel contrasts his own steadfast behaviour as mediator with that of his audience through the use of the emphatic introductory pronouns in vv. 20 and 23: "*You* have done all this evil ... but as for *myself* ..." (Ehrlich 1910:209; McCarter 1980:216). Having criticized Israel's request to the fullest and beyond, Samuel finally responds to their appeal for his prayers. His response—"Far be it from me to sin against Yahweh by ceasing to pray on your behalf"—implies that he has never stopped praying on Israel's behalf because it is part of his God-given task as mediator. The people might be fickle, but not Samuel or Yahweh.

Samuel's reassurance about his continuing prayers for Israel is paralleled in ch. 7 by Israel's request that Samuel not cease crying to Yahweh for deliverance (7:8). His statement here is a conscious allusion to that request, a celebration of his personal victory. Threatened with retirement, Samuel has emerged from the crisis with a public vindication of his integrity (v. 4) and public recognition of the necessity of his intercession. He crowns his successful return to power by electing himself to the role of spiritual director, leading Israel in the good and upright path.

Samuel's pledge so abounds in solicitude for Israel's well-being that Israel seems not to deserve it. He promises his special provision for the succour and preservation of the people, even while they stand, in the hour of need, on the very brink of disaster (so McCarter 1980:219). With Samuel as teacher, the people need not worry that they will foolishly turn away from Yahweh in pursuit of some chimerical end. He will selflessly undertake to keep Israel on the straight and narrow, which in

---

47 This same adamant reiteration of Israel's status as covenantal people of Yahweh is the basis of Yahweh's revelations to Samuel in 1 Sam 9:16, where Yahweh revealed his real design for the new kingship to Samuel.. Halpern (1988:185) goes completely astray on the covenantal implications of ch. 9 with his hypothesis of two separate accounts of Saul's rise to kingship: 9:1–10:12 and chs. 8; 10:17–27; 11; and 12. According to Halpern, it is only the Philistines, not the covenantal constitution, that is cause of the crisis and the institution of the monarchy in 9:1–10:12. Such a reading completely ignores the force of Yahweh's rhetoric in 9:16 and the preceding narrative context of ch. 9.

view of the ominous threat of divine punishment must be accepted as a valuable and necessary service to Israel.

The reader cannot help but notice that the installation of the theocratic mediator as the official censor, dictator of the "good and upright path," is the final blow to Israel's idea of a political system unfettered by the unreliable theocracy. Israel's quest for independence has only strengthened the theocratic hand on this people whom it has pleased Yahweh to make. Whether the people will always accept this imposition, and whether the king will be satisfied with his subordination remain as questions that the reader must carry into the subsequent scenes of the monarchic history (cf. Gunn 1980:65).

One thing is certain about v. 23: it marks the end of the movement for a king like all the nations. Just as the request for a king was sparked by a recurrence of a previous circumstance, the dangerous state of affairs in the mediator's family, so the conclusion to the chain of events resulting from the request is marked by the recurrence of the scene at the end of ch. 7. In both scenes Samuel has brought Israel through a crisis and stands ensconced as mediator, faithful shepherd of the people of Yahweh. Both the request for a king and the conclusion of the issue illustrate the narrative technique of using scenic parallels and allusions to add commentary to scenes that otherwise appear to lack narrative exposition (cf. Alter 1981:7). With Samuel's remarks in v. 23 and the parallel situation in ch. 7, it is almost as though the request had never been made. Under Samuel's direction, with special effects by Yahweh, the pursuit of a king like the nations is only a bad dream (*hattōhû*).

Verses 24-25

Samuel finishes his presentation with a yet another reminder of Israel's duty to balance his descriptions of Yahweh's and his own roles (vv. 22f). Of the exhortations only the addition of the adverb *beʾᵉmet*, "sincerely," is not a repetition of what he has already said in vv. 14f, 20. The penalty, on the other hand, for continued disobedience is that both they and their king will be swept away. The people had said about their proposed king, "Even we (*gam-ʾᵃnaḥnû*) will be like all the nations" (8:20), to which Samuel responds here "Even you and even your king (*gam-ʾattem gam-malkᵉkem*) will be swept away."

The installation of a king has changed nothing with regard to Israel's theocratic obligations. They are still governed by the same theocratic duties in their binding covenant with Yahweh. Regarding the Israelite monarchy, Samuel is right: it has become *hattōhû*.

CHAPTER 5

KING SOLOMON'S PRAYERS

And Solomon stood before the altar of the Lord in the presence of all the congregation of Israel, and spread forth his hands toward heaven (1 Kings 8:22).

1 Kings 1–11

Nowhere is there more discongruity between narrator and character, between the ideology of one of the great orations and that of its larger narrative context, than in the case of King Solomon's prayers in 1 Kgs 8. Here the reader meets with a character utterance laced with the theology and language of the book of Deuteronomy.[1] Solomon's prayer is a fount of deuteronomic piety that would do any preacher proud. Given the phraseological concord and the pious tone of his prayer, how could it and the narrative that contains it be anything but in agreement with the "deuteronomistic" narrator's views on the subject matter of the prayer?[2]

---

1 M. Weinfeld's comprehensive catalogue of deuteronomic phraseology lists 59 entries falling within the verses that constitute Solomon's prayer in 1 Kgs 8. Oddly, if one were to accept the notion that it is the narrator (redactor) who shares the deuteronomic (more properly Mosaic) ideology in vv. 1–11 and vv. 62–66, the narratorial exposition that brackets the prayer, Weinfeld's indices record only one instance of deuteronomic phraseology in v. 5, which is itself an anomalous usage (Weinfeld 1972:326). Solomon waxes more deuteronomistic than the deuteronomist himself, suggesting that if we are going to be more alert to the voice structure of the Dtr, we need to be more careful about deciding what role of deuteronomistic phraseology in the narratives plays. Hitherto such language has straightaway led to the conclusion that here the Dtr author/redactor speaks unaffectedly in his own mother tongue, from his native conceptual universe. If, however, the author puts the phraseology at the service of a character and keeps it from the narrator, with whom he identifies and speaks directly as here in 1 Kgs 8, it behoves the reader to be chary of any such simplistic and automatic equations. The narrator himself is, after all, completely silent in the book of Deuteronomy, which is almost exclusively constituted by the speech of another very

Contrary to common deuteronomistical knowledge, a deuteronomic locution does not a deuteronomistic locution make.[3] Should it be the narrative's aim to expose a conniving abuse of deuteronomic piety, something like Solomon's prayer, the scholarly reader must brace himself to hear the abuse correctly as deuteronomic intonation and stifle the urge to raise the redactor's cry: "deuteronomistic"! Solomon is quite able to voice the deuteronomic pieties without subscribing to them, or if he does subscribe, to be misguided in his understanding. And the narrator is even more capable of allowing Solomon to make his speech without for one moment agreeing with its propriety or unctuous piety. If we are going to get past simplistic deuteronomists—however many they might be—then we must get past simple equations. It is time for our reading of biblical narrative to develop beyond the simple, common-sense arithmetic of source and redaction criticisms to the more comprehensive algebraism of narratology.

As throughout biblical narrative, the narrator's views are usually not presented explicitly. Especially they are not confined to direct expositional address. To share the narrator's comprehensive understanding the reader must take in a wider expanse of context. In the case of Solomon's prayer, its deuteronomistic tones have a radically different colour when studied carefully in the light of their narrative setting. It is not

---

involved and biased human character (against Polzin (1981:57), who errs in hearing a melding of the voices of narrator/author and Moses through the ontological structuring of voices in and subsequent to the book of Deuteronomy. A study of evaluative language in the book of Deuteronomy (see ch. 7, "Explicit Evaluation in the Dtr Narratives") shows that the narrator separates himself absolutely from the numerous value judgements voiced by Moses, who presents them as the normative definitions given by God himself.

2 So Martin Noth makes it a matter of fact that the prayers belong to the Dtr author (1968:174). Cf. S.J. De Vries (1985:121), "1 Kgs 8 is especially crucial in Dtr's overall plan because he here takes advantage of an opportunity to make Solomon the mouthpiece of his theology." As De Vries' remark shows, the conventional reading of the prayer ignores the central role of narrative ontology and voice structure in creating narrative meaning.

3 The reverse assumption is amply evident throughout historical-critical work on these narratives. De Vries, for example, says of the deuteronomistic vocabulary in 1 Kgs 8, "we are able to put to good effect what we already know of the diction, style, and ideology of Dtr in order to isolate what actually belongs to him ...." (1985:122). Given such assumptions there can be nothing but an indiscriminate, uni-dimensional reading of allusions to the book of Deuteronomy in these narratives.

the narrative context that must be interpreted in the light of Solomon's isolated prayer: quite the contrary. It is the contextualized prayer that must be heard both in the light of actions leading up to it and in the light of the consequences of Solomon actions done in reliance on the assurances that he sought and thought he had gained through his prayers.

Light from the Preceding Context

1 Kings 2

Solomon begins his royal career in 1 Kgs 2. Here the narrative grants the reader a privileged audition of David's deathbed instructions to Solomon. David's plan, a revealing glimpse into his dark heart (cf. S. Bar-Efrat (1989:182–84) is presented in a stark narratorial light; no mitigation is stated or implied. David's revenge is cold, calculated,[4] and most importantly for present purposes, unquestioned by the young Solomon. The only narratorial comment on the series of arranged murders that follow is, "and the kingdom was established in the hands of Solomon." If this is how it begins, how will it end?

Political expediency will rule. Solomon ruthlessly strengthens his hold on the throne. Murder is piled upon murder, all on the slightest of pretexts (cf. L. Rost 1982:72). "And the kingdom was established in the hand of Solomon." As Fokkelman has observed, the narrator's closing comment does take up, by repetition, v. 12: "and Solomon sat on the throne of David, his father. And his kingdom was well established" (*wattikkōn malkutô me*ʾ*ōd*). In v. 12 the narrator explicitly states that, at that point, Solomon's kingdom was assured. The statement bears the narrator's authority and is reliable. But Solomon goes on and executes the superfluous series of contrived murders. But the

---

4 "We cannot but draw the conclusion that it is chiefly the dark side of David's life and personality which is made visible here" (J. Fokkelman 1981:386). See especially n. 5 on p. 386 for Fokkelman's clear view of the difference between the narrator's presentation, essentially negative, and possible positive socio-cultural interpretations such as J. Pedersen's (1926:424ff.). A good example of the critical implications of the text is found in vv. 8–9. There the author has David allude to his promise not to kill Shimei (cf. 2 Sam 19:18–23). But whereas in the actual instance David, reveling in his victory, only says, "you shall not die" to Shimei, here he adds that "he swore to him by Yhwh." And then, immediately following this stronger vow David says to Solomon, "you are a smart fellow and know what to do ..." A vow by Yhwh was not part of the deal; its introduction here makes David's plan and Solomon's implementation all the darker.

murders make no political gains: "and the kingdom was established in the hand of Solomon" (*wᵉhammamlākâ nākônâ beyad šᵉlōmōh*). The only difference is that the establishment of the kingdom now bears the imprint of Solomon's bloody hand.[5]

In 2:4, prefacing the murderous instructions, David adds a strange condition to the unconditional promise of dynasty that God made to him in 2 Sam 7. He instructs Solomon to obey the Law (v. 3) so that God will keep his dynastic promise (v. 4). Why?[6] A clue to David's rhetorical strategy here lies in the order of his last comments, which can be outlined as follows:

- I am dying.
- Be strong and obey the Law so that God will maintain our line.
- Here is what you must do:
    - Joab
    - sons of Barzillai
    - Shimei

The structure of the scene that extends from 1 Kgs 2:1–10 also supports this reading:

v. 1 (narratorial summary), David's death approaches
v. 2 (David), stengthen yourself; be a man
vv. 3–4 (David), keep the conditional covenant
vv. 5–9 (David), settle old accounts with my enemies
v. 9 (David), you are a wise man
v. 10 (narratorial summary), David is dead

David's instructions to Solomon are symmetric with references to the latter's manhood and adult intelligence bracketing the injunctions to a murderous covenantal obedience.

The suggestion, fostered by David's agenda, is that the prescribed actions will fulfil the Law, implying even that they are

---

5 Fokkelman also notes that v. 12 establishes the security of Solo-mon's reign, but differs in finding irony in the repetition of v. 46; "only when Solomon feels the kingship firmly in his grasp is the kingship then firm for him. But he feels it securely only after three executions by which he allays his feelings of being threatened" (1981: 409). The main point seems to be the manner of establishment and the forebodings that such an establishment bears.

6 The usual explanation (e.g. J. Gray 1970:100) is that a Dtr redactor has conditionalized this reference to the unconditional covenant recorded in 2 Sam 7 by inserting vv. 3–4 (cf. Noth 1968:30; Montgomery/-Gehman 1951:87). Campbell (1986: 84 n. 43) criticizes Veijola's attribution of the passage to a Dtr redactor but offers essentially the same explanation when he shifts attribution to his "Prophetic Record." R.D. Nelson (1981:100–6) provides an extensive discussion of the redactional reading of this conditionalization but also fails to consider the possibility of local rhetorical reasons for the change.

necessary fulfilments.[7] At this point, in view of what has just come before and in view of how Solomon behaves immediately thereafter, Solomon is not in any position to feel secure on his throne. David plays on his son's insecurity to secure the death of his enemies even after his death. The conditionalized dynastic promise is designed coercion or allurement: either it forces an insecure successor to do what is bidden with a view to gaining God's blessing or it reveals a sinister rationalization to the man who would be king.

Twice in David's remarks to Solomon he refers to Solomon's wisdom (vv. 6, 9). Do according to your wisdom, (*keḥokmāteká*) he tells Solomon as he instructs him to kill Joab (v. 6). Again in v. 9 in regards to Shimei's end he says, "you are a wise man (*ʾîš ḥākām ʾāttâ*) and you will know what to do—a bloody end for Shimei." Again the narrator makes no specific comment about what David says. But the narrative's presentation of one murderous character instructing his son in the ways of bloodthirsty revenge and calling that wisdom does not seem designed to promote a high view of this particular quality as venerated by David or demonstrated by his son, Solomon.[8] Only a foreshadow at this point, it will have important bearing on the narrative's presentation of the wise Solomon and his future actions

---

7 Against De Vries (1985:30), who says that vv. 3–4, which he attributes to the Dtr redactor, have little to do with David's instructions for revenge. Once again ignoring the narrative's voice structure leads to extreme incomprehension of the narrative and the character's rhetoric within it. Characteristically, for historical-critical readings of the narrative, De Vries mistakes David's manipulation of deuteronomistic language, in vv. 3–4, for language employed by the Dtr narrator/redactor himself (p. 34; cf. Gerbrandt 1986:174). It is impossible for characters to voice deuteronomic sentiments that are independent of, or worse contradictory to, the narrator's point of view in De Vries' reading.

Ironically De Vries, commenting on the grammatical structure at the beginning of v. 5, says that the words, "and now," function to draw a logical consequence from the preceding (p. 35). He sees the rhetorical point on a grammatical level but does not understand it on the level of narrative semantics.

8 Of course this bears no implication whatsoever for the author's wisdom affiliations or lack thereof. A high or low view of Solomon's wisdom cannot be immediately translated into a socio-historical syllogism such as:

Solomon was a wise man
Solomon was wicked
Therefore all wise men are wicked.

The reverse is just as impossible—substituting "good" for "wicked"—though that conventional reading of the Dtr's attitude towards Solomon's wisdom has often been taken as an indication of a "wisdom affinity" (e.g. M. Weinfeld 1972:256). H.A. Kenik (1983:94), who maintains a high view of Solomon's wisdom throughout 1 Kgs 1–11 makes no comment on this negative contextualization of this attribute in Solomon.

founded on this same quality.

1 Kings 2:15

Adonijah's remark—that the kingdom reverted to Solomon even though the people wanted him, Adonijah, because "it was his from Yahweh"—is an example of character ignorance about historical events and divine causality, not dramatic irony. (The reader knows that it was political maneuvering that got the throne for Solomon.) In no way should this statement be construed as the narrative's way of approving Solomon's accession to the throne.

1 Kings 2:24

Here Solomon actually makes the connection, suggested to him by David, between killing off the opposition and thus obeying Yhwh. He will kill Adonijah for Yhwh, who gave Solomon the kingdom and made him a house. Solomon makes it his God-given duty to kill his own enemies. His logic: they are threatening the anointed of the Lord, a position that David worked long and hard to secure.

1 Kings 2:26–46

Using the heat of the occasion, Solomon turns to the rest of the adversaries mentioned by David. He kills them one by one, sometimes trapping them first. Vv. 31–4 are chiastic in structure:

Fall on him and bury him
Blood be on his head because he killed Abner and Amasa
Blood be on his head; to David's line let God grant peace
Benaiah fell on him and buried him.

Solomon's comments in v. 33 are bathed in irony. In the same breath in which he gives instructions for the desecration of the sanctuary of Yahweh's tent and the murder of Joab,[9] he

[9] Commenting on Solomon's action which oversteps the bounds of sanctuary laws and customs (e.g. Exod 21:13–14) Montgomery says, with tongue in cheek, "royalty here assumes a superior right" (1951:94). It is difficult to understand how Halpern can say, "Solomon nowhere initiates a cycle of violence and guilt" (1988:146). Who, if not Solomon? Again (p. 150) Halpern says, "From 1 Kings 1, then, through 1 Kings 10, the historian homogenizes inherited materials on his personal palette: Solomon is the passive, prudent king, whose first real act is the construction of the temple." Solomon

claims a distinction between the line of David, i.e. himself, hopefully ever blessed with peace as the reward for their peacefulness, and bloodthirsty men such as Joab.

The narrator's comment on Solomon's behaviour? "And the kingdom was established in Solomon's hand," the inclusiastic end (on the basis of *kûn*) to what began in 2:12. The implication of this dry comment on Solomon is that these actions, these lame justifications and this *modus operandi* are what can be expected under this administration (cf. E. Würthwein 1977:31, against Gray 1970:105).[10] And if Yhwh has indeed used Solomon and his wisdom to complete a series of actions begun long before (2:27) then it would seem either that Yhwh's hands are also fouled by Solomon's actions, or else his ends—whatever they may be—justify the use of means such as Solomon and his Machiavellian wisdom.

1 Kgs 3

Hard on the heels of the ironic presentation of how Solomon went about establishing his kingdom, ch. 3 presents the odd business about the wisdom of Solomon. Immediately after reporting that this is how, "the kingdom was established in Solomon's hand," the narrator goes on to describe the next step, a pact through marriage, with Pharaoh. Solomon strikes a deal with the arch-villain, the Pharaoh, "king of Egypt," of whom the last two recollections have been associated with the Bondage (1 Sam 2:27; Deut 7:8), and who can never be mentioned in the Bible with neutrality. The Pharaoh is, after all, anathematic opponent Yahweh. Could Solomon have chosen a less appropriate ally? Not only does he ally himself with Pharaoh, he even goes so far as to marry Pharaoh's daughter, contravening the commandment of Deut 7:3–5 (cf. Josh 22:5; 23:7–8).[11] And

---

may be David's dupe in settling old scores but he is anything but passive after ch. 1. A rough count of verbs and their subjects in 1 Kgs 1–10 shows a total of 278 with Solomon holding title to 131: a full 47% of the total. Hardly the most passive character in this tale!

10 Cf. Noth (1968:39), "*von einer Sympathie des Haupterzählers für Salomo kann offenbar keine Rede sein.*"

11 Any ambiguity over the narrative's implications in v. 1 is disambiguated a few chapters later, in 7:8, 9:16, and especially 11:1, each of which in its own context shows how the Egyptian alliance is true only to Solomon's own personal preferences and

where does he bring her? To David's (not Yhwh's) royal city![12] And what is he doing there? Building, in order, his house, Yhwh's house, and the wall of Jerusalem—first self, then God, and last his subjects' needs.

Meanwhile the people are still sacrificing at the high places while Solomon pursues his own priorities in which the Egyptian alliance and construction of his own house, not to mention the obliteration of his political enemies, come before the temple. The placement of this description of Solomon's priorities here, is as obvious an indication of the narrator's view as his "exposition-by-implication" expositional strategy allows.[13]

It isn't just the people who sacrifice at the high places. Solomon too shares in the odious behaviour.[14] The chiastic

---

ambitions and anathematic to the behaviour that Yhwh desires of his people and their king. Given the strength of Egyptian symbolism throughout the Bible—a biblical archetype if there is one—the subsequent confirmation is really superfluous (part of what Sternberg calls "foolproof composition" (1985:234).

12 The Greek translators were vexed by Solomon's actions to the point of rearranging the text in order to ameliorate them (D.W. Gooding, *Relics of Ancient Exegesis* , pp. 9–12, cited by De Vries 1985:50).

13 The connection is syntactically foregrounded by the connections between vv. 1 & 2:

- He takes the daughter of Pharaoh
- He brings her to the city of David
- "until" (*ʿad*) he finished building: his house, the house of Yhwh, and the wall of Jerusalem
- "howbeit" (*raq*) the people were still sacrificing at the high places
- for the house of Yhwh wasn't built "yet" (*ʿad*), at that time.

Though Solomon is building the house of Yhwh it isn't first on his list; in the mean time (*ʿad*) the people continue a religious practise that is offensive to Yhwh.

14 Once again, the narrative takes pains to ensure that the reader sees the connection between the peoples' behaviour and Solomon's:

"only" (*raq*) the people were sacrificing at the high places
for the house of Yhwh wasn't built yet.
Solomon loved Yhwh, to walk in the statutes of David
"only" (*raq*) at the high places he sacrificed and burnt incense.

There is even a chiastic pattern within this pattern, between its first and last lines:

raq hāʿām mᵉzabbᵉḥîm *babbāmôt*

raq babbāmôt hûʾ mᵉzabbēaḥ ûmaqṭîr

The syntactic inversion in the last line reveals the narrator's light touch as he works to highlight the similarity and thus, the incongruity. It is, after all, also Solomon's priorities that create the situation in which the people continue to sacrifice at the high places. Solomon, on the other hand, has no such excuse.

Montgomery (1951:104) notes the incongruity—"It is not so remarkable that the king

juxtaposition of vv. 2 and 3 is designed to highlight the incongruity. Like the people, Solomon worships at the high places. Unlike them, he is in a position to change the fact that a temple does not exist by expediting, as he does not, work on the temple project. He could, after all, transfer all the construction workers to the temple project.

Chiastic incongruities continue as the narrative's focus in vv. 3–5:

Solomon loved Yhwh
but he worshipped at the high places.
He went to Gibeon, to the great high place &
offered a thousand burnt offerings in that altar.
At Gibeon, worshipping at the high place
Yhwh appears in a dream and offers to grant a request!

The ironic juxtaposition of the two phrases, "Solomon loved Yhwh," "but he worshipped at the high places" jars the sensibilities of the reader, who knows that God does not look favourably on such behaviour.[15] In v. 2 the narrator has alluded

---

went to Gibeon to sacrifice at its high-place, as that the story has been so artlessly preserved"—but misreads it as the mark of clumsy composition. For Kenik (1983:203), whose careful reading of Solomon's dream is marred by indiscriminate attributions of all major character utterances to the Dtr (an attribution endowed to her by conventional wisdom about the Dtr's compositional methods), Solomon's cultic celebrations at Gibeon were intended, by the Dtr, to portray legitimate, pre-Temple worship. But there is nothing in the context that implies that Gibeon was one of the places where Yahweh had caused his name to dwell. To the contrary, the structure of vv. 2–3 and 3–5 implies that worship at Gibeon impinged (*raq*) on the love of Yahweh and legitimate Temple worship. Kenik notes the negative implications of context (1983:186 n. 30) but fails to pursue the implications for the worship at Gibeon. Furthermore, although she is aware of the connection between vv. 3 and 15 in the narrative (1983:191–5), a connection that focuses on Solomon's mercenary attitude towards worshipping Yahweh in Jerusalem, she does not see anything odd about Solomon offering sacrifice at Gibeon, when Jerusalem was obviously an available and fitting place of sacrifice (v. 15). Why does Solomon travel to Gibeon, some 15 km. distant, when he could have offered the same burnt offerings before "the ark of the covenant of Yahweh" (v. 15) in Jerusalem? Or even more interesting, because the narrator raises this question through structural implication, why does Solomon return to Jerusalem to make those same burnt offerings, though less of them, along with peace offerings before "the ark of the covenant of Yahweh" (v. 15) after Yahweh has granted him a boon? Solomon's behaviour is presented as a textbook case of religious mendacity.

15 De Vries (1985:51; cf. e.g. Noth 1968:49) does not hear the irony (first pointed out to me by David Gunn). Instead he believes that the narrator was forced to admit that Solomon participated in foreign religious observance in order to include the story about the dream at Gibeon. The narrator's emphasis, says De Vries, is on Solomon's love for Yahweh. How inept a redactor to have so foregrounded the irony he was trying

through the deuteronomic phrase "a house for the name of Yhwh," to the law on cultic segregation from other religions (Deut 12:1–14). The point of v. 2 is that the people continue practices that God finds offensive, because they have no temple. With this allusion recently planted in the reader's mind, what is so odd about vv. 3–5 is that God should appear to Solomon at this important high place, which according the Deuteronomy 12 he should thoroughly detest along with any Israelite that might favour it over the place where God chooses to establish as his name's place. That there is a choice for Solomon to make and God to see, is clear enough from Solomon's sycophantic switch (v. 15) of his chosen place of worship.[16] Why does God let him get away with it?[17] Nothing is provided in the immediate context to answer this question. Neither the narrator nor God make any comment on the dissonance of God granting a boon to anyone at this great high place. And why does God go even further and grant Solomon anything he wishes?[18] The narrator

---

to hide! Gerbrandt (1986:176) cites the verse as an adulation of Solomonic piety but cuts the verse off, in his citation, before the part about Solomon's ecumenical tastes. Halpern seems of two minds on Solomon's behaviour here: that it is implicitly critical (1988:155) or that it is neutral because of the Dtr's view of the history of Israel's cult (p. 146). Kim Parker, who concentrates his analysis on a larger structural parallelism in 1 Kgs 1–11, also takes the narrator's statement about Solomon's love for God at face value (1988:22). His reading of the parallels would, in fact, be strengthened along with his persuasive formal arguments for the unity of this passage if he had seen that there is no Dr. Jekyll and Mr. Hyde characterization here. Solomon is pure Hyde, albeit without prejudice.

16 Montgomery (1951:108) follows Hölscher in viewing v. 15's removal of Solomon to Jerusalem as an insertion (cf. Gray 1970:127). Having done so, Montgomery also fails to see the implications for Solomon's character that are drawn only by means of the parallel between v. 15 and v. 4.

17 The Chronicler offers a good example of a reader who sees the problem. His innovative solution to it is one of many examples of his greater concern for maintaining piety and propriety where Kings offers provocation and puzzlement. The solution: to split the legitimate focal points of cultic observance, the tent and the ark, placing the tent at Gibeon and the ark in Jerusalem. "Then Solomon and all the assembly with him went up to the high place at Gibeon, for there was the tent of meeting of God, which Moses, servant of Yhwh, made in the wilderness" (2 Chron 1:3). In this version Solomon gets away with nothing and there is no dissonance at all in God's appearance and offer to Solomon at Gibeon. Keil (1982:41) gratefully accepts the Chronicler's pious rendition of the episode, subverting the narrative rhetoric of Kings with that of Chronicles in the mistaken belief that both must accord with the one historical reality and that the Chronicler's version is most correct because it raises no questions about God's motives in this most unusual incident.

18 This is the only place in the Bible where God says "ask what I should give you" (*šeʾal mâ ʾetten-lāk*), allowing complete leeway for Solomon to respond as he pleases. (A close

does nothing to answer these questions at this point and so makes the dissonance as imposing as possible. Nothing is allowed to distract attention away from it or the questions that it raises. Consequently, when answers are forthcoming later they too make a much stronger impact on the reader's senses.

In vv. 6–9, the narrative introduces, for the first time, Solomon's unctuous rhetoric, which will play such an important role in the prayers to come.[19] Throughout there is a heavy emphasis on past promises that God has fulfilled: in vv. 6–7 Solomon repeatedly alludes to the promise to David made in 2 Sam 7; in vv. 8–9 it is the promise of numerous descendants to Abraham (cf. Deut 7:6–8) and the mighty acts of the exodus with which Solomon exercises his speech (cf. Gen 13:16; 32:13; Exod 19:6). The point of these allusions? 'I am Solomon, the fulfilment of your promise to David. Israel is your great people, the fulfilment of your promise to David.'[20]

---

parallel is Elijah's instruction to Elisha just before he is taken up (2 Kgs 3:9).

As Kenik has pointed out (1983:45–6), within the parameters of the literary form on which Solomon's dream report seems to be based, the so-called *Königsnovelle*, the leeway granted by God for Solomon's response is unique and striking. Normally in such dream theophanies the god will dictate what he will do or give; here, as Kenik notes, the verb "ask" is repeated several times, highlighting the fact that God allows Solomon to choose his boon. Kenik interprets this peculiarity as a reflection of the Dtr redactor's covenantal interests, in which the Israelite king, unlike other kings of the A.N.E., has a dialogic relationship with the god (1983:46).

I agree with Kenik's observations about the prominence, in God's offering, of leeway for Solomon to respond, but find the reason for this emphasis not in the narrator's wish to describe a dialogic covenantal relationship but in God's wish to expose Solomon to temptation and ultimately ruination. Why else add wealth and reputation to the boon when Solomon has successfully avoided these pitfalls in his request?

19 Noth (1968:50) mistakes Solomon's manipulation of deuteronomistic usages for late redactional expansions. The result is a failure to comprehend this aspect of Solomon's rhetorical machinations.

20 Kenik (1983:71, 88–96) correctly hears the unmistakable emphasis on divine obligation in Solomon's petition, but attributes it the the Dtr redactor, who writes the entire narrative. When God replies with a conditionalization of the Davidic covenant (v. 14), placing a contrary emphasis on the obligation of his human partners in the covenant, Kenik also finds the Dtr redactor speaking in chiastic opposition to what he said through Solomon in v. 6 (1983:165–6). She resolves the apparent conflict within the Dtr's views by suggesting a balanced tension, in which the Dtr reinterprets pre-Dtr royal theology (Solomon in v. 6) in the light of Torah, which requires obedience even from the Davidic monarch (Yahweh in v. 14).

This solution to the conflict that only begins to brew here between Solomon and Yahweh over the question of who is obliged to whom is very perceptive and well supported by structural observations. (Kenik finds a chiastic structure underpining the semantic oppositions between vv. 6 and 14 (1983:53–6).) But it brings the narrator—

The singular emphasis in these allusions? This king and this kingdom are the consummation of Israel's divinely guided history. This, along with the flattering tone and self-effacement,[21] aims to encourage God to foster and preserve his accomplishment and so, to maintain Solomon's monarchy. Finally, in v. 9 Solomon presents himself to God as a new Moses, quoting with appropriate alteration from Deut 1:9–16. Whereas Moses addressed his concerns about governing God's burgeoning people to them, Solomon speaks directly to God, playing on the latter's sense of covenantal obligation, which Solomon obviously hopes to have excited.[22]

It is in the context of emulating Moses for the benefit of his divine audience that Solomon slips in, almost unnoticed, his surreptitious request. 'So that I can play my Moses-role for you and "judge" (*špṭ*)—not "rule" (*mlk*), though that is my hidden

---

Kenik's Dtr—too close to the views expressed in the narrative. The conflict is not the narrator's. He sees it; he sets up the chiastic structure that highlights it. But he does not identify with either side, a truly conventional reading, or with both together, Kenik's innovation. There is no real resolution of this conflict in the narrative. Solomon sticks to his view and God to his. In the end, God prevails and any notion of divine obligation to the promises to David is deflated. 2 Kgs 25:27–30 is not a hopeful conclusion (cf. Noth 1981:98).

Throughout, the narrator keeps his detachment from the views expressed by characters, God included. He does not say that God should have kept the promises that he made to David; Solomon does. He only reports that God did not and even then he does not criticize God for reneging. Neither does he say that Solomon must now, against 2 Sam 7, obey in order to receive the Davidic reward; God does. And when Solomon does not obey the narrator does not criticize, though he supplies plenty of allusions to Deut 17 to highlight the disobedience. The narratorial situation is external and unconditioned; the narrator maintains an objectivity that, however much a literary convention, remains unsullied by the issues within the story world. Comprehension, not partisan involvement, was the goal of this reporter.

21 In the context of ch. 2 Solomon's oily efforts at humility ring false. Isn't this "innocent little boy" (*wᵉʾānî naʿar qāṭōn lōʾ ʾēdaʿ ṣēʾt wābōʾ*) the same person who just wiped out his political opposition? Solomon may think he can put this over on God, but only the most jaded of readers could swallow such bilge.

22 M. Weinfeld (1972:256) notes the connection between the two passages, but confuses Moses' and Solomon's rhetoric with that of the author/narrator of each passage (cf. Kenik 1983:143–6). "Like the author of Deut. I:9–18, the deuteronomic editor of I Kgs. 3:4–15 regards the possession of wisdom as the principal requisite for the competent functioning of the judiciary." Unfortunately this confusion leads Weinfeld to believe that the narrator supports Solomon's request and favours its outcome—Solomon's acquisition and employment of wisdom. The context of the request, and it is in the narrative context that we hear the narrator's own voice and views, is objectively neutral about Solomon's acquisition of wisdom, pointing to several anomalies and problems in its procurement.

purpose (cf. 2:12, 46)—this, your glorious people, give me a hearing heart to "perceive" (*byn*)—not "know" (*ydʿ*), for God might recall my predecessors' desire to know good and evil—the difference between good and evil' (cf. Gen 3:5, 22; Deut 1:39). Under the guise of innocence Solomon asks for the knowledge that makes man like God, the pursuit of which cost Adam and Eve their Edenic lifestyle.[23] Although there can be no certainty about Solomon's hubris here, for he has carefully couched the request in a studied naïveté, an Eve-like will to power is not beyond the man we have watched in ch. 2.

Even more surprising than God's appearance at the great high place is his overwhelming response to the request. The narrator specifically points out that *the content*[24] of Solomon's request pleased God (v. 10). Usually this narratorial comment is taken to mean that God is innocently pleased with Solomon's innocent request for theological-political sagesse. It is more probable, more in keeping with the divine character sketched so far, that God too has seen through some of Solomon's subterfuge and that he may have other reasons for being pleased with the request. He has, after all, taken the initiative to approach Solomon at the high place, where Solomon is not (cf. v. 3, *raq*) worshipping Yhwh, and to grant him *at that very place and time* anything Solomon names. Is this not ominous?[25] God is fully capable of being privy to the events of ch. 2. Why might God be pleased with the request? Does he foresee some utility, in his larger scheme of things, for Solomon's veiled grandiosity? Clues to the divine intent are provided by his further discussion of the matter in vv. 11–13.

In his response to Solomon God rephrases what Solomon has asked for—discernment of good and evil—and calls it "discernment to hear judgement" (*hābîn lišmōaʿ mišpāṭ*), an obvious twist of Solomon's request for a "hearing heart to judge your people and to discern between good and evil" (*lēb šōmēaʿ lišpōṭ ʾet-ʿammᵉkā lᵉhābîn bên-ṭôb lᵉrāʿ*). And, in fact, what

23 T.N.D. Mettinger opts for the judicial sense of the expression "to discern good from evil," but admits that "this faculty to discern "between good and evil" grants the king a quality of incomparableness on earth (1 R 3,12), it renders him to some extent "like God" (cf. 2 S 14, 17.20; Gn 3,5.22; 1 R 3,28)" (1976:244).

24 "And it was good, in the Lord's view, that Solomon had asked *this thing*" (*haddābār hazzeh*).

25 Cf. Hos 13:11 for an example of the potential for disaster in God's acquiescence to human requests.

Solomon gets is simply a "wise and discerning heart (*lēb ḥākām wᵉnābôn*, v. 12). The contrast reveals both character's differing aims.[26] Solomon wants more—discernment of good and evil—than he wants to let on, thus the humble couchment, "to *judge your* people." And God does affirm the request, with the proviso that the wisdom given will lead Solomon to *hear* judgement and with total disregard for the elevating discernment of good and evil. The ambiguity of God's response—does hearing judgement mean that Solomon will have a better sense of justice or does it mean that this gift will lead him to hear a judgement on account of it and his use of it?—will become clearer when we see, in subsequent events, how two-edged the gift can be. Solomon's wisdom does bears bountiful fruit, but that same fruit will be his undoing (chs. 5–11).

In v. 13 God adds wealth and honour to Solomon's boon. It is significant that of the items he applauded Solomon for not requesting (v. 11) he does not pick up on "length of days" or "the lives of your enemies." The enemies are, after all, dead so their absence here (v. 13) is self-explanatory. But why honour instead of an extended life span? And why add either of these potential traps for human weakness when Solomon seems so nicely to have avoided them?[27] The logic of these additional fringe benefits is clear from the covenantal rider that accompanies them.

Yahweh goes on to demand obedience to the covenant as his price for extending Solomon's days on earth. Here is the answer to the question raised by the disparity between v. 11 and v. 13. "Many days" are withheld in v. 13 because such longevity is conditional to obedience. The reason for the addition of wealth and honour to Solomon's prize also comes into clearer focus. Like David before him (2:4), Yhwh conditionalizes his promise to David. By putting temptation in Solomon's way, as storyworld history surely indicates (cf. chs. 4–11) and adding this

---

26 Kenik (1983:44) regards the phraseological variations between Yahweh's and Solomon's versions of what he is to get as the same content said four different ways. Such a reading ignores the common biblical device of contrastive characterization through such subtle variations (cf. Alter 1981:72–6). The differences between the characters is significant and revelatory: what Solomon wants is not what God wants to give. (Compare, for example, 1 Sam 8:5, where the people ask for a profane king "like all the nations," to which God responds with a designate (*nāgîd*) "over *my people* Israel.") This is not the same thing said twice but differently.

27 Cf. C. Meyers (1987:197), "... the riches and honor which characterized his realm were not of his choosing."

subversive reiteration of his promise to David, God has set Solomon on a tight-rope that would take a saint to negotiate. Solomon, as chs. 2 and 3 to this point have shown, is no saint. Is this God's way out of his obligation to David?

Neither the narrator nor God offer any explicit comment on this radical adjustment to the promise to David (2 Sam 7). The narrator does offer some structural implication that spotlights the developing struggle between the views of the human and divine characters on the issue of the Davidic covenant and its conditionalization. Standing within the outer brackets formed by v. 5 and v. 15, vv. 6 and 15 are also linked in an inclusio (Kenik 1983:53–4). In v. 5 Solomon, speaking of the Davidic covenant, gushes incessant reminders of how God was faithful to his covenantal obligations (and promises) to David. In v. 15 God, alluding to the same subject, fends off the implication of Solomon's reiterations—that God ought now to continue in his promised obligation—belabouring the notion of necessary obedience, performed by David and expected of his descendants as well.[28]

The only other insight afforded to the reader is David's own adjustment to the terms of the agreement, described just one chapter back (2:4). There David presented Solomon with a conditionalized version of his dynastic contract to push Solomon to carry out his revenge. Here God himself presents Solomon with another conditionalized version of the Davidic covenant. But his purpose is not so clear as David's. If all that God truly wanted was an able tight-rope artist of saintly obedience, then why unbalance Solomon with temptation that the latter had avoided? From Solomon's morally questionable performance in ch. 2 we, and presumably God, know that he is no moral giant. The combination of adding temptation where it had successfully been avoided, followed by a radical revision of the Davidic

28 Kenik sees, in the relationship of vv. 6 and 15, a balanced tension established by the Dtr redactor. "Out of this tension, the Dtr's purpose to bring the Davidic covenant into harmony with Torah is effected" (1983:54). As the story develops, however, it becomes very clear that the tension is not balanced at all. Solomon's grand scheme, the Temple and its public inauguration, is a clever attempt to trap God into a commitment to an unconditional covenant, or at least a conditional covenant whose conditions are meaningless. And Yahweh is equally steadfast in his newly imposed conditionalization of the Davidic covenant. Here there is no balanced tension; to reduce it to such is to dull the edge of character strife and to ignore the subsequent sequencing of interactions which lead to open confrontation and ultimate imbalance of the tension. Yahweh does, after all, win the dispute (ch. 11).

covenant is a trap. And like David's own conditionalized version of 2 Sam 7 the terms of the agreement are rearranged to suit the aims of the interpreter. Here we see the beginning of Solomon's end and the end of the unconditional covenant to David and his descendants.

With v. 15 the inclusio of vv. 3–5 is extended:

- Sacrifice and burnt offerings at Gibeon.
- Dream and boon.
- Sacrifice and burnt offerings in Jerusalem before the ark of the covenant!

Ulterior motive in hand, Solomon returns to the cult site in Jerusalem to offer the sacrifices that he could have offered there in the first place. But Solomon's return to cultic orthodoxy illuminates far more than his self-serving religiosity. If Solomon knows what is pleasing to Yahweh, what of Yahweh himself? Shouldn't Yahweh have chastised him for worshipping at Gibeon instead of appearing to make that unparalleled offer?

The entire affair bodes ill. The place of the dream foreshadows the fact that this promise plays to Solomon's sinful side; it is made while Solomon is out "fornicating" with other gods. Mercenary that he is, Solomon returns from the high place to offer worship and sacrifice to Yahweh, a false show of fidelity in response to the apparent boon in the dream's promise. Yahweh's failure to address either Solomon's unprompted heterodoxy or his subsequent obsequious orthodoxy is particularly ominous. Does he have it in for Solomon already?

The tale that closes ch. 3 demonstrates how Solomon uses his new-found wisdom. It seems a positive beginning: he is human, not demonic in this narrative. Yet it also raises questions about what wisdom Solomon does possess after the dream theophany. Few readers have noticed that it is the mother, not Solomon, who saves the child. If the mother had not spoken out, Solomon's verdict—to cut the child in two—would have been enacted.[29] The story gives no indication that Solomon himself

---

29 M. Sternberg follows the conventional reading in attributing the end result to Solomon's good planning and wisdom. "Lest the snare be mistaken for a fluke, he [the narrator] establishes it as the judge's design all along by the brilliant twist given in verbatim repetition to the mother's outcry. What judge caught off guard would have the presence of mind to transform a shriek of renunciation ("Give her the living child and by no means kill him") into a verdict of restoration ("Give her the living child and by

had any other plan. It is only an assumption, receiving no explicit confirmation in the narrative, that the different turn events take was Solomon's plan. Only the mother's outburst halts the proceeding.[30] What kind of wisdom is this? Certainly events do turn out right, but is it because of Solomon or inspite of him?

The conclusion of the tale has also been misread. In v. 28 the narrator says, "all Israel heard the judgement that the king adjudged. And they feared on account of the king for they saw that the wisdom of God was in him to do judgement." It is significant that the narrator couches the perception in a character observation; he does not lend even this limited observation any of his own authority. The people, viewing the outcome, assume that Solomon planned it that way. But the narrator does not confirm their assumption and readers who accept the observing characters' point of view do so in the face of narratorial silence on the matter. The people do indeed see the wisdom of God operating, but it is not a wisdom controlled by Solomon.[31] It is a wisdom that operates through Solomon, but it is not operated by Solomon. Rather, the divine wisdom that resolves this difficult case is accidental to Solomon's own wisdom; it appears in the events more through the intercession of the mother of the live child than through Solomon's decree. And even operating through Solomon, what are we to think of this wisdom? Is it the kind of decision that any human being would like to face? The

---

no means kill him") by a simple shift of reference?" (1985:169).

The only support that Sternberg marshals to support his reading is an extra-textual supposition, itself supported only by psychological analogy, assumed verisimilitude and probability—"What judge caught off guard would have the presence of mind ..." The repetition, which commits the narrator to nothing, either in favour or rejection of Solomon's wisdom, can just as easily be read as Solomon's vocal reaction to his awakening to the reality of the situation and his grave error. Hearing the real mother's outburst, Solomon is dumbfounded and shouts, as the sword falls, the only words in his blasted mind, namely the words of the stricken mother, the only character here that can or will vocalize a true feeling about the proceedings.

The fact that the narrator subsequently affirms the fact that the whore who renounced her rights to her child is the real mother does not, as Sternberg says it does, remove doubts about the correctness of Solomon's solution. The narrator does nothing but state the obvious and that does not show at all that Solomon knew, aforehand, what result his decision would provoke.

30 De Vries (1985:61) notes the key role played by the mother's intervention but ignores his observation in favour of the conventional reading.

31 Against Halpern (1988:146), who says that "Solomon *demonstrates* that "the wisdom of god was in him to perform justice"" (his emphasis).

response of the characters in the story is to fear—not to love, honour, or admire—Solomon. This manner of operation is more divine than human, more likely divine than Solomonic in origin.

The tale of two whores does show that Solomon takes his new wisdom and responsibility seriously; it does not show that Solomon has god-like prescience or insight. Responding to his show of wisdom the people fear Solomon and see "the wisdom of God in him, to do judgement." The phrasing picks up from similar words in vv. 9 and 11. The proven result is unlike v. 9 (Solomon's perception) in which Solomon would be an agent of judgement (*špṭ*). It is more like God's perception (v. 11) in which Solomon himself is only witness to judgement (*špṭ*).

And so, Solomon's story is also fatefully tragic. Both David and God play on his human frailty to achieve their purpose through him. In both employments, Solomon is a tool in the conditional qualification of the unconditional covenant. In the second, he is also a tool in his own undoing.

1 Kings 4

Chapter 4 emphasizes three things: the shape and extent of the Solomonic bureaucracy (vv. 1–19, 22–23, 26–28), the fulfilment of the promises to Abraham in Solomon's reign (vv. 20–21, 24–25), and the growth of Solomon's wisdom and reputation (vv. 29–34), this last fulfilling the promise of 3:12. Like Samuel's speech in 1 Sam 8:10–18, the description of the royal administration is two-edged: it implies both the benefits of government, here by associating the evils of taxation with the fulfilment of the Abrahamic promises, and the burden of support through taxation, which nevertheless occupies the bulk of this narrative description. The balance thus achieved is typical of the neutral narratorial stance in the Dtr.

The most striking part of the chapter, however, is its description of the fulfilment of the Abrahamic promises and the connection between that and Solomon's reign:

Judah & Israel, numerous as sand, eating, drinking, rejoicing
Solomon reigned over all kingdoms from the River to Egypt
Inventory of Solomon's daily requirements
Solomon dominated all kings from the River to Gaza
Judah & Israel, each under his vine and fig tree

The chiasmus points to the connection between the fulfilment of the promises and Solomon's rule: in Solomon, the fulfilment is at hand. This same connection is prominent in another distinctive parallel in the chapter. The enlargement of Israel and of Solomon's wisdom are linked in their allusion to the fulfilment of the promise to Abraham (progeny [v. 20; cf. Gen 22:17; 32:12] and land [v. 21; cf. Gen 15:18]). The allusion characterizes this point as the height of Israel's political existence. It also points to the problem, given Solomon's personality, of this wisdom. On account of the latter, people from all the kings of the earth begin to come to Solomon. God is as responsible for the aggrandizement of Solomon's wisdom as he is for the fulfilment of the Abrahamic covenant here. The narrative will soon show how those contacts affect Solomon and lead him astray.

1 Kings 5–7

These chapters describe an important part of Solomon's building campaign: construction of the temple of Yahweh and the house of the king. One should say, rather, the house of the king and then the house of Yahweh, for this is the order and the priority of construction described by the narrator. Here as in other lists in the Bible, ordering indicates priority. As before (3:4, 15) Solomon's priorities put his personal goals before Yahweh's.

In 6:1–11 the narrator describes the house Solomon built for Yahweh. The description is paralleled in great detail by the description (ch. 7) of the house that Solomon builds for himself. He and Yahweh have much the same house plan and they live in the same neighbourhood (cf. De Vries 1985:103).

In the midst of the construction Yahweh issues an ominous warning to Solomon about the significance of the temple (6:12–13). Once again (cf. 3:14) the gist of the message is a conditional qualification of the unconditional promise to David.[32] But a comparison of this second iteration with the first reveals a growth in the applicable conditions:

---

32 The qualification of the Davidic covenant here frequently leads historical-critical readers to label God's warning as a subsequent addition (e.g. Noth 1968:118). There is, however, nothing in the immediate context that suggests any inappropriateness about the warning. In the wider context of 3:14 and 9:3–9 it is, in fact, eminently suited as a timely warning against Solomon's growing aspirations by means of the temple that he so doggedly seeks to complete (e.g. 6:14).

3:14	*6:12*
If you will walk in my ways, to keep my statutes and commands as David your father walked, I will lengthen your days.	*[Regarding] this house that you're building,* if you will walk in my *statues and my commands you will perform, and you will keep all my* commands, *to walk in them, I will establish my word with you, which I spoke to David your father. And I will dwell among the Israelites and I won't forsake my people, Israel.*

All italicized items are new to the second instance of the conditional qualification. There is a much stronger emphasis on the necessity of obedience to God's requirements. There is also an explicit reference to the consequence of disobedience: divine withdrawal from Israel.

Though the direction of this new rhetoric is clear, the reason for it is not. The narrator does not reveal why God interrupts the construction at this point, making the heavy-handed tone stronger. When Solomon gets into his public prayer for the temple dedication the reader will appreciate the reasons behind God's warning here: Solomon tries to establish the temple as the guarantee of Israel's survival and his dynasty. For the moment, however, the narrator hides the Solomonic initiative to foreground this glaring conditional qualification of the promises to David.[33]

Yahweh steps in with even stronger provisos and the reader is left not knowing why, just at this point. The question that is raised by both 3:14 and 6:12–13 is why God is altering the terms of the agreement. The net effect of the modification is a return to the pre-Davidic Sinai agreement in which continuation de-

33 For a literary-historical reading of the significance of Yahweh's interjection see Würthwein (1977:65), who posits an exilic redactional insertion that makes for a prophetic warning against over-reliance on the Temple as the surety of covenantal security (vv. 11–12 are DtrN, v. 13, "*spätdtr*"). Clearly a historical-critical reading such as Würthwein's agrees with mine in understanding the tendency of the character's speech; it only differs in resorting to hypothetical socio-historical contexts rather than the existing narrative context for the overall framework of interpretation.

pends on obedience. This modification, combined with the questionable and odd temptations that have been put in Solomon's way in ch. 3, contains within it the shadow of disaster to come. The question, "Could God get away with such a modification, knowing that David might have told Solomon of the agreement?", is easily answered in the affirmative. For David has already imbued Solomon with the idea that the covenant is conditional (2:3–5). Yahweh simply picks up where David left off, though ultimately Yahweh's ends are far more sinister than David's petty revenge. Both David and Yahweh prey upon the fact that Solomon is new to the position and so at the mercy of superiors who legislate the terms of his appointment, a situation that many readers can appreciate.

There is, nevertheless, in ch. 6 some indication of Solomon's strategy and therefore also some hint at the reason for Yahweh's forceful proviso. In 6:14 we read, "So Solomon built the house and finished it." This is the second time he has finished it (cf. 6:9). As usual, such resumptive repetition indicates a connection between the surrounding story and the piece that is inserted between the repeated items. Here the repetitive notice surrounds Yahweh's proviso:

A Solomon built and finished Yhwh's house (guarantee accomplished)[34]

B Yhwh: I won't live in it unless you obey my covenant

A' Solomon built and finished Yhwh's house (guarantee accomplished?)

This notice is like the double notice that Solomon's kingdom was established (1 Kgs 2:12, 46), a biting ironic comment on how it was that Solomon sought to guarantee his political security.

34 Note that the building of the Temple is closely connected to the unconditional covenant made in 2 Sam 7. There David wants to build a house for God because he lives in a better dwelling than God (v. 2). God declines, but announces that David's descendant, to whom an eternal throne is promised, shall build the house: "he will build a house for me and I will establish his throne forever." The link here between an eternal throne and the Temple is what Solomon is counting on as he builds the Temple. He sees the Temple, quite reasonably on the basis of what Yhwh says in 2 Sam 7, as a guarantee of his own dynasty.

An interesting side line is the comment in in 1 Chron 28:2–3 that David wasn't allowed to build the Temple because he was a man of war, with blood on his hands. And what was Solomon after his measures to establish his throne? Solomon's own remarks on the reasons for David not having built the Temple are also revealing. He says (1 Kgs 5:3) that David was too busy in warfare to build the Temple. But so was Solomon until he did whatever was humanly possible to put any human rivals out of the way, and until he got the dream from Yhwh, he was busy worshipping at the high places. Only after the dream did he proceed to try to guarantee his relationship with Yhwh.

Here, the same irony exists in the double description of how Solomon sought to guarantee his reign through the cultic institution. Yhwh's interlude, between the double notice of the temple's completion, is formally parallel to the descriptions of how Solomon eliminated the human threats to his royal security. The difference, which contrasts strongly through this comparison, is that the divine threat is uncompromising and cannot be dealt with so easily. Solomon's efforts to complete the houses, to establish himself even more securely are highlighted even more when this description of completion is repeated again in 6:38 and 7:1, which are chiastically linked. The repetition reflects Solomon's concern to complete the houses, both of which are supports for his government. This same concern is reflected in 7:51, also a description of Solomon's efforts to complete the project.

At this point in the narrative the reader cannot be sure about the motive behind Solomon's building program. There is some hint, provided by the structural parallelism between 6:9–14 and 2:12–46, that Solomon seeks to secure his position. But until he makes public, as he does in ch. 8, his views about the role of the temple in his regime, the reader is left to speculation. Given the attention that the narrative pays to the construction of the temple, a reflection of its importance to Solomon within the story, there is no doubt, however, that it is an important part of his program to secure himself.[35]

The Subsequent Context of the Prayers

The first item that the narrator draws attention to, following Solomon's great prayers, is once again the completion formula (cf. 6:9, 14, 38; 7:51). Each repetition of the completion formula highlights this focal point and Solomon's concentration on it. The reason for Solomon's concentration on the completion of the temple is made clear in his prayers (ch. 8), where the reader is allowed to hear how Solomon wants everyone, but most especially God, to see the temple: a guarantee of the Davidic monarchy's security. Almost every time the notice of completion occurs Yhwh's response to it is recorded and he rejects the assurance that Solomon seeks, in direct contradiction to the

[35] Cf. C. Meyers (1987:189–93) on the real world, utilitarian motives for constructing a temple. Solomon is certainly a character who would have appreciated such considerations.

assurance he grants Solomon's father in 2 Sam 7:13. Whatever Solomon knows about the terms of the Davidic covenant—and he seems to know something about it (8:17–21, 23–26)—Yahweh chooses to ignore his words to David in 2 Sam 7:13–16. How God can get away with ignoring, reneging on, or denying his promise to David is explained neither by God within the narrative nor by the narrator without. It is left as a significant and verisimilar enigma.

In ch. 9 Yahweh responds directly to Solomon's prayers. Solomon has called on Yahweh to honour his commitment to David (8:26). The prayer is Solomon's attempt to win an ironclad guarantee from God, such as he had once offered to David, with the temple as the physical evidence of the arrangement. God responds to Solomon's focus on the temple by saying that even that symbolic edifice will become a heap of ruins (cf. 2 Kgs 25:9) should strict covenantal obedience not be forthcoming.[36]

The prayer seeks great leeway for human sinfulness, with the temple as mechanism and focal point for the proposed forgiveness (8:31–53). Yahweh's response is an embellished reiteration of what he said in 3:14:

> "If you will walk before me, as David your father walked, with a pure heart and rectitude, to do all that I command you, and my statutes and judgements you will keep, then I will establish the throne of your kingdom over Israel forever. As I said to David, your father, "there will not be cut off for you a man on the throne of Israel."

In this response Yahweh brushes aside all of Solomon's prayerful aspirations for the temple. Solomon isn't the only one who can cite the Davidic covenant. Here God quotes his own words in the same breath in which he conditionalizes that agreement. Again this strict requirement for obedience from Solomon, coupled with Solomon's penchant for excess and the temptation that is being put in his way does not paint a bright picture of Yahweh's intentions for the Solomonic monarchy. Solomon's pleas for clemency (ch. 8) have backfired. Or rather,

36 McCarthy (1978:134) understands the rhetoric of Solomon's prayers—to claim the fulfilment and establishment for all time of the unconditional promise to David in 2 Sam 7—but mistakenly reads Solomon's claims as those fostered by the overall narrative and its structure. "... the account of Solomon's reign is so structured as to come to a climax in 1 Kings 8, that is, in the completion of the temple, at once the fulfilment and the guarantee of the promise." Yahweh's response to the prayers in ch. 9 unequivocally shows that such could not be the case and subsequent events confirm their divine engineer's assertion.

having brought his own plans to the light of day, Solomon has forced Yahweh into a more explicit revelation of his own purpose. Though Yahweh is not forced to make his own requirement of total obedience stiffer—it is infinitely stiffer than what he promised David (cf. 3:14; 6:12–13)—Solomon's rhetorical moves in the public prayer force him to make an opposing, more explicit statement of the necessity of obedience and the severe consequences of betrayal.

In response to Solomon's effort to ameliorate the curses of Deut 28, Yahweh reaffirms them in 9:7–9, alluding to Deut 28:37, 45, 63; and 29:23–26 (cf. Keil 1982:139):

> And I will cut off Israel from on the face of the land
> that I gave to them
> and the house that I sanctified to my name
> I will cast off from before my face.
>
> Israel will become a proverb and a saying (cf. Deut 28:37) among all the people
> and this house will be a heap.
> All passing by it will be astonished and exclaim, "For what did Yahweh to such a thing to this land and this house?" (cf. Deut 29:23).[37]
>
> And they will reply, "Because they forsook Yahweh, their God, who brought their fathers from the land of Egypt. And they embraced other gods and worshipped them and served them. Thus Yahweh brought upon them all this evil" (cf. Deut 29:24).

The transferral of the curse of Deut 29:23–26 from the land to the temple is especially significant. Solomon's prayers focus on the role of the temple in the forgiving pattern that he proposes for the future. Because the temple is so central to Solomon's proposal, Yahweh singles it out for special damnation in his rebuttal. God is as able as Solomon at creative re-interpretation of the laws of Deuteronomy.

Subsequently (9:10–11:8) the narrative focuses attention on the relationship between Solomon's wealth and his religious lapses, the actual provocation for the looming disaster. The narrator does not condemn Solomon; neither does he accept the theological line of Solomon's prayer. Rather his interest seems to be the following problematic: Solomon's propensity to excess is aided and abetted by the boon that Yahweh grants him so that his downfall is inevitable. Why does Yahweh aim at bringing Solomon down? How is Solomon's demise part of the di-

---

37 Here Yahweh adds "and this house" to the verse from Deuteronomy to take account of Solomon's temple ploy.

vine plan? What is the divine plan? What is made certain about the divine plan is that it is not to support or extend the "golden age" of Solomon.

Neither Yahweh nor Solomon are criticized in the narrative.[38] That Solomon sinned and that Yahweh helped him along his road to ruin are simple facts in this narrative, neither requiring nor receiving any explicit comment. The focal concern is the pseudo-synergistic impetus that the God/man interaction gives to Israel's history. Israel's history moves according to a divine plan, of which the human characters in the story are almost totally ignorant and of which, if they could be aware, they would most certainly disapprove.

The reader's awareness of the divine plan is only slightly greater, and that thanks to the narrator's selective implicit illuminations. What the narrator reveals is not where God is taking Israel's destiny; he only reveals that God is purposefully shaping it. Thus we see God methodically puts temptation in Solomon's way with one hand while exacting a heavier tribute in obedience with the other. When Solomon tries to gain a little more breathing room for himself, God only becomes more adamant. Solomon is unable to meet the requirements—his human frailty is already evident in ch. 2—and his monarchy, along with the eternal dynasty promised to David, is doomed. Neither the narrator nor God says anything explicit about the aim of this plot. It is left to the reader to draw conclusions from the trajectory that events take. It does not take any meticulous exploration to see that what God does in and through the reign of Solomon is to end the unconditional promises that he made to David; this is, from God's point of view, the single accomplishment of the entire Solomonic era. After Solomon, it is only a few quick steps to the ultimate end itself, the Exile.

In 9:10 we read again that Solomon completed his building projects (cf. 6:9, 14, 38; 7:51; 9:1). This notice is followed by more detailed descriptions of Solomon's administrative practices (vv. 11–18), especially as affected by his Egyptian contacts (vv. 15–19). The inclusiastic connections between 9:11–15 and 5:6–13 imply that nothing has changed, despite all that has inter-

---

38 Parker's reading (1988:25)—that with ch. 9 the narrative description is hostile to Solomon—picks up on the blatant implications of waywardness but errs in imputing a new negative valuation where the narrator is as neutral, if not as subtle as he was in chs. 1–3.

vened. Though it would be unreasonable to expect that Solomon's prayers would have led him to change his behaviour, it would only be natural for him to respond somehow to the strictures that God had imposed in 9:4–9. He does not. By way of literary allusion, the references to his "store cities" (*kol-ʿārê hammiskᵉnôt*) and his "chariot cities" and his "cavalry cities" (v. 19) all foreground the Egyptian aura that pervades his administration (cf. Exod 1:11; 14:9, 23–8; 15:1, 4; Deut 17:16; 1 Kgs 5:6). All is presented for the reader's edification without one comment; only the implication of allusion hints at the trouble that is brewing under the surface. And this is only the beginning of all that he would do, fairly mild by comparison to the later phase of his Egyptian-style rule.

Vv. 20–23 also provide some allusive insight into the manner of Solomon's kingship and the direction in which God is taking Israel's history through Solomon. Despite the emphasis, also by allusion, on the fulfilment of the Abrahamic promises in chs. 4–5 and the post-conquest peace that descended on Israel under Solomon (5:5; cf. Judg 21:44; 23:1) there are still nations unconquered living in Israel's midst (vv. 20–21). We know, from Judg 1 and 2:23 that God has spared these nations from conquest and reserved them as a test to prove Israel's loyalty.[39] As in Judg 1, many years earlier in story time, these nations are still being subjected to forced labour in Solomon's time because Israel was unable to exterminate them completely (*lōʾ-yākᵉlû bᵉnê yiśrāʾēl lᵉhaḥᵃrîmām*). All other appearances to the contrary, Yahweh has not committed himself without reservation; he maintains his trump. The allusion shows that the pattern that the narrator revealed back in Judg 2 is still working; God's plan is still in effect and should continue right to the end.

In v. 22 the allusion to 1 Sam 8:11–18 is obvious. Solomon enslaves the peoples who remained, not the Israelites as Samuel had predicted. But the Israelites have, nevertheless, been put to the work that Samuel mentioned in his tirade against kingship. Samuel's warning was misguided insofar as it predicted that the monarchy would result in a situation as intolerable as the Egyptian enslavement for the Israelites. But as Solomon's reign is proving, Samuel was correct about the way in which the monarchic bureaucracy would engulf the people. He was also right about an Egyptian style of rule in Israel's monarchy (cf. E.

---

39 See above, "These Nations That Remain," "A New Generation In Israel."

Speiser 1971:283), though at this point in the narrative there is no indication that the people are finding it as onerous as Samuel predicted in 1 Sam 8:18.

1 Kings 9:24–28

Sandwiched between Solomon's marriage to the daughter of Pharaoh, who comes up to the city of David, to the house that Solomon "built" for her (v. 24, the formula again), and Solomon's ship-building activities for the pursuit of gold (vv. 26–8, in contravention of Deut 17:17) is another of Solomon's efforts at cultic orthodoxy (cf. 3:15). It takes a back-seat to Pharaoh's daughter, and appears simply as one in a list of his mercenary aims. For Solomon, cultic activity is an insurance policy, not something worthwhile in and of itself. Once again there is a repetition of the notice about "building" at the end of v. 25, which invites comparison with v. 24 and v. 26. Solomon builds:

- a house for Pharaoh's daughter.
- a house for Yhwh, the insurance centre where he offers sacrifice.
- a fleet of ships for the purpose of collecting gold.

The incongruity is sharp and requires no comment from the narrator. Solomon's cultic behaviour continues in its utilitarian track (cf. 3:3–4 followed by 3:15).

Chapter 10 has two focal points, both related to Solomon's God-given wisdom. First there is his relationship with the queen of Sheba; second, the consequent matter of accumulating heaps of gold, silver, and cavalry. The multiple allusions in this chapter recall Deut 17:14–20 to the reader's mind. The queen's visit is a model that explains, at least partially, the manner in which Solomon accumulates wealth. Hearing of his wisdom and then experiencing it (vv. 1–9) the queen of Sheba feels compelled to honour him with her wealth (vv. 2, 10). The pattern repeats itself again and again (vv. 11, 14, 15, 22, 24–5). All the while the reader recalls that it was God who gave Solomon this fabulous wisdom. Hence it was also God who created this occasion for Solomon's Midas-like touch. To ensure that the reader does recall the narrator makes the connection explicit in vv. 23–5:

And king Solomon became greater than all the kings of the earth
in wealth
and wisdom.
And all the earth was seeking the presence of Solomon to hear
his wisdom, which God had put in his heart.
And they were bringing, each his gift,
articles of silver and gold, garments, weapons, spices, horses and
mules, year after year.

The narrator's description of the queen's visit to Solomon is modeled on the description of victims who succumbed to the conquest in the book of Joshua. Hearing of Solomon's wisdom, the gift of God, Sheba comes to test Solomon. When she sees all that Solomon's wisdom has accomplished (vv. 4–5) she is left "without spirit" (*wᵉlōʾ-hāyâ bâh rûaḥ*). This sequence, given appropriate contextual modification, is exactly that already manifest in the conquest stories of the books of Exodus (cf. 15:14–6), Deuteronomy (2:30–33) and Joshua (2:9, 11). The queen's confession is like that of Rahab in Josh 2; both characters confess to the glorious action of God through Israel (or Solomon), which affects most everyone who hears about it, leaving them "without spirit" (cf. Josh 2:11; 5:1). Such behaviour is, needless to say, divinely guided.

The parallel re-asserts the fact, known already from God's promise to Solomon in 3:13, that Solomon's wealth comes to him as God's bequest. The queen of Sheba is as much a conquest as the inhabitants of Jericho, Rahab excepted. The emphasis draws the reader's notice to the paradox that the piles of gold in ch. 10, so offensive to the sensibilities of all[40]—God included (he wrote the text)—schooled in Deut 17, are God-given. It is the confluence of this stream of divine influence and the other—the conditional qualification of the Davidic covenant—in the person and reign of Solomon that will bring the Solomonic monarchy to its abrupt conclusion. It is in short a setup, a biblical Trojan

40 Carol Meyers' interesting suggestion (1987)—that biblical scholars' have mistaken the text's description of Solomon's treasures for criticism by applying western puritanical values in their reading of the text—misses the damaging implications by way of allusion. Of course the narrator is not criticizing Solomon himself, but he is pointing out how adversely the God of Deut 17 and his supplicants might view Solomon's lucre. Her proposal to redress the imbalance in our perceptions of King Solomon by using comparative social scientific methods paves the way to even less attention to the fine literary detail of the text that gives us a very clear view of the narrator's perceptions. And I doubt that even social science can take us, with any exactitude, much further back than that.

horse story, and the queen's "conquest" serves much the same purpose as Rahab's conversion in the book of Joshua.

The queen's speech (v. 10) proclaims what Solomon's wisdom should do for Israel, i.e. "justice and righteousness." This piece of dramatic irony—the queen is unaware of it—contrasts markedly with the actual results of Solomon's reign, which have just been foregrounded in vv. 4–5, where Solomon displays the gains of his wise action:

> And when the queen of Sheba saw all the wisdom of Solomon:
> the house that he built,
> the food on his table,
> the attentiveness of his servants,
> the dutifulness of his servers,
> and their attire,
> and his cupbearers,
> and his stairway [to heaven] by which he could go up to the house of Yahweh,
> she was deflated.

This is the fullest description, anywhere in the narrative, of the fruits of Solomon's wisdom: justice and righteousness are conspicuous only by their absence. To read the queen's remark in v. 10 as dramatic irony requires no great stretch of imagination. All that the narrator has described so far, with the possible exception of the tale of two whores, is Solomon's incessant efforts at material gain for himself and his monarchy, of which the temple is a functioning part. As to the positive remarks made by the Queen about Solomon, his kingdom and Yhwh, we should notice that hers are the only positive remarks in the chapter. By contrast, the narrator offers one negative evaluation (11:7) and Yhwh three (11:6, 33 [2X]).

In vv. 10–23 the narrator describes, in detail, how Solomon's wisdom and reputation magnetically attracts wealth and prestige from around the world. Throughout this section the narrative conveys a vivid impression of the grandeur of Solomon's wealth and reputation, the two things that God added to his request for wisdom in 3:13. The narrator explicitly draws the connection between Solomon's vast accumulations of wealth and his wisdom in v. 23, and there is a chiastic relationship between vv. 23 and 24, which explicitly points to God as the ultimate author of this exponential largesse:

23. And the king, Solomon, became greater
    than all the kings of the earth for wealth and wisdom
24. And all the earth was seeking Solomon's face to hear
    his wisdom
    which God had put in his heart.

The link between the first and last lines alludes again to 3:14. What has come to pass is exactly what God promised at that point. And since the special focus of the chapter is on Solomon's contravention, thanks to his wisdom, of the legislation in Deut 17,[41] these two verses highlight the fact that it is God who ultimately affords Solomon the opportunity and means to contravene the law. The question that the narrative raises for the reader is why?

Verses 24–25 also highlight the connection between Solomon's wisdom and the wealth that it attracts:

> 24 All the earth was seeking (*mᵉbaqšîm*) Solomon's face to hear the wisdom that God put in his heart.
>
> 25 And they were bringing (*mᵉbîʾîm*) each his gift: articles of silver & gold, garments, weapons, spices, horses and mules annually.

The parallel between the two verses is designed to reveal how Solomon's increasing prosperity is the product of the divine intervention.

Solomon's response to the flow of wealth is predictable. He proceeds to sin in horses and horsemen, even to the extent of bringing them from Egypt (vv. 26–9), a direct contravention of Deut 17:16:[42]

> Moreover he shall not multiply horses for himself, nor shall he cause the people to return to Egypt to multiply horses, since Yahweh has said to you, 'You shall never again return that way.'

Anyone with any real intelligence would have enough with quietly sneaking some fine Egyptian horses past the all-seeing eyes of Yahweh; not Solomon. He has the guts to turn around and sell them to the Hittites and Arameans. Once again the nar-

---

41 The recent effort of A. Millard (1989) and K.A. Kitchen (1989) to defend the plausibility of the quantity of loot acquired by Solomon are well-intentioned and, from a non-specialist's perspective, persuasive. But they miss entirely the point being made in ch. 10 and only impede a reader's understanding of it by distracting attention from it onto the irrelevant matters of historical possibility. Biblical verisimilitude here, as so often for modern readers of the Bible, only gets in the way.

42 Montgomery marks the connection with Deut 17 here (1951:228), but gets caught up in piling up delightful historical analogies and misses the point of the allusion.

rator withholds any explicit comment on Solomon's behaviour, preferring to let the allusions do the talking. If there were any doubts about the propriety of Solomon's wealth and wisdom they have dissipated by the end of the chapter. In the person of Solomon the gifts that God has granted are a deadly pitfall, leading to wrack and ruin. The narrator's cool detachment throughout the chapter, in descriptive statements like, "the king made silver as common as stone in Jerusalem," aims at eliciting the appropriate emotional response from the reader —"how could he be so ignorant of Deut 17?" Such commentary by implication increases the impact of the narrative by making the reader a co-author through the strong responses that are evoked. The author impresses the reader with his own perspective by eliciting a response through implication, a far superior rhetorical technique to the explicit bombasms that historical-critical readers find the so-called Dtr redactors capable of.

1 Kings 11

Solomon's deterioration accelerates in ch. 11. The narrator begins by bombarding the reader with descriptions of Solomon's un-deuteronomic marriages in vv. 1–8:

> 1 Kgs 11:1 And king Solomon loved women, foreign and numerous: the daughter of Pharaoh, Moabitesses, Ammonitesses, Edomitesses, Sidonitesses, and Hittitesses.
>
> Deut 17:17 Neither shall he multiply wives for himself, lest his heart turn away (cf. Exod 23:31–33; 34:12–16; Deut 7:3).

Set beside the regulations of Deut 17, to which the narrative so obviously alludes in ch. 11, the sharp irony of the narrator's description stands out. Solomon not only breaks the command, seemingly tailored to suit him, but he goes it one better by marrying the very daughter of the arch-rival whose name and country stand for everything that Israel is to be separate from (cf. Deut 17:16; 28:68).[43]

---

43 For those readers who have failed to appreciate the charlatanic nature of Solomon's rhetoric in the prayers, the narratorial description that opens ch. 11 has often proved a problem. "The idolatry into which Solomon fell in his old age appears so strange in a king so wise and God-fearing as Solomon showed himself to be at the dedication of the temple, that many have been quite unable to reconcile the two, and have endeavoured to show either that Solomon's worship of idols was psychologically impossible, or that the knowledge of God and the piety attributed to him are unhistorical. But great wisdom and a refined knowledge of God are not a defence against the folly of idolatry ..." (Keil 1982:166). When the reader understands the euphuistic rhetoric of the prayers' piety, an

Not willing, at this point, to risk any misunderstanding on the part of the reader, the narrator includes an explicit cross-reference to draw the reader's attention to the fact that Solomon is in contravention of the book of Deuteronomy (v. 2; cf. Deut 7:3). Having provided the relevant proof text, he goes on to elaborate on Solomon's mixed marriages: he had no less than seven hundred wives and three hundred concubines! "And his wives turned his heart."

Further to prevent any misunderstanding about the great King Solomon, the narrator goes on (v. 4) to describe the first instance of somebody committing one of the offences for which Solomon sought clemency in his prayers of ch. 8. It comes as no great surprise that the offender is Solomon himself. His heart is not "whole" with Yhwh (cf. 8:61). His wives have turned his heart away, towards other gods. This correspondence of action and aim, as expressed in the prayers, exposes Solomon's prayers for what the are: not the pious expressions of the so-called deuteronomistic narrator (or narrators, if you will) but the conniving rhetoric of a cunning king trying to win allowances for himself under the guise of altruistic religious concerns. Unfortunately for Solomon, God is not so gullible. In fact Solomon's state of temptation, from which he seeks the allowances in his prayers, is divinely ordained so that it is no surprise that God should respond to the prayer as he does.

There is some ambiguity in the latter part of v. 4: "his [Solomon's] heart was not perfect with Yahweh like the heart of David, his father." Does the narrator mean that Solomon does not measure up to the peerless standard of David, his father? Or does he mean that, like David's, Solomon's heart was afflicted by sinful human infirmity? The structure of v. 4 gives a hint:

And at the time of Solomon's old age
His wives
turned his heart after other gods
and his heart was not wholly with Yahweh
like the heart of David, his father.

---

understanding granted by the narrative's contextualization of the prayers, is this conflict resolved without recourse to psychology or historical-critical literary analysis.

In the verse structure, David is positioned parallel to the wicked wives of Solomon. The whole is introduced by a strong temporal reference to the king's age. This combination recalls to mind 2 Sam 11, a famous incident, also introduced by the same strong temporal reference[44] and also a case of a king gone astray on account of a woman. Given the strong negative aura that surrounds the prior episode in the narrative about David (cf. Sternberg 1985:186–229) is it possible to read the comparison to David's heart as anything but sarcasm? Vv. 5–6 expand on the statements of v. 4, reiterating the same structural pattern and thus a similar response from the reader. The narrator ensures that there is no mistake over Solomon's behaviour and its reception by Yahweh.

In vv. 9–10 the narrator reminds the reader about Yahweh's previous appearances, in response to Solomon's temple building project, in which Yahweh warned Solomon that the temple could be no substitute for obedience (cf. 6:12–13; 9:3–9). We have seen Solomon's efforts to win allowances for sin and we have seen his consequent sinful behaviour. We have also seen Yahweh's rebukes of Solomon's efforts with the temple and now we see his response to the sins themselves.

As in the case of David's sin with Bathsheba, it is not Solomon who is forced to suffer for Solomon's sins, but his son (v. 12). Yahweh's radical qualification of the Davidic covenant is only granted passing notice, in Yahweh's words to Solomon, when he says that he will not tear the kingdom away from Solomon for David's sake. The conditionalization is, in Yahweh's eyes, a *fait accompli.*

The struggle between Solomon and God over the covenant is over at this point. Solomon has lost. His prayers have been answered, but not in the way that he expected. God wastes little time in raising enemies against the Solomonic regime, both from without (vv. 14–22, 23–25) and within (vv. 26–40).

1 Kings 8

Solomon's prayers are among the most impassioned intercessions in the Bible, ranking right alongside those of Abra-

44 The same, in fact and also to David's discredit when compared to 2 Sam 11:1–2:

lᵉʿēt ṣēʾt hammalʾkîm ... wayᵉhî lᵉʿēt hāʿereb wayyāqom dāwid

ham, Moses, and Jesus.[45] His fundamental theme: 'no matter what the sin, no matter who the sinner, please Lord, forgive and forget.' All amelioration is tied to the temple, which Solomon proposes as the clearing house for human repentance and divine forgiveness. A major theme in his plea is the reversal the ominous curses of Deut 28. Throughout, both the reader and the implied reader of Solomon's prayers—God—gets a sense of a powerful hidden agenda underneath the pious overtones.

The reader's first clues about Solomon's rhetorical purpose come, not in the prayer, but in the preceding context. We have already seen how both David (2:3–6) and even Yahweh (3:5–14; 6:12) play on Solomon's insecurities to bend him to their purposes. Solomon's main response to Yahweh's conditional qualification of the Davidic covenant is the temple. His plans for it avert to the Davidic covenant of 2 Sam 7 (5:3–5). Solomon envisions the temple as a means to win back the freedoms that Yahweh had granted to David in 2 Sam 7 but revoked, first in 3:14, under Solomon. Yahweh, a character known for his perspicacity—though it doesn't take omniscience to understand the point of Solomon's reiteration of the Davidic promise (5:3–5) *after* Yahweh's conditional qualification of the same (3:14)—sees Solomon's purpose for the temple and warns against it (6:11–13). At that point, Solomon is left with a very costly building whose prospective tenant refuses to sign the perpetual lease that Solomon envisions on account of the unacceptable terms that he seeks. Whatever can he do? The building is up, completed (over and over) and, one expects, the opening ceremony is scheduled.

> And all the work that the king, Solomon, did on the house of the Lord was finished (cf. 6:9, 14, 38).[46] And Solomon brought the Sanctified of David, his father, and the silver, and the gold, and the vessels, and he put them in the treasuries of the house of the Lord (7:51).

What next?

---

45 The force of Solomon's rhetoric has impressed many readers. So taken in by the power of the prayers, however, scholarly readers have been wont to attribute them to the author instead of leaving them as the relativized statements of the character to whom they have been granted by the narrator (e.g. Montgomery 1951:194, "these prayers attributed to Solomon compose one of the noblest flights in sacred oratory from the deuteronomic school").

46 The continual narratorial allusions to the completion of the work on the Temple culminate here. Solomon's bid, so heavily dependant on the edifice in the process of being built, ends with its completion in failure.

Anyone else might have boarded up the temple, sold it, or demolished it. Not Solomon, that was not his style. He has a fall-back plan, a public ceremony in which he will call upon God to honour his commitment to David and forcing Yahweh to accept the temple, in front of witnesses, on his own terms. The plan has its merits. Yahweh has a history of avoiding public scandal or besmirched reputation because such would defeat his larger revelatory purposes (cf. Exod 32:9–14; Num 14:11–20; Deut 9:13–19, 23–28; Josh 7:7–9). Public knowledge of the Davidic covenant along with an official restatement, to which a few clever Solomonic riders have been attached, might just force the divine hand. Yahweh's move to revise the Davidic promise could be defeated by the wiles of his cunning opponent.[47]

Solomon's plan is, in fact, effective. He does force the divine hand. But the result is a disaster, exactly the opposite of the hoped-for concession (9:3–9). Looking at the surreptitious rhetoric of Solomon's public prayers, it is easy to see why Yahweh responds as quickly and adamantly as he does.

A new scene opens in ch. 8 for Solomon's daring scheme. The narrative offers a detailed description of the grand spectacle that Solomon orchestrates (v. 1, "*then*[48] Solomon assembled ..."). The detail offers, like the continual references to the completion of the temple before, a revealing insight into Solomon's plans. Pomp and circumstance are necessary ingredients in this plan because it brings public notoriety to bear on Yahweh: the bigger the occasion the more attention focused on what Solomon has to say about the temple and its new role in Israel's theological-political economy. The narrator devotes all

---

47 The fact that the rhetoric of the prayers is so well-suited to Solomon's predicament warns against attributing it to a contrary redactional layer in the text. Pre-exilic or exilic hands cannot be distinguished in a text where characters are allowed the liberty to dispute points of obvious personal interest as the issues of dynasty and covenant were to Solomon and Yahweh. But for readers who reject the notion that the biblical authors could have created a narrative with conflicting opinions expressed by its characters, the case for a pre-exilic as opposed to exilic redactional layer in 1 Kgs 8 is made by Halpern (1988:168–74).

48 The narrator emphasizes the causal connection between these ceremonies and the stalemated Temple construction by using the strong adverb *ʾāz* with the imperfect, rather than simple parataxis (cf. GKC §107b, c; König §137, 138). Isaac Rabinowitz's study of *ʾāz* followed by an imperfect verb supports this reading. "Referring to the foregoing context of narrated past events, *ʾāz* + imperfect indicates this context as approximately the time when, the time or circumstances in the course of which, or the occasion upon which the action designated by the imperfect verb form went forward: this was when [then?] ... so-and-so did (imperfect) such-and-such" (1984:54, cf. 59).

of the first eight verses of ch. 8 to describing the pageantry.

In vv. 12–21 the narrator records Solomon's address to the people. In his speech Solomon maintains a thematic focus on one thing: 'what you see before you—this temple and myself—are the fulfilment of God's promise to David. The age of the Davidic covenant is upon us.' Solomon's purpose—to confine the divinity to the temple to Solomon's and Israel's advantage—is poetically introduced at the start: "Yahweh thought to dwell in the thick cloud, but I have indeed built a high house for you, *a place for you to remain forever*" (my emphasis).[49] How gracious of Solomon and how opposite a view to that voiced by God in 2 Sam 7:6–7! By containing God forever in the temple, Solomon the temple builder will have housed God and done what God previously forbade.

Solomon's review of Israel's covenantal history bears a similar implication. Turning to his audience and blessing them (*waybārek ʾēt kol-qᵉhal yiśrāʾēl*, v. 14), Solomon begins his creative review with David, blessing God (*bārûk yhwh*, v. 15) for having once made and now fulfilled his promise to David. Solomon unites his human and divine audiences with his blessings and, by convention, calls for their supportive response to their gracious speaker and his message.

The pattern of Solomon's covenantal history reverses the actual historical order:

Promise to David (v. 15)
Exodus recollection; selection of David as king (v. 16)
Temple building denied to David (vv. 17-18)
Temple building promised to son (Solomon) (v. 19)
Solomon rises, fulfilling promise, & builds Temple (v. 20)
Solomon makes a place for the ark,
for the covenant made during the exodus (v. 21)

49 Though vv. 12–13 are very different from the rest of the prayers, a bit of poetry at the opening of an elevated speech is not altogether an unknown rhetorical device (against e.g. Levenson 1981:153, who marks these verses as a separate "address" on account of their literary appearance). How much more informative it is to ask why Solomon should preface his prayers with a bit of poetry than to ask where the author might have gotten this bit from and how old it might be ("... most likely the oldest piece in 1 Kings 8," Levenson, p. 153).

What is Solomon trying to accomplish with this introductory recitation? He emphasizes the perpetuity of the arrangement he proposes through the word "forever" (*ʿôlāmîm*), the force of which can be gauged by the response of a reader such as C.F. Keil, who spends much effort apologizing for Solomon's attempt to constrain God for all eternity (1982:124). Cf. Noth (1968:182), "עולמים *setz das Nochbestehen des salomonischen Tempel voraus.*"

In this review the exodus is both preceded and succeeded by the Davidic covenant; it is encapsulated by the promises to David and supports them, in the end, by being housed in the temple that Solomon has built.[50]

Throughout his review Solomon practices the power of positive thinking. There is no mention of the Sinai covenant, no mention of Yahweh's recent reiterations of the need for an obedient Davidic monarch, and no reference to the dominance of sin and punishment in Israel's covenantal history. Only the propitious divine actions of the past, especially the unconditional Davidic covenant,[51] are recalled as the basis for the petition that Solomon is about to make. All else, especially Yahweh's recent conditional qualification of the Davidic covenant, is ignored. The rhetorical strategy is much the same as Yahweh's: by ignoring the opponent's position and asserting only one's own it looks as though one's own is undisputed and matter of fact.

Having prepared his audience with tendentious optimism about the past Solomon turns, in v. 22, to the real problem facing his temple project. "And Solomon stood before the altar of Yahweh, opposite the assembly of Israel, and spread his palms to heaven." The real problem that Solomon faces, the threat to himself and his reign, is Yahweh's recent conditional qualification of the unconditional promises to David, his father. In his second prayer, one of the longest in biblical narrative, Solomon seeks to reverse Yahweh's conditional qualification of the Davidic covenant by undercutting the original conditional covenant made at Sinai. He tries to do to Yahweh what Yahweh has done to him! If he could be successful—he cannot—the basis for Yahweh's renewed call to necessary obedience would be vitiated, a tour de force for Solomon's God-given wisdom.

Solomon's primary target is the curses of Deuteronomy (ch. 28).[52] He begins his address to God with a heavy reminder of

---

50 Cf. De Vries (1985:123), who calls this first section "a protocol of legitimation," and Levenson (1981:154).

51 De Vries hears the rhetoric (1985:125), but credits the Dtr narrator for the concentration on the fulfilment of the promise to David as one of the "Dtr's priorities." Cf. Levenson (1981:153) "Nowhere is this keynote [2 Sam 7] dwelt upon at greater length than in Solomon's second speech."

52 "The substance of the prayer is closely connected with the prayer of Moses, especially with the blessings and curses therein (*vid.* Lev. xxvi. and Deut. xxviii.)" (Keil 1982:125; cf. I. Benzinger 1899:59).

the divine promises and obligation to David (vv. 23–6). There are a total of ten verbs in these verses that describe or call for Yahweh's faithful action towards David and his descendants. In contrast there are only three verbs describing reciprocal human faithfulness. Once again Solomon uses the argument that God has made a promise to David and that he, Solomon, is its fulfilment. God, therefore, ought to preserve Solomon: "... you spoke with your mouth and with your hand you have, this day, fulfilled [it]" (v. 24; cf. v. 15).[53]

Solomon does not totally ignore Yahweh's conditional qualification of the Davidic covenant, however. In v. 23 he says that God is faithful with those who walk before him with all their heart. And in v. 25 he seems even to include the conditions that God so recently added to the Davidic covenant, feigning a willingness to submit to them. Apparently quoting God from 2 Sam 7 he says, "there shall not be cut off for you a man before me sitting on the throne of Israel only if your sons guard their ways to walk before me as you walked before me." Solomon says that God is unequalled in the way he treats those who walk before him with all their heart, implying that what he has to say will assume that he and his subjects are doing and will continue to do so. He will only ask for a little leeway for all of the faithful, not least of all himself. This, however, is not a quotation of anything God has said to him about conditions (cf. 3:14; 6:12–14) nor is it taken from 2 Sam 7. Rather, Solomon has chosen to quote the conditionalized version of the covenant that David

A prime example of how historical critics have misread the deuteronomistic rhetoric of Solomon's prayers is offered by Gray (1970:213). "The rhetoric and hortatory style of the whole and its theology, strongly impregnated with the conception of sin and inevitable retribution, stamps it as deuteronomistic, and indeed such orations with historical recapitulation and the future prospect at significant crises of the history of Israel are distinctive of the deuteronomistic history ..." Gray hears the allusions to the language of Deuteronomy (he even notes (p. 215) that Burney (C.F. Burney, *Notes on the Hebrew Text of the Books of Kings*) suggested connections to the curses of Deut 28) but he jumps, immediately, to the conclusion that here the narrator/author speaks and we already know what he will say from our knowledge of deuteronomic ideology and deuteronomistic historiography. Such assumptions must inevitably foreclose on careful reading in favour of automatic support for the conventional historical-critical interpretation.

53 In both cases, Solomon's claim is that this day, in which Solomon, son of David, king of Israel, consecrates the Temple, God is fulfilling his word to David. If God accepts this claim, logic dictates that Solomon and the Temple must continue or the promise will be broken and God will have betrayed his servant.

gave him in 2:4. This quotation also reverses, in chiastic fashion, the order of the quotation:

ʾim yišmᵉrû baneykā ʾet-darkām lāleket lᵉpānay beʾᵉmet
/bᵉkol-lᵉbābām ûbᵉkol-napšām lēʾmōr
lōʾ-yikkārēt lᵉkā ʾîš mēʿal kissēʾ yiśrāʾēl
lōʾ-yikkārēt lᵉkā ʾîš millᵉpānay yōšēb ʿal-kissēʾ yiśrāʾēl
raq ʾim-yišmᵉrû bāneykā ʾet-darkām lāleket lᵉpānay
/kaʾᵃšer hālaktā lᵉpānay

The chiastic reversal places the promise of a perpetual dynasty first, in contrast to David's own emphasis on the need for obedience. Solomon also embellishes the promise of perpetuity by adding the phrase, "a man representing you, sitting on the throne" rather than David's "a man from on the throne." The change emphasizes that subsequent *residents* on the throne are there as *representatives* of David, to whom God is obliged by his promise; the emphasis falls on an obligation made at the expense of forthcoming covenantal obedience. Solomon also deemphasizes David's focus on whole-hearted virtue and substitutes for that the model of David himself. The reason for this change is as obvious to the reader, who has witnessed David's entire career including the Bathsheba episode, as it is to Solomon. The standard set by David is far less demanding even than the blood-thirsty regimen that David imposes on the young Solomon.

Solomon's reasons for adapting David's conditional qualification of the Davidic covenant rather than Yahweh's are also open to view when one compares the two conditionalizations to see what is gained or lost. In 3:14 God also proposes only the lesser standard of matching David's behaviour, but it is in accord with "my statutes and commandments" rather than what Solomon proposes here, which is only "to walk before me as you [i.e. David] walked before me." More important is the reward for such obedience. In 3:14 God only promises lengthened days for Solomon, not an eternal dynasty, not a resident representative of David in perpetuity. Clearly that is not what Solomon wants. Solomon's difference from 6:12–13 is equally understandable. There God requires that Solomon "*perform* (*taʿᵃśeh*) the statutes and judgements" and that he *keep* "all my commandments, to walk in them," in return for which God promises to keep his promise to David. Enlarging on the promise God interprets it as dwelling in the midst of Israel and not forsaking his people, Israel (v. 13). Once again it is easy to see that Solomon's version is very different, eclipsing his obligation to action behind his burning vision of the eternal aspect of the promise, which God has sought to depreciate.

Solomon's opening address to God is formally similar to his first address to the people. The parallels are:

8:14–21	*8:22–26*
Solomon blesses the assembly of Israel, who stand [before him] (v. 14).	Solomon stands before the altar of Yhwh, opposite all the assembly of Israel (v. 22).
Solomon blesses Yhwh, "who spoke with his mouth to (!) David my father and with his hand fulfilled ..." (v. 15).	Solomon praises Yhwh to high heaven, the God who keeps covenant and fidelity (*ḥesed*) with his servants ..., who kept with his servant David (my father) what he spoke to him. "... you spoke with your mouth and with your hand you fulfilled, this very day" (vv. 23–24).
Solomon's revisionist review of Israel's covenantal history and the place of the temple within it (vv. 16–19).	Solomon's revisionist view of the conditional qualification of the covenant (v. 25).
"Yhwh has established (*qûm*) his word and I am established (*qûm*) instead of my father, David, and I sit on the throne of Israel,as Yhwh spoke, and I have built the house for the name of Yhwh, God of Israel and I've set there a place for the ark, in which is the covenant of Yhwh ..." (vv. 20–21).	"And now, O God of Israel, confirm (*ʾmn*) your word, which you spoke to your servant, David my father" (v. 26).

The strong formal parallelism is part of Solomon's rhetorical strategy. He makes two points, one in each of the parallel speeches. In the first address, ostensibly to the people but really only using them as an instrument against Yahweh's qualification, Solomon seeks to ensconce the conditional Sinai covenant within his temple. He reconstructs Israel's covenantal history so that it culminates in his reign. In his scheme the ark of the conditional Sinai covenant is archived in his temple, symbol of the new and eternal covenant to the Davidic dynasty of which he happens to be the incumbent. In the second address, this time to God but also publicly rehearsed so that its conclusions cannot be debated behind closed doors, Solomon reiterates the eternal aspects of the Davidic covenant at the expense of both Yahweh's and David's conditional qualifications. He does include a conditional clause, but it is feeble and easily circumvented in practise, given the low standard set by David's behaviour.

Solomon signals a shift in his presentation with v. 27, the humble rhetorical question about God dwelling on earth in the house built by Solomon. V. 28 sets the petitionary tone for what follows: its glossary of petitionary terms is arranged in chiastic fashion, which itself reiterates the call for God to hear.

ûpānîtā
ʾel-tᵉpillat
ʿabdᵉkā
wᵉʾel-tᵉḥinnātô
yhwh ʾᵉlōhāy lišmōaʿ ʾel-hārinnâ
wᵉʾel-hattᵉpillâ
ʾᵃšer ʿabdᵉkā
mitpallēl
lᵉpāneykā hayyôm

Solomon melds vocabulary parallels and syntax together to create a concentrated focus of petition, humble and pious, which God can ill-afford to ignore given the mass of onlookers. Such is the plan, in any case.

Standing at the centre of this chiastic focus is Yahweh, addressed by Solomon as "my God," public testimony to Solomon's claim of fidelity to his divine Lord. Solomon asks "his God" to hearken to the solicitous cry (*hārinnâ*) that he raises in prayer. And just as he has reiterated his claim that God has fulfilled his promise to David "this very day" (cf. vv. 20, 24) he asks God to hear, "this day" (*hayyôm*), the prayer addressed to him. All is carefully crafted as coercive supplication.

The keynote in the requests that follow is "hear and forgive" (cf. vv. 30, 32, 34, 36, 39, 43, 45, 49–50). Here we come to Solomon's main front against Yahweh's provisos to the Davidic covenant. In the very first request, as throughout, the keynote is given a prominence through rhetorical structuring. It occupies the centre position in each of a series of enveloped structures. The pattern is set in this first, innocuous petition:

When a man sins against his neighbour
and is required to make an oath
and brings the oath before your altar in this house
Hear in heaven, act, and judge your servants
condemning the wicked and justifying the righteous

Solomon's first request for clemency is, in fact, not a petition for lenient treatment but a righteous request for justice (vv. 31–2). The request—a minor matter of what we would call civil law—is a pious enough reiteration of Deut 25:1–3,[54] designed to seem as though the prayer is simply going to mouth conventional deuteronomic piety. The innocuous opening must, however, be viewed in the context of Solomon's overall rhetorical strategy. He begins in such a way as to reduce God to inattentive familiarity—'nothing new here; its all in the book of Deuteronomy'—so that subsequent, more radical revisions might go unnoticed or at least with less fanfare.[55] The only innovation in the first petition is the role of the temple as a focal point towards which oaths are to be directed. Clear it is that Solomon seeks to endear the temple to Yahweh's righteous sense of justice and to make it an indispensable part of the justice system. But that, in itself, is hardly anything for God to take offence against. He has, after all, already accepted the temple within such a covenantally ordered context (6:12–13).

The phrase, "hear in heaven ...," which recurs throughout the seven scenarios to follow, is also part of Solomon's camouflaged rhetorical strategy. According to Würthwein (1977:95–6) what we see here is the Dtr redactor's effort to surmount the old and persuasive idea that with Yahweh dwelling in the temple he might be at Israel's disposal. Given the seven-fold repetition of the phrase it is, obviously, an important part of the prayers. The emphasis, however, must be credited to Solomon, not the

---

54 Keil (1982:128) suggests Exod 22:6–12 or Lev 5:21–24 as the text for Solomon's petition. Whatever it might have been, the rhetorical scheme is the same: to reiterate a conventional religiosity and so to set a tone of conventional familiarity as a camouflage for the radical revisionism that follows.

55 The introduction of the enveloping framework here, in an innocent petition, shares the same rhetorical strategy. The structural sameness of all the petitions, headed off by an innocuous request is designed to woo God into thinking that they also share an innocuous content. The pattern of rhetorical similarities between the seven scenarios has been discussed by A. Gamper (1963) cf. B. Porten (1967:108–9).

narrator (redactor). As a result, its significance is quite different from what Würthwein sees in it. Solomon does, indeed, seem to be stressing the meaning that Würthwein suggests for the phrase. But he does so only because, in fact, he wants to implement its reverse. The point of all of his lengthy prayers is to win from God a concession that would make the temple the place towards which one could pray and gain forgiveness and reconciliation for just about any sin imaginable, at least within the conceptual bounds set by the catalogue of sins in Deut 28.

The incessant reminder to God that Solomon does not for one moment think that he could possibly live or even fit into the temple (vv. 27, 32, 34, 36, 39, 43, 45, 49)[56] fulfils the same function as the first scenario about the two litigants (vv. 31–2). It is aimed at allaying any divine suspicions that Solomon might be trying to constrain God through the device of the temple. The message of the rhetoric is that this is a law-abiding prayer, pious and proper beyond reproach. Each time that Solomon puts forward the idea that God should honour all petitions directed towards the temple he adds a qualification like, "hear in heaven, your dwelling place" (v. 49), so that his brazen scheme to undo the curses of Deuteronomy 28 with the temple will not be so obvious.

Solomon gets down to business in vv. 33–34. The opening phrases—"When your people, who have sinned against you, are stricken before an enemy (*b*ᵉ*hinnāgēp* ʿ*am*ᵉ*kā yiśrā*ʾ*ēl lipnê* ʾ*ôyēb*) ..."—allude to Deut 28:25, "Yahweh will have you stricken before your enemies (*niggop lipnê* ʾ*ōy*ᵉ*beykā*) ...," one of the curses in this collection of curses called down upon any future waywardness on the part of Israel (cf. Lev 26:17). Within the frame of Deuteronomy this curse was the sure recompense for an infraction against the covenant by Israel. Now Solomon adds a proviso to the curse. If the curse is invoked, says Solomon, the temple could function as the Mecca of contrite prayer and God could, upon witnessing such focused repentance, forgive the sin and stop punishing his people. In Solomon's representation the unmitigated finality of the deuteronomic curse is dissolved by his new mechanism for repentance, the temple. With his last petitionary breath, with regard to military defeat that is,

56 Against Würthwein (1985:97), v. 27, the strongest assertion of this prominent theme in the prayers, is not an extraneous marginal comment, but a well-placed disavowal of any intention to incarcerate God in the Temple.

Solomon also reminds God of his covenant to make Israel his people (Deut 32:8–9; Exod 19:5–6) and his promises to the patriarchs: "hear in heaven, forgive the sin of *your people, Israel*, and return them to the land *that you gave to their fathers*." The point is leeway for Israel's (and Solomon's) sin and reminders of promises made for God.

Following this bold initiative, Solomon continues with an unabashed revision of a broad selection of the deuteronomic curses, always with the aim of establishing his temple as a source of security, a bulkhead against the conditionality of the Sinai covenant that Deuteronomy reiterates. In vv. 35–36 Solomon seeks to undo the damaging words of Deut 11:17 (cf. 28:23; Lev 26:19):

> "And the anger of Yahweh burn against you and he shut up (*wᵉʿāṣar*) the heavens and there be no rain (*wᵉlōʾ-yihyeh māṭār*) ..." (Deut 11:17).
>
> "When the heavens are shut up (*bᵉhēʿāṣēr*) and there is no rain (*wᵉlōʾ-yihyeh māṭār*) because they have sinned against you and they pray toward this place ..."

Like the first attack against the uncompromising conditionality of the covenantal formulations in Deuteronomy, this one brings a strong structural focus to bear on Yahweh's obligation to his people:

Heavens shut, no rain: they have sinned
They pray towards this place, confess, and repent
Hear, in heaven, and forgive
Teach them the good way in which they ought to walk
Send rain on your land

Supporting the structural focus there is a strong emphasis in Solomon's vocabulary too: "forgive the sin of *your servants*, of *your people Israel* ... send rain on *your land*, which you gave *your people* for an *inheritance*."[57] The point of Solomon's reiterated attention to Yahweh's ownership of Israel and the land hardly requires elaboration: God ought not to forsake what he, in fact, initiated in this business of covenantal alliance with a people. An occasion of unremittent damnation becomes one of reconciliation and harmonious coexistence, *with no obvious end point*. Solomon's temple is the focal point, structurally

---

57 Solomon alludes, by the word "inheritance," to Yahweh's promises of the land, his part of the Sinai covenant (cf. Deut 4:21, 38; 12:9–10; 15:4; 19:10, 14; 20:16; 21:23).

speaking, of an unending arrangement. God and man need never again face the harsh finality proposed by Moses in the book of Deuteronomy. Anyone who doubts the diametric opposition that I am proposing between Solomon's prayer and Moses' rhetoric need only read the two passages one after the other.

Solomon grows bolder yet in his third similitude (vv. 37–40), which deals with the plagues meted out to a sinful Israel according to Deut 28:21–2, 38, and 29:21 (Eng. 22) (cf. Lev 26:19, 20, 26 on famine; 26:25 on plague). Solomon hypothesizes the following:

> "Perchance there be famine (*rāʿāb*) in the land [or] plague (*deber*), perchance there be blight (*šiddāpôn*) [or] mildew (*yērāqôn*), locust or grasshopper (*ʾarbeh ḥāsîl*), perchance there be an enemy besieging him within the land of his gates: whatever the calamity (*negaʿ*), whatever the disease (*maḥ*ᵃ*lâ*) ..."

If Solomon's were the only scenario his intended reader had, one might wonder why such terrible things would happen. Pure happenstance? Inexplicable divine wrath? Deuteronomy supplies the missing material in its list of covenantal curses, wherein Moses describes the punishments to be accorded to Israel's disobedience and sin:[58]

> Yahweh will stick the plague (*hāddāber*) on you until he has consumed you from the land that you came to possess (28:21).
>
> Yahweh will strike you with consumption and with fever and with inflammation and with fiery heat and with the sword and with blight (*šiddāpôn*) and with mildew (*yērāqôn*) and they will pursue you until you perish (28:22).
>
> And the next generation, your sons who will rise after you, and the stranger who comes from a far country—they will see the devastation (*makkôt hāʾāreṣ*) of that land and the disease (*taḥ*ᵃ*luʾeyhā*) [with which] Yahweh has diseased (*ḥillâ*) it (29:21).

A comparison of Solomon's review of the curses with the actual curses quickly reveals his rhetorical emphasis. He admits the possibility of the calamities but avoids any reference to their causes and avoidance. The shifted emphasis is in complete accord with the general tendency of his prayer. 'If such terrible things should happen—who knows how—and if your people, Israel, should pray towards this house, then hear and forgive ...'

58 On the covenantal literary form of the book of Deuteronomy and its resemblance to ancient near eastern treaty forms see M. Weinfeld (1972) or D.J. McCarthy (1978).

As in the previous two petitions, Solomon structures this scenario in concentric fashion, with pride of place accorded to divine attentiveness and forgiveness, even though in this case no particular sin has been mentioned.

If there are famine, plagues, or enemies in [the land]

and your people, each [knowing] the affliction of his [heart], pray and spread out their hands towards this place

Hear, in your heavenly dwelling place and forgive;

render to each, whose [heart] you [know], according to his ways, for you alone [know] the [hearts] of man.

That they may fear you all the days that they live on the face of [the land] that you gave to our fathers.

(Boxed items indicate *Leitwort* connections within the unit.) Once again Solomon's covenantal vocabulary is marshaled to support the structural argument of his rhetoric: "... your people, Israel (v. 38) ... that they may fear you ... in the land that you gave to our fathers." In the middle of all of these reminders about God's covenantal obligation to preserve Israel, as they pray towards "this [earthly] house" Solomon aims to conceal his ultimate purpose—to tie God to an eternal dwelling in "this house" and an unending polity for Israel and the Davidic line—beneath an ingratiating piety, apparently overcome by the majesty of this God's heavenly dwelling place.[59]

The fifth scenario in the series is most revealing of Solomon's rhetorical maneuvering against the curses of Deuteronomy. Having treated, in vv. 37–40, the destruction at which future generations and "the foreigner from afar" are supposed to marvel (Deut 29:22), Solomon now transforms the foreigner himself. He takes this "foreigner from a far land" (*hannokrî ʾᵃšer yābōʾ mēʾereṣ rᵉḥôqâ*) and makes him into someone who, having heard about Yahweh's mighty arm (not, however, that arm as it destroys Jerusalem and Judah), comes (in the Gibeonite manner, cf. Josh 9:3–9) to Jerusalem not to marvel but *to pray in Solomon's temple*! How efficacious the prayers of vv. 37–40 must be and how central the role played by "this

59 Solomon makes this same rhetorical flourish in each of the scenarios; cf. vv. 32, 34, 36, 39, 43, 45, 49, and, in context, especially v. 27.

house"! Again, there is a concentric structure with the same rhetorical emphasis:

> Concerning the foreigner who is not of your people, Israel
> who, having heard of your name and your might,
> comes from afar to pray towards this house
>
> Hear in your heavenly abode and do his bidding
>
> So that all the earth may know your name and fear you
> like your people Israel, and that they may know that
> your name is called on this house, which I have built.

There is a twofold rhetorical goal in this scenario. First Solomon aims to defuse the dangerous rhetoric about the foreigner from afar in the book of Deuteronomy. The foreigner becomes a pious God-fearer who, having heard about the mighty deeds that Yahweh has done on Israel's behalf,[60] comes to Solomon's temple to worship.

The second goal is more insidious. One of the main purposes of the exodus, perhaps even its main purpose, was the education of the nations. Pharaoh is emblematic of the learning experience of all non-Israelites. "I will harden Pharaoh's heart that I may multiply my signs and wonders in the land of Egypt ... and the Egyptians shall know that I am Yahweh" (Exod 7:3–5). "For this purpose have I set you up—to show you my power and to proclaim my name through all the earth" (Exod 10:16). To protect his name and reputation, which was of such great importance to the overall plan of the Israelite God, Yahweh was convinced several times that he had to forbear destroying Israel, even though they deserved it (cf. Exod 32:9–14; Num 14:11–20; Deut 9:13–19, 23–28; Josh 7:7–9). In the inevitable destruction promised in the book of Deuteronomy, and especially concerning the role of the foreigner from afar as a witness, the problem of a ruined reputation is removed by prediction (e.g. Deut 4:25–26; 28:15–68; 31:16–32:47). If Israel is destroyed in accordance with Yahweh's prediction, on the basis of disobedience to his divine commandments, then it is clear that he is in total control. Far from casting doubts on Yahweh's reputation, such disastrous events confirm it. What the for-

60 As always, references to Yahweh's great name, his mighty hand, and his outstretched arm are strong allusive references to the foundational exodus events in Israel's history. Cf. e.g. Deut 4:34.

eigner from afar witnesses, unlike the hypothetical witnesses who might see weakness in Yahweh's unpredicted destruction of Israel (e.g. Num 14:16; Deut 9:28; Josh 7:9), is a confirmation of the power made known in the exodus. Even though the historical accomplishment of the exodus is destroyed and undone, Yahweh's reputation—from the divine perspective, the most important concern in the exodus events—is vindicated (Deut 29:22–28). Obviously Solomon's plans for the temple cannot bear such a role for the foreigner from afar.

Having removed any potential for witnessing a disaster on the part of the foreigner, Solomon, ever felicitous for his divine auditor's sense of well-being, creates a substitute. The foreigner will come from afar by reason of having heard of the old, established reputation of Yahweh, a reputation established by the exodus events that benefited and brought Israel, "your people," into existence. This God-fearing foreigner comes to pray at the temple, which Solomon has built (v. 43) and which is called by Yahweh's name. He is merely one example of the many that can be so affected and converted through the agency of the temple, "upon which your name is called and which I have built." The temple and the continuing preservation of Israel are new and powerful means to accomplish what Yahweh set out to do in the exodus. And the foreigner from afar is the symbol of a new, blessed age in which all the peoples of the earth[61] will come to know Yahweh through worship at Solomon's temple, not the symbol of death and destruction that Moses made him out to be in Deuteronomy.

The sixth scenario is short and undeveloped. It functions primarily as a neutralizing footing for the more controversial seventh, and concluding scenario. Again there is the concentric structure, no reference to any sinful activity on Israel's part, and a petition for God to honour his covenantal obligation to Israel.

61 One wonders whether Solomon's solicitude for the cultic needs of the foreigners might not also be a back-door route to allow for the foreign cults of his wives (cf. 11:4–8, esp. v. 8).

When your people go out to battle against an enemy
on the way that you send them
And they pray to Yhwh,
toward the city you have chosen
and the house I have built to your name

Hear in heaven the prayer and the supplication

And perform the obligation [owed to] them

The first half (v. 44) of the larger envelope structure is itself chiastically organized:

Israel (acting for God)
divine choice and action
prayer to Yhwh
divine choice (and action)
Solomon (acting for God)

The subunit mirrors, on a smaller scale, the structure of the larger envelope. All works together, as previously, to de-emphasize human sin or error while simultaneously calling for Yahweh to be true to his covenantal obligations. Solomon's call for God to "do their justice" (*mišpāṭām*) is a call to the divine king and lawgiver to honour his commitment to protect Israel in battle.[62] Again, the temple, about which Solomon is ever ready to mention that *he built it*, serves as the clearing house for all future covenantal correspondence between Yahweh and Israel.

The final scenario in the series is also the most impassioned and the most controversial. It treats the case of exile, well-known as the capital punishment for sins against God and his covenant. The scenario follows the structural convention now well established in the preceding prayer: it is chiastic, with the key request for divine flexibility and sympathy set at the pivotal midpoint.[63]

---

62 Weinfeld (1972:150–5) discusses the phrase *ʿśh mišpaṭ* with regard to David in 2 Sam 8:15–18. He suggests that it means to "establish justice," following a suggestion from A.B. Ehrlich. In both passages, the phrase emphasizes the legal obligation of the king to his subjects.

63 The stylistic divergencies of the last scenario from the previous six led Jepsen to posit the existence of an exilic addendum (vv. 44–53) to the prayers (1956:15–16). It is, however, equally possible to interpret the variations as integral to the rhetoric. It is the culmination of Solomon's effort, after all, and stands out for length alone. The stylistic divergencies to which Jepsen points have significance in Solomon's argument; explanation in terms of literary history is therefore unwarranted and destructive of the

A When they sin against you and you deliver them to an enemy who takes them captive to a land far off or near (v. 47).

B If they repent in the land of their captivity and make supplication (*wᵉhitḥannᵉnû*) to you (v. 48).

C If they return with all their heart and soul and pray to you, toward their land that you gave to their fathers, the city that you chose, and the house that I have built for your name (v. 49).

D Hear their prayer and supplication in your heavenly dwelling place and do them justice; forgive your people and make them objects of compassion (v. 50).

C' For they are your people, your inheritance (cf. Deut 4:20; 9:29, which you brought out of Egypt from the midst of the iron furnace (v. 51; cf. Deut 4:20).

B' May your eyes be open to the supplication (*tᵉḥinnat*) of your servant and of your people Israel, to listen to them whenever they call to you (v. 52).

A' For you separated them for yourself as your inheritance from all the peoples of the earth, just as you said by the hand of Moses your servant when you brought our fathers out of Egypt (v. 53; cf. Lev 20:24, 26; Deut 32:8).

The chiastic patterning, in this case, is less prominent than previously and more dependent on thematic connections on the covenantal topic. These connections can be abbreviated and mapped as follows:

A Divine action against Israel—scattering—for infraction of the covenant.

B Repentance and supplication (*ḥnn*) on the part of Israel.

C Portrait of Israel's repentance combined with reminders to God of his past benefactions and promises to Israel, especially with regard to the Davidic covenant as symbolized by the chosen city and the temple built by Solomon.

D "Hear and forgive ..."; meet "transgression" (*pšʿ*, 2X) with "compassion" (*rḥm*, 2X).

C' Reminders of God's past benefactions to Israel, the work that is begun but which would not be finished if Israel were not treated with compassion.

B' Call for divine attentiveness to Israel's supplication (*ḥnn*).

---

prayers' semantic structure. Jepsen observes the divergencies and, without further investigation of their significance, assumes that they are the telltale signs of a second hand.

A' Reminder of past divine action—separating—on behalf of Israel, which initiated the special covenant relationship.

Abstracted in this way, Solomon's characteristic focus on divine duty is clear. He does not say that God owes Israel because Israel has lived up to expectations. On the contrary, he frankly admits Israel's sin: it is a matter of fact. His argument, rather, is that God owes it to himself to continue the project that he began so long ago, provided of course that Israel should be truly contrite for its sins. And how is God to know? Quite simple: when they pray towards the holy city, in the centre of which is the temple, "which I have built for your name," then God can rest assured that they are truly desperate and in need of his compassion.[64]

The deuteronomic clause to which Solomon addresses himself this time is found, again, in the curses of the book of Deuteronomy (28:49): "Yahweh will bring against you a nation from afar (*mērāḥôq*) ..." (cf. 1 Kgs 8:46, "to the land of the enemy, far off (*rᵉḥôqâ*) or near"). Once again, Solomon does his best to ensure that even the ultimate punishment, the exile that should spell the end of the covenant relationship, can be remitted on the basis of prayer towards the temple (v. 48). Unlike the "foreigner from afar," who was transformed in Solomon's version, this allusion maintains the same thought and tone as the deuteronomic curse. Solomon's tactic here is candid admission of the cause of the curse's invocation—Israelite sin—combined with a reiterated emphasis, complete with supporting allusions, on God's promises and past actions on Israel's behalf. Solomon's temple plays a critical role in his proposal both as a focal point for Israel's contrition and supplication and as a visible reminder to God of his promises to David: "the city that you chose and the house that I have built to your name." In Solomon's presentation God's promises and his covenant are too historic and too progressive to be deterred by Israel's sin. Capital covenantal punishment—exile away from the land—is transmuted into a life sentence with the possibility of parole at any time the guilty confess and repent of their sin.[65]

---

64 Solomon's portrait of Israel's experience in exile is much milder than that of Deut 28:64–8. In Deuteronomy, Israel is destitute and despairing; according to Solomon, they are full of contrition and desire for reconciliation. Exile spells the end in Deuteronomy; in Solomon's prayer it is only a stage in a domestic quarrel.

65 Levenson (1981:158) dates vv. 44–53 to the exile, reasoning that only in such a context does the hope of return from the exile make sense. In the overall context of the

Solomon concludes his prayers with a second address to the people (vv. 54–61). Like his first address to the people, his concluding remarks are an exercise in assertive optimism. By rewriting the past so that it becomes a record of success and total divine commitment to Israel, Solomon encourages his human audience to expect more of the same in the future. And God, if he accepts the acclamation awarded by Solomon for his past benificence, is thereby compelled to fulfil the equally optimistic promise of the future.

For the reader, Solomon's choice of phrasing, awarded to him by the narrator, is less than propitious; for his human audience, it may have been more impressive. He opens in much the same manner as he did in v. 15, "Blessed by Yahweh ...," but goes on to quote Joshua instead of reiterating his prior assertions about the fulfilment of the promises to David. The quotation is taken from the narrator's ironic comments and Joshua's dramatically ironic comments on the success of the conquest at the end of the book of Joshua:

Narrator (Josh 21:43–45)

And Yahweh gave to Israel all the land that he swore to give to their fathers and they possessed it and lived in it. And Yahweh gave them rest (*wayyānaḥ* ; cf. Joshua in Josh 22:4) on every side, according to all that he had sworn to their fathers. Not one of all their enemies stood before them; Yahweh gave all their enemies into their hand. There fell not a word from the entire good word that Yahweh spoke to the house of Israel; all came about.

Joshua (Josh 23:14)

... you know in your hearts and souls that there fell not one word from all the good words that Yahweh, your God, spoke concerning you; all came about.

Solomon (1 Kgs 8:56)

Blessed be Yahweh who has given rest (*mᵉnûḥâ*) to his people, Israel, according to all that he spoke. There has not fallen one word from all his good word that he spoke by the hand of Moses, his servant.

---

prayers, however, in which Solomon does his best to undo the curses of Deuteronomy, the ultimate curse—exile—is obviously an important subject, not to be omitted. For Solomon to speak about return from exile, therefore, tells us little about the date of this piece of rhetoric. And from a historian's point of view, there is every reason to believe that just as "Israel knew of and dreaded exile long before she experienced it" (Levenson 1981:157), it could also entertain the hope for reprieve should that terrible eventuality ever come to pass.

Whereas these sentiments, which are always incorrect wherever they occur, were previously set in an ironic frame in the narrative Solomon uses them here to convince his audience that God has, indeed, fulfilled all and that he, Solomon, is the peak of fulfilment. The dissonance between Solomon's representation and the ironies of the book of Joshua heightens the reader's sense of the emptiness of all Solomon's rhetoric. He has played many rhetorical tricks through his allusions and references to tradition. Here he gets caught and it is the narrator's own irony that catches him. Like Joshua's similar assertions, however, there is no indication that the human audience was privy to the vacuity of the assertions. Solomon's rhetoric aims to compel God by saying that he has done the very things that the narrator and the narrative have shown he has not done. The ironic implication of this allusion to the ironical judgments at the end of the book of Joshua is that Solomon's rhetoric cannot succeed. It bears within it the seeds of its own destruction.

The remainder of Solomon's public address is primarily taken up with exhortations to God: to remain with Israel and to incline their hearts to obedience to his commandments. The latter is significant because it reveals Solomon's efforts to put almost all the weight of allegiance to the covenant, even Israel's allegiance, on God. Twice more (v. 59) does he reiterate his request for God to "do the right" of Israel, his servant. In v. 60 he alludes to the larger purpose of the exodus events—knowledge of Yahweh throughout the world—claiming that by maintaining Israel as Solomon has suggested, God will accomplish what he once sought to accomplish through the exodus. "... that he might do the right of his servant and the right of his people Israel, day by day, so that all the peoples of the earth will know that Yahweh is God; there is none other." With this argument, Solomon augments Moses' embarrassment argument (God must preserve Israel or be shamed before the nations) with God's demonstrated concern for international reputation. God can only win!

Only in his last exhortation does Solomon finally call for action from Israel. "Let your heart be whole (*šālēm*) with Yahweh, our God ...."[66] By keeping exhortations to Israel minimal—actually they are insignificant in comparison to all those

66 Ironically it is Solomon himself who is first to fail in "whole-heartedness" with God (cf. 11:4, *wᵉlōʾ hāyâ-lᵉbābô šālēm ʿim-yhwh*).

directed to Yahweh—Solomon has, on a larger scale, also inverted the overall emphasis of the deuteronomic curses (Deut 28:15–68), which overbalance fifty-four verses of cursing in case of Israelite sin against fourteen verses of blessing in case of obedience.[67] Even on the less obvious structural level, everything in the prayers is devoted to undermining this key passage from the book of Deuteronomy.

The crowning glory of the prayers is the public sacrifice, a physical manifestation of the rhetorical spirit and ploys of the prayers. The sacrifice is, by design, all encompassing. It lasts for seven and seven days, a perfect and whole period twice extended to ensure completion (v. 65).[68] It includes, within its geographical purview, all Israel from its northern (the entrance of Hamath) to its southern most extremes (the brook of Egypt) (v. 65). "All Israel" celebrates with Solomon (v. 65). And no less than 22,000 oxen and 120,000 sheep are slaughtered (v. 63). These numbers and for that matter the entire account may seem fantastic (so Montgomery 1951:199–200; De Vries 1985:127) but such is the nature of this affair in the story world of the narrative. It is fantastic that Solomon should so try to coerce God. The prayers and the sacrifices are at once subtle and heavy-handed in the manner in which they aim to extract divine assent to Solomon's proposals.[69] But then Solomon, as the narrator shows in chs. 9–10, has an extravagant nature.

The Role of the Prayer in the Dtr Narrative

Martin Noth and most other interpreters of the Dtr saw the numerous literary connections between Solomon's prayers and the book of Deuteronomy as a sign that here the deuteronomistic ideology of the author of this history was shining through clearly. "Finally, after the completion of the

---

67 Against A. Šanda (1911:221), "*Das Ganze klingt in der Aufforderung der Gemeinde zur treuen Anhänglichkeit an Jahve aus.*"

68 The seven days twice done are the perfect complement to the seven scenarios of the perfect prayer. The parallel numerical symbolism counts against those who wish to disallow vv. 44–51 as original to the main prayer (e.g. Würthwein 1985:97).

69 Cf. Keil (1982:135), who is innocently taken with Solomon's rhetoric of word and deed, "The thank-offering consisted, *in accordance with the magnitude of the manifestation of divine grace* of 22,000 oxen and 120,000 sheep" [my emphasis]. Keil correctly sees the point of the exceptional offering as a response to the tremendous leeway that Solomon seeks in the prayer. He fails to see, however, that the grace is something sought by Solomon but rejected by God.

temple in Jerusalem—an event that was of fundamental importance to Dtr.'s theological interpretation of history—King Solomon makes a detailed speech in the form of a prayer to God, which thoroughly expounds the significance of the new sanctuary for the present, and especially for the future" (Noth 1981:5–6; cf. Noth 1968:175, 182).

Noth's interpretation is wrong. The reasons for his error are twofold. First his belief that the Dtr redactor had inserted, at key points, his own ideological exposition into the narrative led Noth to read these insertions at some remove from their narrative context. Treating the speeches as redactional insertions, Noth never gave any serious consideration to the subtle contextual moorings of the speeches. Consequently all of the powerful narratorial exposition through implication, which completely relativizes the propositions set out in the prayers, was overlooked. Second, Noth read the narrative in total neglect of its voice structure. He made no distinction between the voice of Solomon and the voice of the narrator. Once again he was misled by the assumption that the high ratio of deuteronomistic vocabulary and ideology in Solomon's prayers was a certain indication that 1 Kgs 8 represented the views of the Dtr author/redactor. This lack of depth perception regarding the voice structure led Noth to interpret the obvious concentration of highly charged deuteronomistic language as a nugget of authorial exposition, concentrated commentary lodged in a mass of traditional narrative material. Given that the supposedly traditional material appeared so bereft of commentary, what else could such a vein of evaluative discourse be than the persuasive rhetoric of the redactor trying to breath his own meaning into the bare historical facts of tradition? Presuppositions about the evaluative stance of the redactor combined with the sheer weight of Solomon's charged rhetorical valuations inevitably led Noth, and others, to the simple equation between the views expressed in the prayer and the views of the redactor(s)/author.

Solomon's prayers and speeches are, together, one among a series of character utterances in the Dtr narratives in which there is an abnormally high evaluative content. In each case (e.g. 1 Sam 12; 1 Kgs 8) a character in the narrative is given the floor and makes a series of strongly evaluative statements. The narrator never explicitly contradicts what the character says, allowing context and implication to do a more effective job of relativizing and so undercutting the character's assertions. That is exactly why this narrative is so subversive of the ideology presented in the character's gushing evaluative discourse. The impersonal irony of this narrator depends for its success on a spartan evaluative silence at the explicit level. Of course there are unambiguous signs, usually part of the narrative structure and organization, that show how the narrator regards the views that are ironically, perhaps even sarcastically exposed. Such signs are the essential tools of the literary ironist, taking the place of intonation which works so well for the oral expression of irony or sarcasm.

The prayer is Solomon's attempt to gain some leeway for his political and religious undertakings. The attempt earns a sharp rebuke from Yhwh, who is not taken in. The narrator could not possibly be taken in; nor could he every agree with the prayer, which he sets as one in a series of peak character evaluations. Each member in the series exposes the limited understanding of the human characters in the story and sometimes, as in the case of Solomon's prayer, reveals how the character's understanding of God's intention, especially as made known through Moses' rhetoric in the book of Deuteronomy, leads inevitably to confrontation with God and disaster for the nation.

There is no question that the covenant granted to David in 2 Sam 7 gets a radical alteration before it is passed on to Solomon. God has changed the rules and no one in the story can gainsay it. When Solomon tries to use the temple, with all of its associations from 2 Sam 7, to pull God back to a view closer to that he originally expressed to David, he meets only a stony divine refusal to listen and a dogmatic emphasis on the necessity of obedience. For God, the temple will never bear the expiatory weight that Solomon would like. Solomon tries to make Deuteronomy's foreboding "foreigner from afar" (Deut 29:22–28) into an itinerant pilgrim coming to Jerusalem to worship in the temple because he has heard about the great deeds that Yahweh had done *formerly* (1 Kgs 8: 41–43) and God responds (1 Kgs 9:6–9), not only reiterating the threat of Deuteronomy, but adding to it a new threat of destruction for the temple. Far from ameliorating the threats of Deuteronomy, the temple, as Solomon has presented it, only aggravates them.

In all cases, the narrator maintains the distance built into his external, unconditioned viewpoint, which separates his views from the characters in the narrative by at least the same distance that separates divine and human characters in it. Nowhere is there any indication that the narrator (= the author) shares any part of Solomon's actual or rhetorical views. He simply reports them, showing how they derive from Solomon's ambitions and lifestyle. Far from being a statement of the narrator's (= author's, Dtr redactor's) views about the temple and the future, Solomon's prayers are the tendentious rhetorical peregrinations of a desperate king seeking to outfox his divine overlord.

Neither does the narrator express any support for Yahweh's apposite rebuttal to Solomon's impious prayers. Having exposed their impiety, he is not at all concerned to decry it. Rather, the narrator's concern seems to be to show how all of Solomon's efforts to retrieve the promises that Yahweh has revoked end up putting him at loggerheads with Yahweh. And that is all that he is concerned to do. He provides a history of the difficulties through which the covenantal relationship moves. Since it is the narrator's special talent to include revealing information about God's behind-the-scenes schemes and manipulations of his human partners, it is safe to say that assumptions of agreement between narrator and divine character are sure to go astray.

Neither is the narrator a railing critic who chastises God for having changed the terms of his agreement with David. He simply tells his story in which Yahweh does, in fact change, the terms when they are handed down to Solomon. Here there is no need for the extended description that is provided to show the extent of Solomon's perfidy. The simple fact that God does renege on his promise to David is provocative enough, a provocation only made stronger by the fact that no explicit excuse or condemnation is made for the divine character. Any implication on the divine action at this point is not critical but objective, at least conventionally so. God is not presented as immoral for having changed the terms of the Davidic covenant. He is, rather, amoral. The divine end justifies the divine means. Or does it? The result is a narrative presentation of divine action in human history that is very much like that of the exodus narratives, in which God does things that would be reprehensible if performed by a human and yet comes away with clean, amoral hands.

For an interpreter such as Noth, who hears the Dtr redactor speaking through the voices of the characters in the narrative, there is an obvious self-contradiction in this story between what the Dtr says through the voice of Yahweh in ch. 9 and what he says through Solomon in ch. 8.[70] Through Solomon there is a strong affirmation of the unconditional Davidic covenant; through the voice of Yahweh there is an equally strong conditionalization. According to Noth, the way the Dtr resolved the contradiction was through a scheme of development within the life of Solomon himself. "Dtr portrayed, as the position of 9:1–9 shows, the ambivalency of the figure of Solomon in a simple chronological sequence....In this manner he allowed the beginnings of Solomon's reign up to the completion of the temple to appear in a good light, followed by the grave divine warning, which could not have been unfounded, and finally by the open defection of Solomon" (Noth 1968:199).

Noth's solution fails to deal with the fundamental issue between the characters in the narrative, which is covenantal: did the Davidic covenant alter the effect of human sinfulness on Israel's and the Davidic monarchy's continuation or didn't it? Noth's solution also neglects the characterization of Solomon prior to the prayer, which is less than a shining example of the ideal monarch. Finally, Noth ignores the fact that Yahweh, following David's example, emended the Davidic covenant with the addition of the stiffer conditional requirements already prior to the prayer (3:14; 6:11–13), long before the turning point that Noth proposes.

1 Kings 1–11 shows how the temple serves as a key breaking point between God and Israel in the events leading up to the Exile. Both sides quote Deuteronomy in support of their claims about what the temple should mean for the covenant relationship. The winning side, the divine, wins by virtue of strength alone. On rhetorical grounds, Solomon's efforts are more polished than God's. Perhaps that explains why scholarly readers have identified Solomon's prayers rather than God's rebuttal as the voice of the redactor, even though the two character voices are in radical opposition.

The narrator takes no sides in the dispute; the linguistic affinities between Solomon's prayers and Deuteronomy are certainly not to be used as tags to identify his own narratorial views. The narrator's purpose is to show the irreconcilable differences between God and Israel, as represented by Solomon, over the significance of the temple. It is the ultimate

---

70 "*Dtr sieht die Gestalt Salomons in einem Zwielicht stehen*" (Noth 1968:199).

result of those differences—the Exile—that it is his purpose to explain.

CHAPTER 6

THROUGH THE FIRE

And they caused their sons and their daughters to pass through the fire, and used divination and enchantments, and sold themselves to do evil in the sight of the Lord, to provoke him to anger (2 Kings 17:17).

Introduction

In quantity of explicit narratorial evaluation 2 Kings 17 stands almost alone. The chapter presents one of the most difficult passages in the entire narrative. Only once before (Judg 2:11–14) has the narrator heaped up a similar, though smaller collection of explicit evaluations all seemingly critical of the Israelite people's behaviour. Much reading space and story time has passed since Judges 2, which turned out to be more neutral than it first seems; the reader staggers under the weight of the authoritative evaluations with which the narrator burdens him in ch. 17.

The result is, in terms of the reading history of this chapter, a rhetorical failure. Without exception, so it seems, readers have understood the evaluative commentary in 2 Kgs 17 as an unconditional condemnation of Israel. This censure is read as the author's (narrator's/redactor's) etiology of Israel's demise in the Assyrian exile (e.g. J. Gray 1970:646–50; F.M. Cross 1973:281; J. Van Seters 1983:315).

Grown accustomed, through the books of Samuel and Kings, to the narrator's expository reserve, especially when it comes to evaluative commentary on the behaviour of the general Israelite populace, the reader is brought up short by the evaluative torrent in 2 Kgs 17:7–23. What does it mean? Has the narrator changed his mind about his story? Is he dropping his objective guise just here, near the end, because now he really wants to blame Israel when ever since the rise of the monarchy he has almost entirely omitted Israel's sins from view? Or, to adopt a different manner of reading biblical literature for a moment, are we reading the thoughts of a different narrator (redactor)? Has he decided that it was not really the kings' waywardness from the paths deemed acceptable by Yahweh that led Israel to its end? If so, one wonders why he did not retrace his steps to erase, expunge, or otherwise diminish his repetitive descriptions of how the kings' leadership disturbed Yahweh and corrupted Israel (so, 1 Kgs 14:15–16; 15:3, 14, 26, 30; 16:2, 7, 13, 19, 25–6, 30; 21:22, 51–3; 2 Kgs 3:2–3; 8:16–19, 26–7; 10:29–31;13:2–3,[1] 11; 14:24; 15:9, 18, 24; 16:2–3; 17:2). 2 Kgs 17:2 is especially odd, since it presents an immediate contradiction to vv. 7ff. on the cause of the northern kingdom's exile (compare vv. 2–6 with vv. 7–18).

All the blame for the exile of the northern kingdom is placed squarely on the Israelites' collective shoulders in 2 Kgs 17:7–23: they sinned—an ingrate slap in the face to the redeemer God who delivered them from Egypt (v. 7)—walked in the customs of other nations and the kings of Israel, did secret, unethical things, participated in the cultic practises of the nations, served idols, stiffened their necks just like their unbelieving fathers against the warnings of prophets, refused the statutes and covenant of Yahweh, went after the surrounding nations, forsook the commandments of Yahweh and made the two golden calves, made an Asherah, worshipped the host of heaven, served Baal, made their sons and daughters pass through fire, practised divination and enchantments, and sold themselves to do evil in Yahweh's sight (vv. 7–18)! What more could they do?[2]

The list is without parallel in the Dtr narrative. Stranger yet, it is almost completely unsupported by any preceding narrative description showing Israel engaged in these practises. Yet, there are important vocabulary and thematic linkages between 2 Kgs 17 and what precedes. These links invite the reader, as

---

1 2 Kgs 13:1–7 is reminiscent of the descriptions in the book of Judges of cyclical apostasy in Israel. It differs in attributing a strong apostatizing leadership to Kings Jehoahaz (v. 2) and Jeroboam (v. 6, a continuing effect of his reign).

2 A. Šanda (1912:221) is an example of a reader who hears the breathless rhetorical effect ("*langatmigen Schilderung*"), but he neglects the ironic incongruities between the rhetoric and the narrative realities to which it refers and so the force of the rhetoric is lost on him. "*Der Schreiber ringt hier mit dem Ausdruck. Er möchte den Abfall Israels recht eindringlich schildern und strebt nach Effekt. Er zieht deshalb alle möglichen termini und Ideen herbei.*"

always, to investigate the significance of the connections and the contradiction between what the narrator now says, in review, about what happened and what he previously said, in the course of narrating events, actually happened.

Whenever such a conflict exists between what a narrative voice asserts and the narrative description of what happened, the reader must make a choice: to accept the evaluation and reject the veracity of the narrative description or to qualify, somehow, the evaluation by contextualizing it within an interpretive framework in which the conflict is subsumed within some larger unity of vision.[3]

Irony

If it is a character's evaluation that creates such a contradiction it is an easy move to comprehend the discrepancy as the difference between the reality of the story world and the character's personal existential bias. But when, as in 2 Kgs 17, it is the narrator that provokes by contradicting the reality that he has already established, things are more difficult. There are two common reading strategies to deal with such a situation. Either the narrator's voice is judged to be unreliable—it is itself contextualized within the narrative as a relative, unauthoritative voice projected from a biased existential context that is either described by the narrative or at least betrayed within the narratorial voice itself—or it presents such evaluative discrepancies in an ironic vein to expose their fraudulence when they are thus counterpoised to narrative reality that this same voice has already secured.

Given the dearth of information about the narratorial situation from which the external unconditioned narrator narrates, information usually supplied so that the narrator's views have a context and can be understood and judged on that basis, the strategy of finding the narrator unreliable is out of the question. Here as elsewhere in the Bible, so-called "third person"[4] narration is from an external, unconditioned perspective, reliable by ontological definition and by the conventions of this

---

3 Cf. "These Nations That Remain," n. 3.

4 I am aware of the problems involved in using "person" as an all-encompassing description for the characteristics of this narratorial situation. M. Bal (1985:121–6) summarizes the problems. It will do here, however, as a familiar short-hand description with precision enough for present purposes.

mode of biblical narrative discourse. We have already seen how many times the narrator has consistently demonstrated his total reliability, which is anchored in an unconditional access to information about the characters and events he describes.

In both Judges 2 and 2 Kings 17 it seems at first (and also usually in the end) that the narrator offers a untrammeled view of his attitude towards Israel's behaviour and his comprehension of its ultimate historical demise. But these narratorial comments need to be measured against the reality they claim to describe. The subtle theological vision of the Dtr narrative provides an overpowering setting in which the flimsy artificiality of of conventional wisdom leaps at the reader's eye.[5] And as the reader has already seen at least once before, in the case of the ironies of the conquest narrative, in biblical narrative the facts, the realia of the story world, are directly accessible to the reader only in the narrative description of the story world.[6]

---

5 Robert Polzin's suggestions about the ideology of the Dtr narrative apply just as well in 2 Kings as they do to the narrative in Joshua-Judges: "... we have attempted to show how the Deuteronomistic History, contrary to the prevalent view of scholars, is not representative of an orthodox retribution theory carried to its most mechanistic extreme ..." (1980:126–7). I would extend Polzin's remarks on the narratorial subversion of what he calls "authoritarian dogmatism" to cover examples such as 2 Kgs 17:7–23 In such passages, as Polzin has demonstrated for the book of Joshua and its relationship to the book of Deuteronomy, the stock theological phrases and conventional piety are undercut by a narrative that presents such views as though they were its own but sets them in a context that exposes their hollowness.

6 It might appear an arbitrary distinction to say that the context preceding 2 Kgs 17:7–23 describes the actual events in the story world while the verses in question are presented only as summary evaluations of those same events. But what distinguishes 2 Kgs 17:7–23 as evaluative commentary is the fact that it is a compressed overview, a summary rehearsal that does not attempt to describe events as they happen and lead on to other, future events. Here the narrator stops the flow of story world time to review the past in order to explain the significance of an event that is just then current in the on-going plot of the narrative. Here, Israel's history of convenantal defection is reviewed to explain why the Assyrian exile occurs. The difference in time ratio too, between the events described and the space of narrative that is expended in their description, shows that here the narrator engages in abstract exposition rather than blow by blow description (cf. Sternberg 1978:19–34).

A different objection might be based on S. Sandmel's suggestion that the ancient mind was less troubled by apparent contradiction that the modern and that it was a common enough practise for subsequent interpreters such as redactors to allow contradictions to stand as creative elements in the on-going life of sacred tradition (1972). The contradictions between 2 Kgs 17:7–23 and its preceding context, then, could be explained as unexceptional differences between one or another of the Dtr redactors and the traditional material, their ancient minds being so much more accommodating than ours. What this resolution would mean, however, is the impossibility of irony, for them or us, in ancient writing. I would submit that there is ample evidence of irony and of

What is most difficult about the narrator's evaluative commentary in 2 Kgs 17 is the manner in which its overt, overbearing rancour controverts the subtle implication and objective tone that inspires the narratorial voice both before *and* after 2 Kgs 17. Here, nearly finished his story, the narrator seems to step out into the open, shamelessly flaunting views that he has kept so private up to this point. Having avoided such a direct confrontation with the reader since Judges 2, he spews an inflammatory tirade that targets the Israelite people as cause for the exile.

Many readers have drunk this draught to the dregs, allowing their intoxicated perceptions to blur the subtle and sobering implications that precede. Under the influence of this evaluative grog the reading consciousness becomes foggy and memories of delicate, theologically indelicate implications fade away. Here at last, it has seemed, is an interpretive framework of conventional theological lineage (Polzin's "authoritarian dogmatism" [1980:132]) within which all the unorthodoxy and uncertainty evoked by the narrative can be subsumed. It is, so the conventional reading, simply the harsh reality of a world filled with sinners and ruled by an exacting Judge who administers the beating that Israel so richly deserved.

For those readers able to resist the temptation of an easy inebriation that assuages uncertainties about sin, exile, and divine justice in this story, there are here as in Judges 2 some submerged, but strong underlying contextualizations of the bald evaluative statements. The implicit undertones of the explicit evaluations are provided through allusions to prior events in this story and especially through linkages to Judges 2, which set the implicit agenda for 2 Kgs 17. When these prior events are implicated through the allusions, the evaluations take on a very different coloration from the black hues in which they are explicitly cloaked. The rhetorical ploy of the narrative here is no different from that already played in Judges 2, to which 2 Kgs 17 is so closely tied by conceptual and vocabulary linkages.

There are two main buttresses supporting an ironic reading of the evaluative statements of 2 Kgs 17: a. the literary linkage to Judg 2, in which the narrator used a similar vocabulary to ex-

perception of contradiction and incongruity within the Bible to undermine such a psychological distinction. We do, after all, share enough similarities with the ancient mind to continue reading and re-reading their writings with interest and understanding.

plain, from his conventionally objective viewpoint, how and why Israel sinned against God and why God responded as he did; b. the allusions and connections between 2 Kgs 17 and the narrative that precedes. This last support for the ironic reading is formed out of the incongruity between the strong evaluations that the narrator makes about the Israelite people's behaviour in 2 Kgs 17:7–23, and the description of what they have actually done in the preceding context.[7]

Reading 2 Kings 17

Verses 1–6 are patterned on the cycle, known well to the reader from the book of Judges, of sin against God by Israel followed by divine punishment of Israel through a historical agent (cf. Judg 2:14–23). There is no explicit statement here that Yahweh sold Hoshea into the hand of Shalmaneser, but there is no need. When the narrator says, in sequence, that Hoshea did "evil in the sight of Yahweh," and this description is followed immediately with a view of Shalmaneser "coming up against" Hoshea, we know that Yahweh stands behind Shalmaneser's campaign. The direct concatenation in the narrative description of the two character actions evokes this causal understanding from the reader, in whom it has been thoroughly implanted by every book since the book of Judges.[8]

Yet, vv. 1–6 departs from the pattern established in the book of Judges to follow another pattern, equally well-established,

---

7 An alternative understanding of the disparity is proposed by T.R. Hobbs (1985:240) who understands the evaluative commentary of 2 Kgs 17 as a summary of actions previously described: "He does this by listing ***again*** the actions of the people which stand in stark contrast to the standards of behavior and worhsip expected of them" (my emphasis). The problem, of course, is the "again," since these actions have not been described, for the most part, before. One might go on, however, to suggest the here the narrator is simply filling in gaps left in the prior narration of events. The narrator pauses here to add information now relevant, on account of the exile, but previously not that important. Given that the entire Dtr narrative is viewed as a historical theodicy, supposed to explain over its extent the rationale for the exile, and given the numerous literary connections between this summary and its preceding context, contacts that foreground the incongruity of the summary with its preceding context, it seems more fitting to comprehend the dichotomy as purposeful and itself significant.

8 Cf. Ruhl's algorithm describing reader-response and perception of causality in narrative literature:

> If a structure A-and-B can be analyzed as a temporal sequence, it will be. If it can be further analyzed that A is a precondition for B, it will be. And if A can be analyzed as a decisive condition—that is, a cause—for B, it will be. Only if the first stage—the temporal sequence—is not reached, will the co-ordinate structure be analyzed as symmetric (cited in M.L. Pratt 1977:156).

that dominates the narrative in 2 Kings. Over and over the narrator introduces the reign of a king with the description that introduces Hoshea's reign here: 'In the __th year of King X, King Y, son of Z became king and reigned __ years. And he did evil in the sight of Yahweh ....' Unlike the book of Judges, in the books of Kings, with one mitigated exception,[9] it is the kings who offend Yahweh by their own behaviour and who lead Israel to similar offence.[10] But the narrator does not even show any pressing concern to evaluate even the kings. His aim, rather, is to show that throughout the monarchic period the irritation that provokes Yahweh to impose the exile is located in the monarchy; the behaviour of the general populace, described so fully here in ch. 17, is almost totally ignored. So he has not blamed the kings for the exile and far less provided a chronicle that pin-points the people for the disaster. If he had, in 2 Kgs 17, made the kings target to his vituperations it would be far easier for the reader to accept the claims; the fact that it is the people whose presence has been less than obvious all the way through the narrative is the key to the irony of the presentation in this chapter.

Chapter 17 opens with a description of monarchic offence to Yahweh that follows a combined genealogical-evaluative pattern encountered many times before in the books of Kings. A major development in this instance is that the historical consequence of the offensive behaviour is exile (v. 6). This turn of events touches on the event towards which the entire narrative has been moving: the exile and its implications for the covenant. The implication of this formulaic description of royal offence to Yahweh is that Hoshea's action and the action of his monarchic predecessors provoked God to send Israel into exile: it is the monarchy, not the people, that has a history of doing what is

---

9 In 1 Kgs 14:22–24 the whole tribe of Judah did evil in the sight of the Lord through apostasy and syncretism; see below, pp. 196–98.

10 Cf. Von Rad (1962:338, 339, 344–5). The central formulaic description in the books of Kings sets responsibility for Israel's waywardness right on the kings' doorsteps. "The king is now regarded as the responsible person to whom has been entrusted the law of Moses and who has the duty to see that it is recognized in his kingdom" (Von Rad 1962:339). Von Rad is correct in his understanding of the key role played by the kings according to the predominant formulaic expression of the books of Kings. He errs, however (as does Gerbrandt [1986:190, 192-94]), in attributing this requirement to the narrator rather than to the character, God. In every case, the king's aberrant behaviour is described as offensive to God; the narrator dissociates himself from the evaluation. His goal, rather, is to explain the dynamics of the relationship between God and Israel, culminating in the exile.

evil in the eyes of the Lord. This implication has been building through the narrative to this point. Every time another formulaic introduction to a new king appears the offence to Yahweh grows and with it the likelihood of a confrontation. By the time the reader hits 2 Kgs 17 and the connection between yet another formulaic introduction and the Assyrian exile, the reader is so prepared that the simple combination of the formula and the paratactically joined description of the Assyrian assault is enough to convey the idea that God has finally responded.

There is no strong evaluative tone to the description. The offence to God and its consequence are presented as a simple fact: this is what Hoshea did and that is what it lead to. The perspective, as before, is dispassionate and analytical: the narrative looks like good historiography should, even though the action described is leading to the ultimate disaster.

The formulaic connection between Hoshea's and his predecessors' provocation suggests that the kings of Israel, they who made Israel sin against God (*heḥᵉṭîʾ ʾet-yiśrāʾēl* 1 Kgs 14:16; 15:26, 30; 16:2, 25, 30; 21:22; 22:51–3; 2 Kgs 3:2–3; 10:29–31; 13:3, 11; 14:24; 15:9, 18, 24; 16:2–3) are the human agents who provoked God to impose the capital penalty. This implication gains its strength not by shouting at the reader, but through a long, reiterated description of a repeated pattern of actions—the sinning leadership of Israel's kings—that culminate in the exile. As a result the reader's comprehension of the human provocation for the exile grows naturally out of the historiography of the narrative description. It is a logic to which the reader is habituated. The reader's assent is won, not by coercion or browbeating, but by a subtle camaraderie built slowly but surely between reader and narrator. And nothing in the preceding context has been introduced to subvert this understanding.

Verses 7–23 present a disquieting contradiction between the new explanation in these verses—"and it was because the sons of Israel sinned (*ḥāṭᵉʾû*) against Yahweh ..." and that of the formulaic opening of ch. 17—the sin of the kings provoked the exile.[11] What has happened to the notion that the kings

---

11 Whether the kings are blamed by the narrator or not is an entirely different question. One needs to decide whether or not the descriptive verb "to sin" (*ḥṭʾ*) is neutrally descriptive or pejorative and in what circumstances one can be sure in which sense it is used. Given that the formula always appears in conjunction with a tagged attribution—

"brought Israel to sin" (*heḥeṭîʾ ʾet-yiśrāʾēl*)?[12] Conventional theology and reading might not see the contradiction here: kings of Israel or sons of Israel, what does it matter? All together—one *massae perditus*—have sinned and come short of the glory of God. This is the comforting theological brew under the influence of which a reader may overlook the contradiction.[13] But if the reader reflects on what has been narrated about Israel's behaviour as he imbibes the tirade in vv. 7–23 a sobering realization begins to dawn.

The narrative description that precedes the tirade provides no assuring echos, allusions, or vocabulary linkages to support the assertions of the tirade. One might reasonable expect some broad support for such a condemnation in the preceding context, something at least as important, say, as the formulaic introductions to the wayward monarchs. To the contrary, there has been almost no attention paid to Israel's behaviour, good, bad, or indifferent. All eyes have been directed toward the actions of the kings of Israel and the events in which they are involved. The Israelites, where they have played a repeated role, have only done so as the objects of the kings' action, "making Israel sin" (*heḥeṭîʾ ʾet-yiśrāʾēl*). A review of the narrative since the inauguration of the first king, Saul, quickly reveals how little attention the narrator has paid to the people. Were the rolling rebuke of the tirade actually the narrator's own heart and soul belief, one would expect that he might have had a little more to say in the course of telling his story about these despicable actions and why Israel engaged in them. Sending one's children through the fire is not something to be treated lightly (v. 17), yet nowhere has the reader heard anything of it in the preceding narrative description.[14]

"king X did evil *in the sight of Yahweh* and walked in the way of [king] Y and in his sin which he made Israel to sin"—it seems safest to assume that the description of monarchic sins is objective, in keeping with the conventional objectivity that reigns the narratorial perspective throughout.

12 T.R. Hobbs (1985:231) notes that the beginning phrase of v. 7 (*wayyeḥî kî*) "is extremely rare, it introduces the following explanation, and makes it dependent on the preceding recitation of the events of the fall of Samaria." The phrasing is designed, it seems, to foreground the incongruity between the two different explanations for the exile found in vv. 1–6 and vv. 7–23.

13 Comforting, because it maintains a just God who, so long as the mechanisms for atonement are in place, can be relied upon to save repentant readers and damn and destroy wanton sinners like Israel.

14 In fact, the only one to have done such a thing prior to 2 Kgs 17 is King Ahaz, just before in 2 Kgs 16:3. And subsequent to 2 Kgs 17 the only documented cases are those

Comparing Evaluation to Story World Reality

As L. Dolezel (1980:11–12, 24) has suggested, the reality of the story world that is described in any narrative is found in the narrative description of events, characters and actions. It is against the standard of that reality, however much a literary convention it may be, that assertions such as the tirade of 2 Kgs 17 must be measured. As soon as the reader begins to think about what he has just read there should be a strong reaction to the quantity and tone of the tirade against the Israelites. The story has been about the kings of Israel, their political rivalries, plots, and manipulations. In fact a percentile breakdown of the narrative from 1 Sam–2 Kgs 17 reveals the following allocation of narrative space, analyzed by major focus on character:

Saul	9%
Saul & David	18%
David	29%
Solomon	12%
Kings of North & South	32%
	100%

The Evaluative Pre-Context to 2 Kings 17

Given the question that the strong evaluations of 2 Kgs 17:7–23 raises, one needs to re-examine the preceding context to see whether the condemnation is born out by the facts of the story world. This is not an effete retrenchment nor is it special pleading for an interpretation contradicted by the plain (surface) meaning of the text. Any reader coming to 2 Kgs 17:7–23 with a fair recollection of what has just preceded in the narrative should be struck by the lack of resonance between these evaluations and the preceding context. So struck, it is perfectly natural for a reader to reflect on the disparity between the evaluation and the prior factual description.

---

of Sepharvaim (2 Kgs 17:31) and Manasseh (21:6). That fact that Ahaz's commission of this abhorrent crime comes just before the assertion that the Israelites did such a thing is a sure indicator of the narrator's subtle use of contradiction to subvert the assertions made in the tirade. It was a king, not the common people, who did this thing; the attribution to the people is ironic.

Judges

In 2:11–13, 17, 19 the narrator presents a thematic introduction to the entire book, showing why Israel goes astray, why there are nations left in the land, and why God punishes Israel. This explanation is given to the reader as an interpretive key (cf. D. Jobling 1986:47) illuminating all that follows, especially the subsequent occasions within the book[15] when the narrator uses the same phraseology to supply supporting allusions back to this critical chapter. When the same language surfaces again in 2 Kgs 17:7–23 there is a strong contextual argument, supported by the standard Hebrew narrative technique of commentary by associative comparison (Alter 1981:180–1; Sternberg 1985:365–440), for bringing the associations and perspective of Judg 2 to bear on the new occasion of its use. The consequent distancing from the evaluative tone of 2 Kgs 17:7–23 is supported by the intervening disconfirmation through the factual description of events, which transforms 2 Kgs 17 one step further, from the dispassionate comprehension of Israel's waywardness manifest in Judges 2 to an ironic reversal of the common reaction to the exile.

1 Samuel

In 7:3–4 we read that the sons of Israel serve the Ba'als and Ashtaroth. This is a non-evaluative description from the narrator, who includes an extensive description of the mitigating circumstances that led Israel to this behaviour. (Yahweh seems to have abandoned them and this is their reluctant [cf. 7:2] response.)[16]

In 10:27 some Israelites are described as "renegades" (*b^enê b^elîyā^cal*), who spurn Saul. This description has usually been interpreted as a negative evaluative term, but the contexts of its occurrence suggest a neutral, descriptive usage (Eslinger 1985:356–8). Even leaving this reading of the term aside, the action in question in 10:27 is not action directly against God as is all action evaluated in 2 Kgs 17:7–23.

15 Judg 3:7, 12; 4:1; 6:1; 10:6; and 13:1, all repeat the language of 2:11–13 and thus imply the same explanation as it.

16 The arguments to support this assertion are presented in my study of 1 Sam 1–12 (1985:55–8, 65–236).

In 14:32–33 only Saul seems upset by the people "eating on the blood." This is a cultic transgression that evokes no response from Yahweh and which is not mentioned in 2 Kgs 17.

1 Sam 15 describes a campaign led by Saul in which the ban (*ḥrm*) is transgressed. The reader already knows that this law has been mitigated by its selective enforcement by Yahweh (Josh 2–9, see above, "These Nations That Remain"). Furthermore, David Gunn has raised enough questions about Samuel's authoritarian perspective in 1 Sam 15 for us to wonder whether this is at all a negative characterization of Saul or the people.

> Thus, on the interpretation I have just sketched, it becomes otiose to seek an underlying reason for Saul's failure ... for here in chapter 15, as in chapter 13, there is essentially no failure on Saul's part to be accounted for, no failure, that is to say, for which he can be held seriously culpable (1980:56).

The rest of 1 Samuel contains nothing to support 2 Kgs 17:7–23. What is most strange about 1 & 2 Samuel as the pretext for 2 Kgs 17:7–23 is that no attention at all is paid to the general religious behaviour of the people. Were the narrative the theodicy by way of confession that so many scholarly readers have seen in it, the rhetoric of plot could hardly be more poorly planned. If the intent were to support the evaluative remarks of 2 K17:7–23, why leave the actions of the sinning populace so hidden from view? David and Saul, Saul and David—all eyes are on this pair and nothing else matters. Surely the religious behaviour of the people could not have changed so dramatically without such an important event coming to light (whether in history or story world). Why has the narrator laid things out in such a way as to leave Israel's behaviour out of view and then, in 2 Kgs 17:7–23, to bring it so strongly into view?

Among scholarly readers of the Bible, such inconsistency usually leads to suggestions of multiple authorship in the diachronic perspective of historical criticism. From a narratological point of view, however, it suggests ironic juxtaposition at the expense of the evaluation's credibility.

2 Samuel

2 Samuel describes many wrongs and injustices, all committed by members of the royal family or court of David. In 2 Sam 11 the narrator presents the story of David & Bathsheba. It is the only case thus far in 2 Sam of someone doing something terribly wrong and the culprit is none other than King David! In 2

Sam 13, Amnon, son of David, rapes his sister. In 2 Sam 13, Absalom, son of David, murders his brother. In 2 Sam 15, Absalom, son of David, conspires against his father. In 2 Sam 18:14, Joab murders Absalom. And in 2 Sam 20, Sheba revolts against David. Even though turpitude prevails[17] the general populace comes away clean if only because its actions go unmentioned. The narrator chooses to leave them aside. Immorality does indeed abound but only in the house of David, the house that Yahweh has promised to perpetuate forever![18]

There is one apparent exception to this absence of wrongdoing on Israel's part. In 2 Sam 24:1 the narrator reveals that Yahweh's anger burns against Israel (*wayyōsep ʾap-yhwh laḥᵃrôt bᵉyiśrāʾēl*). The involuntary response of the pious biblical reader, operating within the conventions of religious psychology in which God is angry with no one who has done no wrong, is that Israel must have sinned. Such a response to apparent divine wrath is exemplified by Job's three friends. But when the reader looks for an explanation of the divine wrath in the context preceding 2 Sam 24:1, there is none. Israel has done no wrong. Why does God punish them with the curses of Deut 28?[19] The only hint is found in the divine choice of David, whose family difficulties have occupied so much of the book. Perhaps David is a mechanism by which to afflict Israel. More analysis is required but it seems that Israel suffers evil at the hand of Yahweh here ("Yahweh repented on account of the evil," *wayyinnāḥem Yahweh ʾel-hārāʿâ*, 24:16) because of his displeasure with the house of David.[20] Far from being the source of divine provocation, Israel is the innocent scapegoat. There is nothing in the narrative context to controvert David's appraisal of the situation; everything, in fact, supports it.

---

17 The development of decadence in the character of David, the king chosen for his psychological profile (1 Sam 16:7), and the troubles that his reign brings to Israel have been carefully traced by Fokkelman (1981).

18 The turn that Israel's leadership takes beginning with David himself—Yahweh's hand-picked king—suggests that David's waywardness may itself have played a not unforeseen part in the divine scheme of Israel's history. It is not beyond belief that Yahweh might provide Israel with some institution or holder of that institution in order to lead it astray, the deviation being an integral part of his plan for Israel's historical existence (cf. Hos 13:11; Ezek 20:25).

19 Compare v. 13 with the curses in Deut 28:21, 25.

20 Cf. 24:17, [David speaking] "Lo, I have sinned, and I have done wickedly: but these sheep, what have they done? Let thine hand, I pray thee, be against me, and against my father's house."

1 Kings

As at the end of 2 Samuel, the narrator opens the books of Kings (1 Kgs 1–2) with an insight into even more ills within the royal family and its squabbling over the succession. In 1 Kgs 3–11, the narrator gives a detailed view of Solomon's insidious machinations and his attempt to ensconce Yahweh. In 1 Kgs 12, Rehoboam's pride takes pride of place. In 1 Kgs 12:30, Jeroboam's calves become a trap for the people. In 1 Kgs 13:33–4, the narrator first mentions the sin of Jeroboam, a phrase repeated many times subsequently and in connection with which the people are presented only as pawns whose fate is determined by the behaviour of their kings. It needs saying, however, that the people's gain in virtue is not necessarily the kings' loss. The narrator is no more concerned to chastise the monarchy than the people.

The remainder of 1 Kings presents a parade of royal deviations from the path of correct action delineated by Yahweh. In 1 Kgs 14:15–16 the narrator quotes Ahijah's prophecy of the exile to come. The approaching punishment of Israel, the nation and the people, comes because of the king's wicked leadership, because of the sins that he sinned and made Israel to sin.

This chain of monarchic leadership in sinful behaviour is broken once, in 1 Kgs 14:22–24. Here the narrator presents the tribe of Judah doing evil in the sight of the Lord through apostasy and syncretism. The language used to describe the sin of the Judahites parallels some of the items in the catalogue of sins in 2 Kgs 17 (vv. 8, 10). Could this be the needed confirmation of 2 Kgs 17:7–23?

The vocabulary connections between the two passages are strong and reliable. The reader will, of course, associate this description with that found just before (1 Kgs 14:15) in Ahijah's prophecy, which also mentions the Asherim. There too it is the sin of the people, Israel, that is described. But in the prophecy a clear link is forged between the sin of the people and the leadership of Jeroboam (cf. 14:16) The connection develops further in the form of a parallelism between the report of Jeroboam's reign and its consequences in the north and Rehoboam's in the south. The pattern is as follows:

Reign of Jeroboam	*Reign of Rehoboam*
Introductory description of Jeroboam's reign (12:20–13:34, extended because of the connection between it and the story of the partition of the kingdom).	14:21
Basis of indebtedness to Yahweh:	
election of Jeroboam and grant of the major portion of David's kingdom (covenantal phraseology, 14:7–8).	election of Jerusalem, the place where Yahweh chose to put his name (v. 21).
Sins described:	
Jeroboam's (v. 9), Israel's (v. 15 [Asherim]), Jeroboam's (leading to Israel's) (v. 16).	Judah's (vv. 22–4).
Punishment:	
destruction of Jeroboam's dynasty and exile of Israel (vv. 10–11, 14–16).	defeat at the hand of Egypt (by implication, vv. 25–8).
Concluding formula:	
vv. 19–20.	vv. 29–31.

The parallelism between the accounts of the two reigns suggests that the sin of the Judahites should be viewed, like the sins of their northern counterparts, as occurring under the aegis of monarchic leadership. The same logic underlies the punishment for the sin, which is a punishment that strikes against and is responded to by Rehoboam, king of Judah. The narrator's omission of any explicit description of Rehoboam's leadership stands in stark contrast to the description of Jeroboam's, but that difference is a product of the large role that is played by Jeroboam as the paradigmatic wayward leader. Rehoboam, on the other hand, plays a lesser role, local to the business of the secession of the north. The vocabulary linkages between 1 Kgs 14:23 and 2 Kgs 17:8,10 should be weighed along with a similar, though weaker linkage between 1 Kgs 14:23 and v. 15 of the same chapter. The implication of this linkage is that 14:23 is not the independent action that it might seem to be.[21]

The rest of 1 Kings continues to trace the pattern of monarchic sin and leadership in the sin of the nation . In 1 Kgs 15:3, King Abijam, king of Judah, walks in the sins of his father. In 1 Kgs 15:14, Asa's heart is not whole with Yahweh, even though he did what was right in the sight of Yahweh (v. 11). In 1 Kgs 15:26, Nadab does evil in the sight of Yahweh, walking in the way of Jeroboam, the sins that he did, and the sins that he made Israel to sin.. In 1 Kgs 15:30, disaster comes to the house of Jeroboam because of the sins that he sinned and made Israel to sin. In 1 Kgs 15:34, Baasha does evil in the sight of Yahweh. In 1 Kgs 16:2, Baasha is chastised for walking in the way of Jeroboam, and for the sins that he made Israel to sin. In 1 Kgs 16:7, 13, the sins of Baasha and his son Elah are mentioned again along with their role in leading the people in sin. In 1 Kgs 16:19, the subject is the sins of Zimri, who walked in the way of Jeroboam, the sins that he did, and the sins that he made Israel to sin. In 1 Kgs 16:25–6, it is the unprecedented sins of Omri, who walked in the way of Jeroboam, the sins that he did, and the sins that he made Israel to sin. In 1 Kgs 16:30, it is Ahab's sins; he too walked in the way of Jeroboam and made Israel to sin. In 1 Kgs 21:13–21, Ahab and Jezebel murder Naboth to get his vineyard. In 1 Kgs 21:22, Ahab is said to have provoked Yahweh and made Israel to sin. In 1 Kgs 22:51–3, Ahaziah, son of Ahab does evil in the sight of Yahweh, walking in the way of Jeroboam, the sins that he did, and the sins that he made Israel to sin.

Such a review of 1 Kings leaves little doubt about the narrator's views about who provoked Yahweh to punish Israel. Over and over again it is the kings, northern and southern, whose own actions are "evil in the sight of Yahweh" and who cause the people of north and south to sin.

---

21 In addition the word "Asherim" also harks back to Judg 3:7, where the Israelites served (rather than built) "Asherot" and Judg 2:13 (also serving "Ashtarot"). There is no doubt that the people did engage in this particular cultic practice, at least in the story world of the narrative. But because of the context of occurrences in the book of Judges, just after the narrator has explained why Israel goes astray, there can be no doubt about the neutral, rather than negative, nature of this description there and here in 1 Kgs 14. The variations, in Judges, between *ʿaštārôt* and *ʾăšērôt* (cf. *ʾăšērîm* in 1 Kgs 14:15, 23) are explained as indications of unharmonized redactional variants by Boling (1975:74).

2 Kings

The book of 2 Kings differs little from the pattern established in 1 Kings. In 2 Kgs 3:2–3, Jehoram, son of Ahab, does evil in the sight of Yahweh, clinging to the way of Jeroboam, the sins that he did, and the sins that he made Israel to sin. In 2 Kgs 8:16–19, Jehoram becomes king of Judah and walks in the way of the kings of Israel, doing evil in the sight of Yahweh. But God, for David's sake, spares Judah. In 2 Kgs 8:26–7, Ahaziah walks in the way of the house of Ahab and does evil in the sight of Yahweh. In 2 Kgs 10:29–31, Jehu walks in the way of Jeroboam, the sins that he did, and the sins that he made Israel to sin. In 2 Kgs 12:2–3, Jehoash *does right* in the eyes of Yahweh, only the high places are not taken down and the people still sacrifice and burn incense on the high places. In 2 Kgs 13:2–3, Joash does evil in the sight of Yahweh, walking in the way of Jeroboam, the sins that he did, and the sins that he made Israel to sin. In 2 Kgs 13:3 the narrator describes another historical presage of the exile, once again closely linked to a description of a monarch leading the people astray (v. 2). In 2 Kgs 13:1–7 the cycles of the Judges are revived, along with all of the implications of those cycles from the book of Judges, where the logic of Israel's sin was explained (see above, "A New Generation In Israel"). In 2 Kgs 13:11, Joash, does evil in the sight of Yahweh, walking in the way of Jeroboam, the sins that he did, and the sins that he made Israel to sin. In 2 Kgs 14:3–4, Amaziah does right in the eyes of Yahweh, only the high places are not taken down and the people still sacrifice .... In 2 Kgs 14:24, Jeroboam does evil in the sight of Yahweh, walking in the way of Jeroboam, the sins that he did, and the sins that he made Israel to sin. In 2 Kgs 15:3–4, Azariah does right in the eyes of Yahweh, only the high places weren't taken away and the people still sacrificed at the high places. In 2 Kgs 15:9, Zechariah does evil in the sight of Yahweh, walking in the way of Jeroboam, the sins that he did, and the sins that he made Israel to sin. In 2 Kgs 15:18, Menachem does evil in the sight of Yahweh, walking in the way of Jeroboam, the sins that he did, and the sins that he made Israel to sin. In 2 Kgs 15:24 Pekiah, does evil in the sight of Yahweh, walking in the way of Jeroboam, the sins that he did, and the sins that he made Israel to sin. In 2 Kgs 15:34–5, Jotham does right in the eyes of Yahweh, only the high places weren't taken away and the people still sacrificed at the high places. In 2 Kgs 16:2–3, Ahaz does evil in the sight of Yahweh, walking in the way of Jeroboam, the sins that he did, and the sins that he made Israel to sin. And finally, in 2 Kgs 17:2 Hoshea does evil in the sight of Yahweh, only not like the kings who were before him.

The list includes all descriptions of sinful wrong-doing in 2 Kings. The description leaves no doubt about who God holds responsible for the covenantal waywardness. The people do sin, but it is their monarchic leadership that leads them to it.

The View of the People from the Database[22]

A review of all cases of narratorial evaluation of Israel in the narrative reveals a remarkable state of affairs. Aside from the two prominent evaluative spikes in Judg 2[23] and 2 Kgs 17, the narrator is conspicuously silent on the matter of Israel's behaviour.[24]

---

22 For more information on the database cataloguing evaluative language in the narrative, to which I refer here, see ch. 7, "Explicit Evaluation in the Dtr Narratives."

23 There is, in the book of Judges, a continuation of the same evaluative language in chs. 3, 8, and 10. In all cases the same language and tone are used as introduced by the key passage in ch. 2 (see. Judg 3:7; 8:27, 33–5; 10:6). And in all cases the subsequent descriptions are coloured by the implications that attend ch. 2. This is also true of 2 Kgs 21:9, which shares the language and implicit contextual coloration of 2 Kgs 17.

24 The narrator's explicit evaluative silence between Judg 2 and 2 Kgs 17 is broken only in 1 Sam 14:32 and again in 1 Kgs 14:23 (v. 22 being attributed to Yahweh). In both cases the narrator's comments are more in the way of description, albeit of actions reprehensible to Yahweh, than explicit negative evaluation. Nothing in either context betrays narratorial animosity toward the action described. In the case of 1 Sam 14:32 it is questionable whether there is any evaluation at all. I included in the database so as to err on the side favouring maximal narratorial evaluation, a view that any student of narratorial situations in this particular narrative cannot favour.

Negative Narratorial Evaluations of the People

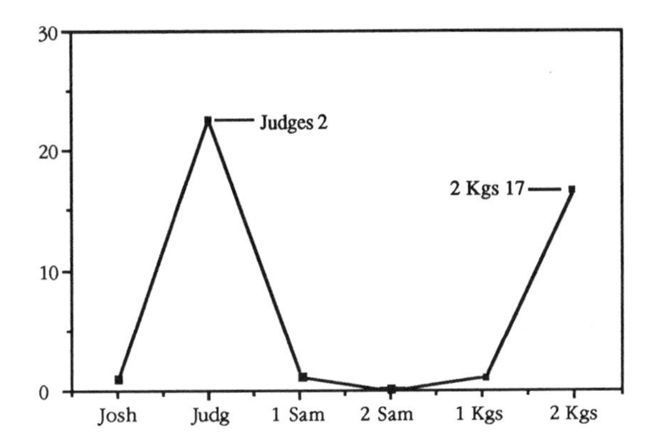

Considering that the graph compresses a range of some 147 chapters along the horizontal axis, the exceptional quantity of narratorial evaluation (the vertical axis records a simple count of instances of explicit evaluation) in these two chapters is obvious. The question is, why would the narrator offer such apparently strong negative criticism of the people in 2 Kgs 17:7–23 when the story he has already told does not support it? Either the narrator is extremely obtuse and inept as a story-teller—unlikely given the sophistication already demonstrated in the narrative—or he means to undercut the evaluative sentiments he expresses in 2 Kgs 17.[25] If he was inept, the graph of negative evaluations of Israel's behaviour shows that he could not have been more so; if he was trying to undercut the evaluations of 2 Kgs 17 by the implications of the preceding context, the graph shows that he could not have done so more strenuously.[26]

---

25 The narrator cannot, after all, mean to undercut the reality of the story world, conveyed in the narrative through his own narrative description. To do that he would have to reject his own narrative, as historical criticism has. The simple fact of the existence of the narrative is testimony enough to the narrator's acceptance of the facts of his story. It is his view of things.

26 Even the pattern of divine evaluation follows the same contours as the narrator's own, though Yahweh will take a leading hand in the negative evaluation of Judah in 2 Kgs 21:15 and 22:17. Yahweh, along with Samuel, does criticize Israel in 1 Sam 8–12 (8:7–8; Samuel in 10:19; 12:9, 17) but his evaluations are set in a narrative context that disaffirms them. The same is true of Israel's own self-censure in 1 Sam 12:10, 19, which the narrative displays as anguished extortions that would not have been made in better circumstances (Eslinger 1985:414–16). Solomon presents some negative criticism of Israel's actions (1 Kgs 8:34–6) but they are only hypothetical and strongly implicated in

The Judges 2 Connection

In both Judg 2 and 2 Kgs 17 the narrator offers unabashed evaluative commentary on the Israelite peoples' behaviour. In the case of Judg 2, the narrator provided enough contextual information to show that the evaluative material is offered in a dispassionate, analytical manner verging on irony. Israel's sin was displayed, but in such a manner that the its mitigating circumstances were prominent. The sins were catalogued in evaluative terms, but the quality of the evaluation and the terms used were radically altered by their context, which showed that the terms could not be taken as simple, self-evident truths. In 2 Kgs 17 the reader faces a similar, though more bombastic collection of evaluative commentary. How does the context, especially that preceding the tirade, affect its understanding?

The linguistic parallels between 2 Kgs 17:7–23 and Judg 2:11–23 are critical to a correct understanding of 2 Kgs 17.[27]

Judges 2	*2 Kings 17*
The children of Israel did evil in the sight of Yahweh, God of their fathers and served the Ba'alim (v. 11).	And it was because the children of Israel sinned against Yahweh (v. 7),

the rhetorical ploys of his prayers (cf. Israel's hypothetical repentant remarks in 1 Kgs 8:47). Athaliah is critical of Israel's behaviour in 2 Kgs 11:14, but then she is about to lose her life at their hands.

There is no voice in the narrative that presents a reliable negative evaluation of the Israelite people's conduct in the narrative between the two great gateways of narratorial evaluative remarks: Judges 2 and 2 Kgs 17. The narrator's own additional negative evaluations of Israel are found in Judg 3:7; 8:27, 33–5; 10:6, and in 1 Sam 14:32. The instances from the book of Judges all fall under the mitigating shadow of the narrator's explanation in Judges 2. And it is doubtful whether the sole case in 1 Sam should be called a negative evaluation at all. But even if all these cases were allowed to stand, the bulk of the narrative would not support the heavy condemnation that the narrator levels in 2 Kgs 17:7–23.

27 A detailed historical-critical analysis of some of the linguistic parallels, viewed within the context of Deuteronomistic speech patterns in general, has been made by R.D. Nelson (1981:49–65). Von Rad (1962:335; cf. Noth 1981:6) noticed the parallelism between the evaluations of 2 Kgs 17:7ff and evaluation of the book of judges but did not pursue it, suggesting only that the linguistic connection betrayed the Dtr redactor speaking his own mind.

And they forsook the God of their fathers, who brought them out from the land of Egypt (v. 11)	who brought them up from the land of Egypt, from under the hand of Pharaoh, king of Egypt (v. 7).
and followed (*wayyēlekû ʾaḥarê*) other gods (*ʾelōhîm ʾaḥērîm*) from the gods of the peoples round about them.	But they feared other gods (*ʾelōhîm ʾaḥērîm*) (v. 7) and they walked (*wayyēlekû*) in the statutes of the nations that God had dispossessed before them (v. 8)...
And they paid obeisance to them and vexed (*wayyakʿisû*) Yahweh (v. 12).	And they set up statues and Asherim on every high hill and under every green tree and they burnt incense at every high place just like the nations whom Yahweh had exiled before them; they did evil things so that they vexed (*lehakʿîs*) Yahweh (vv. 10–11).
And Yahweh's anger burned (*wayyiḥar-ʾap*) against Israel (v. 14)	... to do evil in the eyes of Yahweh to vex him (*lehakʿîsô*) (v. 17). And Yahweh was wrothful (*wayyitʾannap*) at Israel (v. 18)
and he put them in the hand of the spoilers (*wayyittenēm beyad-šōsım*) and they despoiled them (v. 14)	... and put them in the hand of the spoilers (*wayyittenēm beyad-šōsım*) until he cleared them from his presence (v. 20; cf. Keil [1982:418]).
[But Yahweh raised up judges and they delivered them from the hand of the spoilers (v. 16).]	[But Yahweh testified against (*wayyāʿad*)Israel and Judah by the hand of all his prophets, every seer, saying, 'Turn from your evil ways; keep my commandments and statutes and all the law that I commanded your fathers and which I sent to you by the hand of my servants, the prophets' (v. 13).]

But they would not listen to their judges (v. 17),	But they rejected his statutes and his covenant, which he made with their fathers, and his testimonies (*ʿēdôtāyw*) which he testified (*hēʿîd*) against them (v. 15)[28]
but went a whoring after other gods, paying homage to them and turning quickly from the way in which their fathers walked, obeying the commandments (*miṣwōt*) of Yahweh—this they did not do (v. 17).	but they pursued vanity and themselves became vain, and [pursued] the nations that surrounded them about whom Yahweh had commanded (*ṣiwwâ*) them that they should not do as they did (v. 15).

The parallelism of the events and the phraseology used to describe them, while not exact, does reveal the narrator's effort to engage the reader in a stereoscopic view of the two scenes, two complementary perspectival lenses that shape the viewer's perception of all the material intervening between them. Most important is that these linguistic linkages and the general structural parallelism (similar plot sequences) are used to bring Judges 2 and all of the associations developed in reading it to bear on the reading of 2 Kgs 17:7–23. This is, as M. Sternberg has shown, the normal expositional effect of sequentiality in narrative literature (1978:183–235). The reverse of this linking strategy is that the similar implications of 2 Kgs 17:7–23 reinforce the understanding of Judges 2. The connection makes the implication of both passages—the inclusive ironic brackets that envelope the narrative—that much stronger.[29]

28 The parallel is in the fact that whatever God sends to turn Israel, whether judges or prophets testifying testimonies, is rejected.

29 Menakhem Perry describes a reading situation in which an implied meaning survives to the end of a work simply because it is not contradicted by anything intervening (1979:48). And even if there is a piece of information that intervenes to modify, replace, or subvert the original implication and the interpretive frame that a reader has constructed, such original hypotheses, as for example Judges 2 encourages the creation of, still influence the reading of a text (Perry 1979:49). How much more so, when they are reinforced at the end of a narrative by a similarly implicative text such as 2 Kgs 17:7–23.

Notes On 2 Kings 17

Verse 7 begins with a *kî* clause that presents the material that follows as an explanation for what precedes: the exile of the northern kingdom occurred because of the sin of the children of Israel (*wayᵉhî kî-ḥāṭᵉʾû bᵉnê-yiśrāʾēl lyhwh*).[30] This explanation for the exile conflicts with that offered previously, by implication in vv. 2–3 and explicitly in vv. 4–5. This contradiction is exacerbated by another, more wide-ranging conflict: few of the charges listed in vv. 7–12 are confirmed by the preceding context in the narrative. Only the observations regarding the high places, the Asherim, and the incense are confirmed and then each supporting instance is closely bound and credited to the wayward leadership of the king at that time.

Taken one at a time, the charges and their connection to the preceding context are as follows.

2 Kings 17:7

The Israelites "sinned" (*ḥāṭᵉʾû*) against Yahweh, their God (a. divine accusation of sin on Israel's part: Josh 7:11;[31] b. Israel's own confession of having sinned: Judg 10:10, 15; 1 Sam 7:6; 12:10 (Samuel alluding to Judg 10 confession);[32] 12:19, the confession extorted from Israel; c. anonymous report of Israel sinning by "eating with the blood" (the report evinces no comment from either the narrator or God) 1 Sam 14:33). By way of contrast there are a number of narratorial reports of a king "leading Israel to sin" (*heḥᵉṭîʾ ʾet-yiśrāʾēl*) (1 Kgs 14:16; 15:26, 30, 34; 16:2, 13,

30 The reading of the Septuagint (adopted by J. Gray [1970:645, note a], who inserts *ʾap yhwh ʿal-yiśrāʾēl* after *wayᵉhî*) makes explicit what is implied by simple consecution in the Hebrew (cf. J. Montgomery [1951:478]; according to C.F. Keil [1982:414; cf. Montgomery p. 468] the apodosis only comes later in v. 18—"Yhwh was very angry"). But v. 18 only makes explicit what is already quite implicit in vv. 1–6. The connection between the first discussion of the exile and the explanation of it is also marked by an inclusio, which links the two sections:

v. 7 *wayyegel ʾet-yiśrāʾēl ʾaššûrâ*

v. 23 *wayyigel yiśrāʾēl mēʿal ʾadmātô ʾaššûrâ*

31 An accusation that is strongly mitigated by its narrative context. See ch. 2, "These Nations That Remain."

32 The confessions in the book of Judges are governed by the narrator's opening exposition in Judg 2. Though the Israelites do, indeed, commit the sins that they confess, their actions are made comprehensible by the narratorial exposition and the reader is led to understand that the narrator reports the act and its confession neutrally, not to reprehend.

19, 26; 21:22; 22:52; 2 Kgs 3:3; 10:29, 31; 13:2, 6, 11; 14:24; 15:9, 18, 24, 28).

The balance of evaluative discourse regarding the Israelites' sin in the Dtr narrative is heavily weighted in favour of narratorial neutrality. It is far from demonstrating that the narrator holds a strong, negative view of its quantity or severity. On the contrary, the twenty-one-fold repetition of the summary expositional report that the kings led Israel to sin by the narrator suggests just the opposite: that the narrator seeks to exculpate the Israelite people.

The Israelites "feared other gods" (*wayyîrʾû ʾᵉlōhîm ʾᵃḥērîm*): (a. contrariwise, Israel fears God or his representative: Josh 4:14; 1 Sam 11:7; 12:18[33]; b. subsequently foreigners, imported by the Assyrians (presumed agents of the wrathful Yahweh), do not fear Yahweh (2 Kgs 7:25) but are persuaded to do so (2 Kgs 7:28, 32–5). The charge is ungrounded.[34]

In addition to the unfounded and hence ironically voiced charges in v. 7, the narrator supplies an explanation of the continuing misunderstanding between Yahweh and Israel in this same verse. It is the same explanation that he drew at length in Judg 2 (esp. v. 10); v. 7 only alludes to the fuller account. Israel's allegiance to Yahweh, supposed by God to exist on account of the exodus, has long disappeared.[35] Even if Israel were guilty of the charges of v. 7 the grounds for culpability have evaporated.

According to Keil (1982:414), "... to show the magnitude of the sin, the writer recalls to mind the great benefit conferred in the redemption from Egypt, whereby the Lord had laid His people under strong obligation ...." Keil is correct to notice that the allusion to the exodus is set as a reminder to the reader here, but he errs in thinking that it reminds the reader of Israel's obligation. Any allusion to the exodus after Judg 2:10 can only remind the reader of the futility of Yahweh's attempts to

---

33 A case mitigated by the fact that this attitude is extorted by God and Samuel (see Eslinger 1985:412–14).

34 Even if the charge is extended to include instances of following, serving, or going a-whoring after other gods the support from the preceding context is weak: a. "following other gods" Judg 2:12, 17, 19; 10:13: all subordinate to the narratorial exposition in ch. 2; 1 Sam 8:8: mitigated by God's bias (Eslinger 1985:264–7). By way of contrast, royal commissions of such actions are described (by the narrator himself) in 1 Kgs 11:4 and charged (by God) in 1 Kgs 14:9.

35 See "A New Generation In Israel," n. 14.

hold Israel to a covenant to which they no longer feel beholden. The allusion only reminds the reader of why it is that Israel might do what is claimed in vv. 7–17.

2 Kings 17:8

Israel "walked in the statutes" (*wayyēlᵉkû bᵉḥuqqôt*) of the nations (*haggôyim*) that Yahweh "dispossessed" (*hôrîš*) from before the Israelites. In the books of Joshua and Judges, the narrator has already shown that Yahweh *did not dispossess* the nations, though it was his sworn duty (cf. Exod 33:2; 34:11; Deut 4:38; 6:19). God admits as much—to himself alone—in Judg 2:21, "I will no longer dispossess (*lᵉhôrîš*) a single man from before them from the nations (*haggôyim*) that Joshua "left" (*ʿāzab*) when he died"[36] and the admission is verified by the narrator in v. 23.

If Israel were walking in the statutes of these "remaining nations" it would be a defection sponsored by Yahweh himself, an unfortunate (unforeseen?) side-effect of preserving the nations as a means of testing and commanding Israel's loyalty. If he had indeed driven them out, there would be no role models for Israel to defect to. The problem, however, is that there is no prior description of Israel doing what is claimed here.[37] And the irony of the statement that Yahweh did "dispossess" the inhabitants when in fact he did not, is not aimed critically; the reader has already seen, in Judg 1–2, that it was as much a duty of Israel as of Yahweh to "dispossess" the inhabitants.[38] The allusion to the failed dispossession balances the explicit description of Israel's defection with a reminder of the divine initiative that opened the door to such a possibility. The result is that 2 Kgs 17:8 criticizes neither Israel for defecting nor God for not dispossessing. It is another piece in the ironic vision that runs through the narrative, here tying back to the companion piece in Judg 1–2.

---

[36] Cf. v. 23, where he goes so far as to give the remaining nations "rest," (*wayyannaḥ*) something Israel, not the nations, was supposed to get (cf. Exod 33:14; Deut 3:20; 12:9–10; 25:19; Josh 1:13; 22:4; 23:1; "A New Generation," p. 78.

[37] If the reader responds by accepting any description of sinful apostasy as evidence in support of this charge the problem of the mitigating narratorial explanation in Judges 2 remains. Given the established narrative techniques of repetition with significant variation the probability is that the lack of congruity between narrative description and evaluative summary is an intentional disparity. See Alter (1981:88–113) on the rhetoric of biblical repetition.

[38] Cf. "A New Generation," pp. 67–68.

The narrator continues his ironic exploration of a past supposed to justify the Assyrian exile with another assertion contrary to the past and this time, to the entire rationale of Israel's ensconced theocracy. (The monarchy began and remained in absolute subordination to the divinity, at least in narrative fact.) The suggestion that Israel walked (in the statutes) of the kings that they made is controverted by the repetitious formulations that it was the kings who led Israel astray and by the strong emphasis that Yahweh and his servants have placed on the notion that Yahweh and Yahweh alone had the right or the power to confer the royal office on an individual.[39] There is, of course, the case of Jeroboam (as 2 Kgs 17:21 reminds us, *wayyamlîkû ʾet-yārobʿām*) in which the people play a part in making Jeroboam king, but that part comes after Yahweh has indicated his will by making Jeroboam king.[40] The entire history of the monarchy and king-making in Israel is thoroughly conditioned by the first instance of king-making and the sole authorization of Yahweh to do such a thing that is established by that instance. If Israel were walking in the "statutes" of the kings, it would not be possible to blame them for the mere existence of such a pitfall, as v. 8 purports to do.

2 Kings 17:9–12

The narrator's description of Israel's sin parallels his description of the original post-Joshuan sin in Judg 2. Nothing has changed: the parallel to the pace-setting dispassion of Judg 2 provides the same mitigating comprehension for this catalogue as was created for Judg 2.

1. The high places: a. the people build high places (1 Kgs 14:23), the sole incident; the people sacrifice at high places because no house is yet built to Yahweh (1 Kgs 3:2); b. Solomon, pre-eminent king of Israel frequents the high places (1 Kgs 3:3, 4) and even builds one (1 Kgs 11:7;); c. other kings associated with the high places (Jeroboam 1 Kgs

---

39 Hobbs (1985:231–2) notes the awkwardness of the grammatical construction here, which may have been designed to prolong reader contemplation of the proposition and thus to encourage reflection on its ironic incongruity with the mass of preceding contrary assertions. Cf. Šanda (1912:220), who rejects v. 8b as a gloss.

40 1 Kgs 12:20, "And when all Israel heard that Jeroboam had returned they sent and summoned him to the assembly and they made him king over all Israel," follows the divine initiative in 1 Kgs 11:31 in which Yahweh proclaims his decision to give the lion's share of Solomon's kingdom to Jeroboam.

12:31–2; 13:2, 32–3; Asa 1 Kgs 15:14; Jehoshaphat 1 Kgs 22:43; Jehoash 2 Kgs 12:3–4; Amaziah 2 Kgs 14:4; Azariah 2 Kgs 15:4; Jotham 2 Kgs 15:35; Ahaz 2 Kgs 16:4; d. Samuel, confidant of God, is mentioned in association with a high place no less than five times (1 Sam 9:12, 13, 14, 19, 25).

2. The Asherim: a. the people install Asherim (1 Kgs 14:15,[41] 23); b. kings associated with Asherim: Asa (through his mother) 1 Kgs 15:13; Ahab 1 Kgs 16:33; 18:19 (through Jezebel).
3. "Under every green tree": a. the people (1Kgs 14:23); b. Ahaz (2 Kgs 16:4).

   There is a strong allusive contact between 2 Kgs 17:10 and 1 Kgs 14:23. In addition to the arguments already presented for rejecting this connection as conclusive verification of the claims the narrator propounds here, there is also the irony that 1 Kgs 14:23 describes the actions of Judah while here it is Israel, the northern kingdom, that is being sent off for these crimes. Were the allusive connection not taken as ironic, the implication of the connection would be that Israel is unjustly accused and punished with exile for sins accomplished by Judah.
4. "Sacrificing and burning incense at the high places": the people (1 Kgs 22:43; 2 Kgs 12:3–4; 14:4; 15:4, 35).

   There are five instances in which the people sacrifice and burn incense at the high places. In each case the people's action is mentioned immediately after the king's failure to remove the high places is described (above 1c). In each instance the expositional value of narrative sequence is to show the consequences of the king's failure to remove the items so offensive to Yahweh. The people's action is a product of the king's. In any case, the people are not excused nor is the king; neither are they condemned. The action is simply reported.

   There is, hidden within the assertion about incense burning in v. 11, a small irony that surfaces in comparison with the preceding context. The verb *glh* provides the connection. In v. 6 the narrator describes the Assyrian king "exiling" Israel to Assyria; vv. 7ff. are then provided as the explanation of

---

41 A divine claim, unsupported even within the context of the oracle, which suggests that Jeroboam is responsible for leading the people astray.

that event. In v. 11, part of the explanation, the narrator tells the reader that Israel burnt incense in a manner like the nations that Yahweh had "exiled" before them. But the reader knows, from Judg 2:21–3 that Yahweh did not, in fact, exile all of the previous inhabitants. The assertion combines two allusions to the prior context, neither of which is fully confirmed and both of which raise doubts about the validity of the charges raised against Israel.

5. The other terms—*ḥpʾ* (v. 9), *dᵉbārîm ʾᵃšer lōʾ kēn* (v. 9), doing as the nations do (v. 11; contrast Ahaz, 2 Kgs 16:3), doing wicked things (v. 11), and serving idols (v. 11)—are not supported by the preceding narrative context.

2 Kings 17:13

In v. 13 the narrator takes a different tack. Instead of piling more orthodox claims of Israel's waywardness on the high but hollow pile, he turns now to God's counter activity, the warning testimony (*wayyāʿad*) through the prophets.

Since the death of Joshua and his generation, divine recourse to the exodus as a means of compelling Israel's loyalty and obedience had become futile. God does resort to it but to no avail. What he needed and what he developed was a new voice with which to remind Israel of its covenantal obligation to him and a new reality by which to evoke its gratitude and compel its obedience.[42] The divine solution has two corresponding manifestations. First he arranges for some of the original inhabitants of the land to go unconquered. They are used as a goad to afflict Israel, prodding it to turn to the God who wielded these nations for relief (2 Kgs 17:20; Judg 2:14, 21–3 and throughout the book of Judges). The second stage is the introduction of the prophets who were called to the office of testifying against Israel on behalf of the divine covenanter. They were to substitute for the lost experience of the exodus and Israel's consequent lack of any sense of obligation to Yahweh. This understanding of the role of the prophets as substitutes for the compulsive power of the obsolete exodus is conveyed by the narrative structure in 2 Kgs 17.

---

[42] The rise of prophecy in Israel, usually connected in historical studies with the rise of the monarchy, is explained, then, by the demise of the exodus experience as an effective psychological force in the national psychology of ancient Israel.

Structure in 2 Kings 17:7–20

2 Kings 17:7–12 parallels the narratorial description of apostasy that we find in Judg 2:12–19: Israel neglects the duty it owes to God on account of the exodus (v. 7; Judg 2:10–12) and defects to the Canaanite religions (vv. 8–12; Judg 2:12–13). But here in 2 Kgs 17 God no longer appeals to the exodus as an argument to compel Israel's obedience, as he does in Judg 2:1–3.[43] Instead he sends prophets (v. 13) to turn Israel from its sin, knowing as he must that the exodus argument no longer works.

Judges 2:12–19	*2 Kings 17:7–13*
Israel forsakes Yahweh, God of the fathers, who brought them out of the land of Egypt (v. 12a).	The children of Israel sin against Yahweh, their God, who brought them out of the land of Egypt from under the hand of Pharaoh (v. 7).
Israel apostatizes (vv. 12b–13).	Israel apostatizes (vv. 8–12).
God sends a messenger to remind Israel of its obligations to the laws that he made on the basis of the exodus event ("I brought you out of Egypt and brought you to the land that I swore to your fathers and I said I will never break my covenant with you; and you shall not make any covenant with the inhabitants of this land .... What have you done ?" 2:1–3).	God sends the prophets to testify against Israel, telling them to keep the commandments and statutes "according to all the law which I commanded your fathers, and which I sent to you by the hand of my servants, the prophets" (v. 13).

The situation is nearly the same but now it is the prophets and their testimony that are supposed to oblige Israel to God and which form the basis of his claim to just punishment.

---

43 Judg 2:1–3 are, in terms of the passage of time in the story world, temporally subsequent to 2:10–12. See ch. 3, "A New Generation," p. 87.

The structure of 2 Kgs 17 contains this entire record of revelation (through the exodus), obligation, apostasy, and new revelation within itself:

1. The exodus and its burden of obligation.	V. 7.
2. Apostasy.	Vv. 7–12
3. The new prophetic revelation and its new vehicle of obligation.	V. 13
4. Unrelenting apostasy.	V. 14 (15–17)

The problem with this record of divine clemency and goodwill toward Israel, as expressed in the warning voices of "all his prophets and all (his) seers" is, once again, that the preceding narrative description does not support it.[44] There is no case, after Samuel's warning in 1 Sam 12 (cf. 8:9), of a prophet trying to warn the people away from their sin. If the narrator says that God sent his prophets to warn the people off and if such a thing is not documented in the preceding context (cf. however, Judg 6:8–10!),[45] what is the narrator trying to say here? Is it not, rather, a question of ironic gainsaying?

---

44 Šanda (1912:221) hears the blatant over-emphasis but responds to it only with the suggestion that "and all his seers" might be a gloss.

45 It would be even more ridiculous if the assertion of 2 Kgs 17:13 were intentionally linked to Judg 6:8–10 as proof of its veracity. The warning of the unknown prophet of that chapter along with Samuel's warning in 1 Sam 12 would hardly constitute the reiterated warnings, over the years, of "all his prophets, every seer" (2 Kgs 17:13). Keil (1982:416) correctly observes that the appositional phrase "every seer" is included to emphasize the extent of the prophetic revelation. What he fails to accept is that there is no such extensive revelation. He gets round the difficulty by importing a selection of appropriate warnings from the latter prophets (p. 418).

Starting with 1 Kgs 11 there is some communication from God through prophets, but it is directed to the kings that God is making and breaking. The prophets address themselves to the kings' behaviour, potential or actual, not the people's. Ahijah, for example, plans a secret meeting with Jeroboam to designate him king as a replacement for Solomon (1 Kgs 11:29). In 1 Kgs 13:1–2 an unidentified prophet comes to Bethel to decry Jeroboam. In 1 Kgs 14:6–16 Ahijah prophesies against Jeroboam, on account of Jeroboam's behaviour, and predicts the end for Israel because of what Jeroboam has done (see esp. v. 16). In 1 Kgs 16:7 the word of Yhwh comes against Baasha through Jehu, son of Hanani (note that vv. 12–13 reiterate that the prophecy of Jehu was against Baasha, condemning him, among other things, for making Israel sin). 1 Kgs 19:15–18 is an interesting passage since it is, again, a command to a prophet (Elijah) to anoint a replacement for a wicked king. Yet here God makes no distinction between the people and the wicked king. God does not make the narrator's distinction between the people, made to sin by the king, and the king who makes the people sin. All are lumped

2 Kings 17:15

With v. 15 the narrator seems to loop back for another run at the same material already presented in vv. 8–14. The reiterated vision is marked by the opening words of v. 15, "they rejected his statutes (*ʾet-ḥuqqāyw*)," which picks up the opening phrase of v. 8, "they walked in the statutes (*bᵉḥuqqôt*) of the nations." The reiteration is continued in the sequential parallelism between vv. 15–18 and vv. 8–14. The pattern is roughly as follows:

1. Introductory description of apostasy, keyed by the word "statutes" (vv. 8, 15).
2. Allusions to past covenantal history, specifically the conquest (v. 8b) and the early monarchy (v. 15).
3. Descriptions of apostasy (vv. 9–12, 15b–17).
4. Divine response to apostasy (vv. 13, 18).
5. Israel's response to God's response.

Verse 15, like v. 8 before it, alludes to prior events in Israel's covenantal history, presumably for the purpose of showing just how ingratious its apostasy is. By prefacing the apostasy with a portrait of preceding divine constancy, the heinousness of Israel's deeds should be all that much stronger. Verse 15 seems to allude to the events of 1 Sam 8–12. There are several vocabulary parallels: "... they rejected (*wayyimʾᵃsû*; cf. 1 Sam 8:7) his covenant, which he made with their fathers (cf. Judg 2:17, 20) and his stipulations that he stipulated (*ʿēdôtāyw ʾᵃšer hēʿîd bām*; cf. 1 Sam 8:9, the only other location in the Dtr narrative of this expression with a reduplicated stem). And they went after vanity (*hahebel*) and became vanity" (*wayyehbālû*) (cf. 1 Sam 12:21, though there the word describing empty pursuits is *tōhû*). The views represented in 2 Kgs 17:15 are essentially those of Yahweh and Samuel in 1 Sam 8-12, views from which the narrator had already distanced himself in 1 Samuel. Once

together as those who have bent the knee to Baal. In 2 Kgs 9:6–10 a word comes through Elisha anointing Jehu, son of Jehoshaphat, because of Ahab's wickedness. In 2 Kgs 14:25 a prophet delivers a message of relief for the Israelite people, not one of condemnation.

2 Kgs 17:13 seems, therefore, a narratorial assertion, not much supported by story world reality (cf. v. 23). In 2 Kgs 21:10–15 there is another divine interpretation, which says that prophets were sent to warn Israel. Here, however, God does admit that it was the king, Manasseh, that led Israel astray. Finally 2 Kgs 24:2 contains another narratorial assertion that Yhwh had sent prophets ahead to warn of the impending disaster of the exile. Here too, assertion must be weighed against the factual evidence that precedes.

again it seems that he voices evaluative sentiments only to give the lie to them through contextual implicature.

What the reminder of past history does, in fact, is the opposite of its superficial function: to defend Yahweh's past at the expense of Israel's. Like v. 8, v. 15 reminds the reader of a past in which God's part is not without blemish and in which the reasons for Israel's undeniable defection from its covenant with Yahweh become apparent. Since the descriptions of Israel's covenantal defection follow, in both vv. 9–12 and vv. 16–17, right after the reminders about God's equally questionable (though unquestioned here) performances, the ironic implication is that Israel's apparent wantonness may after all be rational or at least comprehensible.

2 Kings 17:16–17

Verse 16 wrongly—and thus ironically, since there is little doubt that this allusive narrator could be mistaken about a matter he so clearly portrayed only seven chapters previously (2 Kgs 10:29)—attributes the sin of the golden calves to the people.[46] The preceding context makes it quite clear that the creation of the calves and their maintenance was the action of Jeroboam (1 Kgs 12:28, 32)and Jehu (2 Kgs 10:29). Always the people are led astray by the kings in this matter. Further to his ironic purpose, the narrator alludes to an act of King Ahab (1 Kgs 16:33) with the assertion that Israel "made an Asherah": it was he, not they, who made it. The worship of the host of heaven along with the construction of another Asherah is the accomplishment, later in the narrative, of Manasseh (2 Kgs 21:3, 5).[47]

The service of Ba'al is something that Israel, in fact, does in Judg 2:13. But that text is presented and read under the aegis of the narratorial exposition that precedes it in Judg 2. Subsequent iterations of such service are performed by Ahab (1 Kgs 16:31), Ahaziah (1 Kgs 22:53), and Jehu, champion of the sacrament (2 Kgs 10:18, "Jehu gathered all the people together and said unto

---

46 Gray (1970:648) simply overlooks the wrong attribution and says that it is the specific sin of Jeroboam that is stigmatized.

47 Keil (1982:417) exemplifies the pious reader who notices that the Israelites have not worshipped the "host of heaven" and seeks to apologize for the ironic assertion that they did so.

them, 'Ahab served Baal a little; but Jehu shall serve him much'").

In the light of the preceding context vv. 17–18 are pure fabrication. The assertion made in these verses is probably the most obvious clue to the expositional strategy of 2 Kgs 17:7–23 There is no place in the preceding context where the Israelites do what the evaluator says they do here. Rather, and this is supported through *Leitwört* connections, it was Ahaz (2 Kgs 16:3–4), son of Jotham, who did these things (cf. Manasseh, later in 21:6–7). Enforcing the attachment of this behaviour to the royal houses, 2 Kgs 16:3 prefaces a description of Ahaz's fire-walking son with the note that Ahaz's behaviour was typical of the royal house of the northern kingdom: "He walked in the way of the kings of Israel." And it is Ahab, not Israel, who Elijah says has "sold himself to do evil in the sight of Yahweh" (1 Kgs 21:20).

2 Kings 17:18

What the reader sees in v. 18 is exactly what he has already seen in 1 Sam 4: the Israelite people suffer for the sins of their divinely appointed leadership. But the emphasis of 2 Kgs 17:7–23 is not so much on the sinfulness of the kings—that is taken for granted and is presented in an objective, dispassionate voice. The narrator is not concerned to judge the kings, only to point out that their actions were the source of provocation that led Yahweh to exile Israel. It is Yahweh, not the narrator, in whose eyes almost all have done evil. The point of 2 Kgs 17:7–23, rather, is to subvert the conventional wisdom, so exhaustively pilloried here, about the national sin.

2 Kings 17:19–20

With v. 19 the narrator loops back a third time to repeat, roughly, the same sequence of description that he has gone through twice already (vv. 8–14, 15–18). The repeat performance is marked, once again, by a primary reference to "statutes": "they walked in the statutes of Israel, which they did" (cf. v. 15, v. 8). Just as Israel had walked in the statutes of the nations (v. 8) Judah takes its turn to walk in the statutes of Israel, which has now assumed the role formerly held by the nations.

Verse 20 alludes to Judg 2:14—"by the hand of the spoilers" (*wayyittnēm bᵉyad-šōsîm*)—but with the difference that the punishment has now advanced from temporary affliction to exile. As in Judges 2, the punishment that Yahweh metes out to Israel is warranted from the divine perspective. But the literary context of both passages reveals that the divine perspective is limited; it does not have the objective balance demonstrated by the narrator. In Judges 2 God punishes Israel because he holds them responsible for knowledge of an experience that they did not share and an obligation that they do not feel. In 2 Kgs 17:20 God punishes Israel for sins almost exclusively originating with the kings. The injustice of punishment allotted to the many for the sins of the few may be lost on Yahweh, but it is certainly not lost on the narrator of 1 Sam 4 (cf. Eslinger 1985:172–5) or 2 Kgs 17:7–23.

In the second phrase of v. 21 the narrator specifically attributes the act of crowning Jeroboam to Israel, whereas the preceding phrase (same verse) implies that he was enthroned by Yahweh ("he [Yahweh] tore Israel from the house of David," (cf. 1 Kgs 11:29–39; 1 Kgs 12:20). Verse 21 raises the issue of who made Jeroboam king because he has become a symbol of bad leadership: "... he drove Israel from following Yahweh and made them sin a great sin." The question of responsibility for having made Jeroboam and his successors king is an important one for the narrator. He has just finished a long ironic discourse that shows how important he sees the waywardness of leadership to have been. If it was Israel that crowned Jeroboam and others of his ilk, then at least some of their blood—there are many other significant actions, divine and human, leading to the exile—might be on their own head. If it was God, on the other hand, then there is something awry, though not unusual as such things have gone previously in the story, with the punishment that God sets out for them.

What v. 21 shows is that there was divine-human synergy at work in the installation of Jeroboam and, by implication, the installation of the other wayward kings. Yes, God did tear Israel from the house of David to give it to Jeroboam (1 Kgs 11:28–33) and yes, Israel did make Jeroboam king (1 Kgs 12:20). This is the same synergism that led to the establishment of the monarchy in the first place (1 Sam 8–12). The monarchy is a problem for Israel and God. Neither is blamed for what has happened but both are implicated in and affected by the chain of events and actions that are described in the narrative. The problem of bad leadership in Israel—a problem that the institute of a "secular" monarchy was supposed to resolve (1 Sam 8:5; Eslinger 1985:254–9)—has been with Israel at least since the Elide priesthood (1 Sam 1–4).

Although it would be possible for the narrator to heap opprobrium on the sinning kings he does not, letting God take the credit for evaluating their behaviour—"king X did evil in the eyes of the Lord." His purpose before and now is to present an analysis of Israel's course of existence. Here, in 2 Kgs 17:7–23 a subsidiary purpose is to expose the shallow, wrong-headedness of the traditional theodicy that placed all the blame for the exile on an incredibly obstinate, foolish Israel. The conventional explanation trades on the common psychology of Israelite religion (and its successors) and so receives almost universal welcome from readers within that religious tradition. The narrator's very different perspective is formulated as a subtle review presented, like the noted intimations in Maimonides' *Guide to the Perplexed*, by implication rather than assertion. The narrator steps outside the conventional view and uses the literary convention of the external, unconditioned narratorial situation to find a more balanced understanding of the problems that led to the exile.

2 Kings 17:22

Verse 21 concludes with the stock phrase, repeated many times before in the narrative, that 'King X caused Israel to sin a sin' (*wᵉheḥᵉṭēʾām ḥᵃṭāʾâ*; cf.*ʾᵃšer-heḥᵉṭî ʾet-yiśrāʾēl*: 1 Kgs 14:16; 15:26, 30, 34; 16:13, 26; 21:22; 22:52; 2 Kgs 3:3; 10:29, 31; 13:2, 6, 11; 14:24; 15:9, 18, 24, 28; [21:16; 23:15]). Having reminded the reader of that strong formulaic description of the kings' leadership of Israel, the narrator goes on to assert that Israel "walked in all the sins of Jeroboam that he did." The contrast could not be greater: Israel is now active where before it was passive.

The narrator has returned to his ironic mode of discourse immediately after his brief sortie into the more balanced view of v. 21. The strength of the conventional view demands that the narrator surround the balanced view of v. 21 with ironic exposure of the conventional views. That such is the purpose of v. 22 is underlined by the other ironic twists in the rhetoric of the verse. The children of Israel are said to have "walked in the sins of Jeroboam"; in the preceding narrative description it is, with one exception (2 Kgs 13:6), only kings who do this.[48] The phrase "they departed not from them [the sins of Jeroboam]" returns like results.[49] The rhetoric has the same ironic logic as the entire review.

2 Kings 17:23

In v. 23 the narrator says that Israel continued in its wayward course until God removed Israel from his sight "as he spoke through all his servants, the prophets." The summary conclusion leads the reader to expect that there had been a series of figures trying to warn Israel away from its folly in the manner of an Isaiah, a Jeremiah, or an Ezekiel. Given the pattern of incongruity that prevails between this evaluative review and the preceding context, it should come as no surprise that the reader will reflect or re-read in vain if he looks for the expected repetitious warnings from "all his servants, the prophets." There are, in fact, none.[50]

Conclusion

As the database of evaluative language in the Dtr narrative reveals, Judg 2 and 2 Kgs 17 are parallel evaluative spikes in the narrative. Both are distinguished by the fact that the narrator breaks his characteristic silence to voice some strong and considerable evaluative remarks about the behaviour of the characters, especially the Israelites, in the story. The parallelism between these two outbursts extends beyond a simple count of

---

48 Abijam, son of Rehoboam, "walked in all the sins of his father" (1 Kgs 15:3); Nadab, son of Jeroboam, walks "in the way of his father, and in his sin wherewith he made Israel sin" (1 Kgs 15:26); Baasha "walked in the way of Jeroboam, and in his sin wherewith he made Israel sin" (1 Kgs 15:34); Jehu "walked in the way of Jeroboam, and in his sin wherewith he made Israel sin" (1 Kgs 16:2); Omri "walked in all the way of Jeroboam, and in his sin wherewith he made Israel sin" (1 Kgs 16:26); Ahaziah "walked in the way of ... Jeroboam, and in his sin wherewith he made Israel sin" (1 Kgs 22:52); Jehoram "walked in the way of the kings of Israel" (2 Kgs 8:18); Ahaziah "walked in the way of the house of Ahab" (2 Kgs 8:27); Jehoash "departed not from all the sins of Jeroboam the son of Nebat, who made Israel sin: but he walked therein" (2 Kgs 13:11); and Ahaz "walked in the way of the kings of Israel" (2 Kgs 16:3).

49 "Departed not from them": Jehoram 2 Kgs 3:3; Jehu 2 Kgs 10:31; Jehoahaz 2 Kgs 13:2; Israel 2 Kgs 13:6; Jehoash 2 Kgs 13:11; Jeroboam 2 Kgs 14:24; Zachariah 2 Kgs 15:9; Menahem 2 Kgs 15:18; Pekahiah 2 Kgs 15:24; Pekah 2 Kgs 15:28.

50 The closest thing to such a warning of exile to come is a private revelation made directly by God to Solomon (1 Kgs 9:7). But the Israelites are not privy to that.

evaluative language to the main object of evaluation: it is the Israelite people in both cases.

A comparison of Judges 2 and 2 Kings 17 shows that the narrator uses parallel phraseology to frame the strong negative evaluations within a narrative framework that mitigates the negative evaluations, whether through understanding in a larger context or through irony. The parallelism binds the two passages and they work together as an ironic bracket for the intervening narrative. These two gateposts on the narrative frame the view expressed in the narrative as a whole. They stand as rejections of the conventional, simplistic understanding of Israel's history and the reasons for its exile. The narrator sets these ironic rejections near the beginning and end of his story. In between the narrative is characterized by a subtle expositional strategy through implication and allusion. The placement of the pair of strong ironic brackets in Judges 2 and 2 Kings 17 is an effort to ensure that the reader does not mistake the subtleties of implication within for passive acceptance of the traditional views without .

CHAPTER 7

EXPLICIT EVALUATION IN THE DEUTERONOMISTIC NARRATIVE

Computer-Assisted Biblical Studies and The Deuteronomistic Problem

More and more biblical scholars are using computers in their work. Though the most common application remains word processing—an invaluable advance for all academic writers—a few individuals have advocated, from time to time, the use of computers to assist the progress of conventional historical–critical research. Statistical analysis of literary works, especially in attribution studies of authorship, is an established way of using computers in studies of the Bible.[1] But the results have often been ignored or given only a passing glance. Often it seems that only a statistician could interpret such analyses, biblical scholars not included. And some statisticians who have looked at the work that has been done have faulted it for lack of a sufficient data sample or for questionable statistical methods.

From a literary point of view, the problem with a computer–based statistical approach to the Bible is that the questions it can address are constrained by the concordance–like orientation of the work. The proliferation of KWIC (Key Word In Context) concordances, at least in biblical studies where good concor-

1 E.g. the studies of Y.T. Radday (e.g. "Genesis, Wellhausen, and the Computer," *ZAW* 94 (1982) 467-81). For more detailed descriptions of the kinds of computer-assisted analysis of the Bible that have been tried see J.J. Hughes (1987:491–602).

dances have been available for many years, has only increased the ease and speed of concordance work. Such gains do not necessarily advance, methodologically speaking, beyond work done with a bound copy of a printed concordance. Frequently the application of sorting and counting tools, the strength of computer assisted analysis of large bodies of text, directly to the naked words of the text results in "answers" that only a computer would find interesting. Before we set our silicon assistants to work that we might regularly find interesting we must provide them with some descriptive categories derived from a hypothesis and set of questions that we are interested in getting information about.

Such categories, informed by any hypothesis one might wish to explore, are at hand in the data "fields" that almost every database program requires before data can be input. Using database software rather than concordance-oriented software, the biblical researcher can create a software research environment that is orented to the specfics of any hypothesis from the very beginning. This framework, supplied by the researcher and not dictated by the structure or abilities of the computer or software, can make for a more exact union between the questions of the researcher, the data available in the biblical texts, and the computer's remarkable capacity for fast and accurate data manipulation. Of course electronic concordance tools are still useful to assist in the work of analyzing the text for entry into the database.

During the years 1985–86 I worked on a research project[2] using database software to assist in the literary analysis of biblical texts. Database software for micro-computers, though not usually written with the needs of humanistic scholars in mind, can be adapted to abstract an interesting and comprehensive collection of literary data from the massive detail of the biblical text. The advantage of database software over simple concordance routines such as sorting, collating, and counting is that the data structure is determined by the questions that the scholar wishes to put to the text. Whereas the analyzed data of the concordance program is almost formless, a distillation of the text unstructured except for having been sorted or counted, the data structure of a data base is already based on a question or ques-

---

2 The project was supported by the Social Sciences and Humanities Research Council of Canada and the Calgary Institute for the Humanities.

tions that the researcher puts to the text. The record structure of the database—the various categories (called data "fields") that one uses to describe the literary text—is an input requirement of the software that at the same time allows for abstract, second order categorizations of textual phenomena. As a result the researcher can enter abstract descriptions of the text, which can then be manipulated in the same ways that a concordance program deals with the raw literary data of the text. The difference is that what the computer sorts and counts can now be *interpreted* data, much of which may not be explicit in the text.

Hypotheses and Database Record Structures

Compared to literary research without the use of a computer, database assisted research has the advantage of requiring that one be very specific about the questions addressed to the text. Before any data can be entered into a database one must create a record structure. Of course, this tight focus also means that the answers one is able to reach will also be tightly circumscribed; it also tends to make the researcher more conscious of the limitations of presuppositions that accompany any interpretation of a text. But the clear focus that is achieved and the greater quantity of data available for analysis offer a research potential not readily available to a scholar working without the assistance of a computerized database.

Each record is a collection of fields; each field, a distinct description of some feature of the text. A record is a collection of related data residing in the interrelated descriptive categories called fields. Each record is a construct derived from the questions that the researcher bring to the text and the raw data in the text itself. Before creating a descriptive analysis of the text one must know quite clearly what features of the text one wishes to analyze. This greater precision and directedness does have practical limitations. Though not impossible, it may not be easy to adapt the database you create to answer questions other than those to which the original data structure was directed. And, if your questions are not carefully drawn it is possible to finish, after many hours of analysis and data input, with an unapt collection of descriptions that cannot meet the original objectives. A well-thought plan is the prerequisite of any successful use of database software.

Software: Reflex™

The database software that I chose for this project is called Reflex. Reflex (published by Borland International) is an MS-DOS™ "flat file" (i.e. non-relational model) database program that offers powerful analytical capabilities through its five dynamically related "views" of the data. The program offers cross-tabulations and flexible graphing capabilities that can be adapted to analyze textual data rather than the business numerics at which the program's publisher aims them.[3] Using the graph "view" of Reflex, for example, one can quickly locate sections of the narrative in which the count of evaluative language is abnormal and then filter the database to isolate the records that contain the anomalous data. In a few seconds the program can display a graph that shows which narrative voices are so active in evaluating and even who it is that they are concerned to appraise. The contours of evaluative language in the narrative, normally submerged and difficult to perceive, are quickly exposed and mapping—analysis of the narrative's voice structure—can begin.

"For Each" & "Intra-Field" Graphic Analysis

One other powerful feature of Reflex for literary analysis is its "for each" option, which automatically categorizes any designated field into clusters of related entries. This is a valuable feature for anyone who needs to see a text field in related subcategories. For example, in the "attribution" field of my database (a field that describes who it is that is doing the evaluating), there are several possible characters in each book who might make evaluative statements. To see a graph that shows a book by book distribution of evaluative language broken down character by character, we issue the following instructions in Reflex's graph view:

1. Attach the "book" field to the graph's X (horizontal)-axis.
2. Attach the "count" field (the single numeric field in the database) to the Y (vertical)-axis.[4]

3 The trick is to include a numeric field with a value of "1" in each record. Reflex™ can then be instructed to use that numeric field as the basis for its graphing calculations on related textual data in the non-numeric fields. See R. Person (1986:112–13).

4 The Y-axis must be numeric.

3. Attach the "attribution" field to the "for each" option attached to field plotted on the X-axis..

The result is:

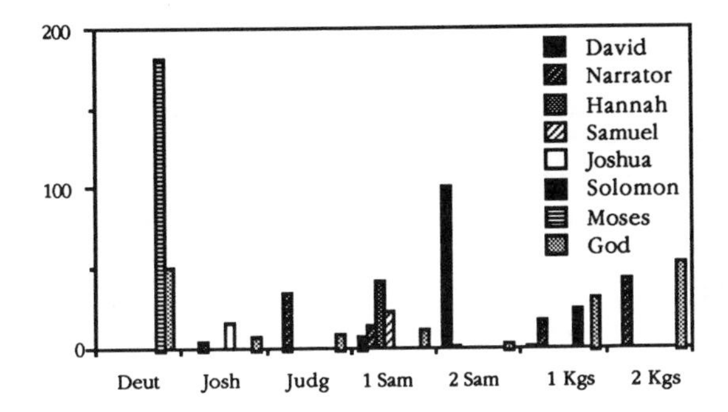

The ability of Reflex to slice the abstracted data into different views is virtually limitless. The graph view is particularly useful for initial surveying because it quickly gives a visual impression of the shape that the data takes when organized according to the search and display criteria supplied to the data manager. By successively refining the criteria the user can, in a few moments, move from the comprehensive view, which only the database could supply, to a close-up view of a specific item (record or records) that is still informed by the overall view. In this way, the user can gain literary insights into the text that would be impossible without the database. Detailed analysis of a specific text in a limited context, a fundamental and indispensable part of all literary analysis, can now be informed by the overall context of the narrative or book that one wishes to analyze. To use a photographic analogy, the literary analyst can zoom rapidly from panorama to detail and back again. Texts that were previously unmanageable for their size can now be studied both in minute detail, still the heart of all literary analysis, and comprehensively, virtually at the same time.

The Problem & History of Scholarship: The "Dtr"

Comprised of the so-called historical books (Joshua - 2 Kings), the "Dtr" is commonly attributed to two or more editors, each successively adding a peculiar slant to the narrative's meaning. The existence of such multiple editions is supposed on the basis of perceived contradictions in the narrative, both factual (referential and internal literary discordancy) and ideological. So, for example, when God unconditionally promises David an eternal dynasty in 2 Samuel 7 but adds the condition of obedience to that promise when he reaffirms it to Solomon (1 Kings 3, 6, 9), scholars see a contradiction between the views of a pre-exilic and post-exilic editor on the subject of the promises that God made to the Davidic dynasty (cf. J. Gray 1970:167). Viewed from a broader historical perspective, such disagreements are ultimately resolved in the traditio-historical perception that the editors shared a basic theological outlook that results in the theodicy that we now read in the narrative. Collectively[5] these successive editions of the narrative produced a work that blames the Exile of 587/6 B.C. on human error—what the Bible calls "sin"—and exonerates God of any wrong-doing. What we have, in the end, is the multi-authored, but broadly unanimous layered anthology of the deuteronomistic school.

Recent studies of biblical narrative have agreed on at least one thing: biblical narrators, who almost universally represent the voice of the author in the narrative, are also uniformly laconic (cf Alter 1981:184; Sternberg 1985: index entry, "Narrator, reticence & self-effacement of"). They consistently refuse to provide a firm evaluative viewpoint from which the reader can survey and understand what is said and done within the story world of the characters. Various reasons for this reticence have been proposed—the illusion of objectivity, the attempt to engage the reader in an active response to the text—but the most important result, in terms of past readings, is that unguided readers can get lost. In the absence of a blatant narratorial (authorial) evaluative standard readers have latched on to the only explicit inter-pretive remarks in the narrative, the characters' observations and comments. They mistakenly allow these *ideas from within the story world* to guide their interpretation of *the narrative that contains them.* Many existing readings of the deuteronomistic history depend on this fundamental confusion of its voice structure and narrative ontology, which Sternberg describes as follows: "God operates within and the narrator without the represented world; so do their respective addressees, the characters and the reader.... The sharp line sep-

---

5 Though each edition is seen to present a certain, particular emphasis, they are all understood to share a common explanation for the political disaster that befell the Israelite nation in the 6th c. B.C. No one, to my knowledge, has suggested that any of the many redactors that have now been supposed placed the blame for the disaster anywhere other than on Israel's or its leaders' shoulders.

arating the privileged [the narrator and reader] from the non-privileged [the characters within the story]—not to mention the variability within the latter group itself—makes for the clearest divergence in representation and interpretive cogency, amounting to an antithesis between the objective and the subjective views of the world" (1985:160). Yet even Sternberg, whose training is in literary theory, not biblical studies, is susceptible to confusion over the question of the stance of the narrator vis-à-vis the divine character, who is, as the preceding chapters try to show, also ontologically subordinate to the narrator in the conventions of this narrative situation.[6]

The conceptual result of reading that ignores the fundamental narratological notions of voice structure and narrative ontology is now accepted as common knowledge about the Dtr. Historical-critical scholarship finds the narrator of the deuteronomistic history to be a strong dogmatic exponent of a rather conventional theological position (e.g. G. von Rad 1966:206), a heavy-handed puritan firm in belief and forthright in expression. He [they] (the Dtr redactor[s]) is the great evangelistic preacher who surveys the past with scathing condemnations for sins accomplished, duty denied. His purpose: to convict his audience in the hope that their contrite heart might open the door to reconciliation with the God who had inflicted the exile upon Israel (cf. J. Gray 1970: 37–43). Or he might be the clever propagandist, striving through his "official" version of Israel's history to legitimate the potentiary that has commissioned the work (e.g. F.M. Cross 1973:284). Either way the Dtr is seen to present a view of Israel's past that is not more privileged than any normal human perspective aside from the privilege of retrospection. Such readings are primarily the result of taking evaluative commentary from characters such as Moses or Samuel and reading it as though it were offered by the narrator: the resulting equation creates a narratorial perspective that is, in fact, fully as limited and conditioned as that of the characters with whose views the narrator's have been confused.

On this reading, a major vehicle for the expression of the Dtr's theological convictions is found in several extended orations given by major characters at strategic points in the narrative. The list of speeches, broken down by attribution, is as

6 This apparent confusion seems to run throughout Sternberg's recent book (1985) but is most visible in ch. 3, "Ideology of Narration and Narration of Ideology."

follows:

- Josh 1:11–15 Joshua
- Josh 12 the Dtr narrator
- Josh 23 Joshua
- Judg 2:11–23 the Dtr narrator
- 1 Sam 12 Samuel
- 1 Kgs 8:14–61 Solomon
- 2 Kgs 17 the Dtr narrator

According to Martin Noth (1981:5), and most interpreters have shared this view, the speeches were set as ideological comments at turning points in the narrative of Israel's history. Their purpose was to provide explicit thematic exposition at all the critical junctures in the history. With these speeches, the Dtr is supposed to ensure that all of his readers got the point, the essential truth about the historical drama that he was representing.

In all cases, these speeches are supposed to be meaning centres, touchstones of interpretation that train the reader to understand the deuteronomist's perspective on these events. In voice, tone, and meaning the narrative and these speeches are identical; they are only formally different expressions of the deuteronomist's singular understanding of Israel's history.[7] The speeches from key characters do not differ in opinion nor does the expositional commentary they provide vary from two other key passages in which the Dtr speaks directly in his own narratorial voice.[8]

On this reading, the message of the Dtr narrative is trite. To paraphrase: "Israel has sinned. See, here is the evidence. Sin upon sin upon sin. And so, God has punished Israel. Rightly so and good riddance to the wicked. Sinners, repent!" This

---

7 Of course those who discover multiple Deuteronomists will disagree with the suggestion of a singular understanding in the Dtr history. But they do not differ as much as it first seems in this respect from those who favour a single Deuteronomist. Depending on how the redactional layers are divided and then aggregated as $Dtr^{1,2,3,...}$, or DtrN, G, P, ..., they will have the speeches associated with one or the other layer and will find *all* the speeches therein to reflect the conventional wisdom of that redactional layer. The fact that some have even divided some of the speeches between redactional layers, as in Levenson's work on Solomon's prayer (1981), has not changed this perception of agreement between narratorial and character speeches at all.

8 Cf. D.J. McCarthy (1978:131), "In the one case as in the other the content is a kind of meditation on Israel's history ... They call attention to the significant changes in Israel's circumstances and serve to explain how these things have come to be." According to Noth (1981:6) the speeches, whether from the narrator or a character express "a simple and unified theological interpretation of history."

canonized reading of the narrative is accepted by scholars and believers alike, an accord that seems more expressive of the common place of contrition and guilt in the Judeo-Christian psyche than of the perspective of the narrative. Unfortunately the collective religious psyche of biblical readers has refused to allow the Dtr's representation to have its own say about the way of God with man. Readers have failed to hear the narrator's subtle insurgent voice because they are so attuned to hear and accept the clamorous pieties of the human characters of the Bible, with whose existential predicament and religious sentiments they can so easily identify. With regard to the great orations in the Dtr narrative, this means that readers have been disposed to hear the narrative in the light of the orations rather than to read the orations in the light of their existing narrative context. Contemporary scholarly readers see one, undifferentiated plane of utterance in the narrative; if there are discrepancies in the views expressed they are to be comprehended in terms of literary history and the multiplicity of writers who have had a hand in creating the narrative.

Because historical-critical readers share, with their own readers, a similar set of theological assumptions and the belief that the authors of the narrative shared the same *basic* set as they themselves hold, their readings of the narratives have occasioned little criticism at a fundamental level.[9] Certainly there have been many disputes over the quantity, dating, and social locale of the editions through which the narrative has passed. And within the same confines there have been small skirmishes over the theology represented by the varying redactions of the narrative. But these all operate within the same large parameters: the work is a theodicy, exculpates God, blames Israel, and varies within itself over the question of Israel's future.

The scholarly consensus about the so-called deuteronomistic history does, however, provide an established starting point for studying the profile of explicit evaluation in the narrative. Many hours have been spent studying the questions of the authors' attitudes and points of view on the subject matter of the narrative. The history of scholarship provides us with a lengthy

---

9 Naturally I am speaking of a fundamental set of values and beliefs that span the history of biblically based religions and the religions that gave rise to them. I doubt that anyone would deny such commonality.

history of scholarly reader responses to the narrative. We should be able to use these same responses as a guide to the profile of evaluation in the narrative. Perceptions of the tone—irony excepted—and content of explicit evaluation are likely to be correct. It is only in the matter of attribution that past scholarship has found itself in difficulty—witness the disputes over the number of redactions—and in which its observations are, from the perspective of narratology, unreliable.

Hypothesis & Record Structure

I chose to examine explicit evaluation in the Dtr narrative as a new entrance to the question of what the author(s) are saying through the narrative. A study of what voice says what about whom should, on the face of it, lead to some insights into the author's meaning comprehended through the narrative rendition of his story. There are two prominent features of evaluative language in the narrative: 1. the very low normal quantity of evaluative discourse coming from any given voice or within any given piece of the narrative; 2. the conspicuous evaluative spikes, usually one per book, spread throughout the narrative.

Without a considered theory of voice structure and narrative ontology from which to interpret the results of the data analysis, we would be no further ahead and might even be more confused about the author's views and where we might encounter them than before. Does the author speak through these prominent evaluative outbursts even when they are voiced by a character in the narrative? Or does he only speak through the spikes when they are voiced by his own identifiable mouthpiece in the narrative, that of the narrator, that is only in Judg 2 and 2 Kgs 17? On what basis can a reader be certain that the author agrees with the sentiments voiced in the evaluative spike? Or, perhaps, all the evaluative spikes are set in such strident contrast to the broader evaluative norms of the narrative in order to expose the sentiments they express against the backdrop of a more distanced, less dogmatic view—a commentary that draws its power from silence.

There are two main questions to which I addressed the record structure of the database. Do these perceived ideological tensions in the narrative lie within the authorial voice (the narrator) in the narrative or are they differences of opinion between characters or between a character and the narrator? Second, and more important, what exactly is the author/narrator saying through this narrative? The index by which I chose to assess the narrative in the light these questions is explicit evaluation, overt assessment of the quality of another's action, in the narrative. The record structure of the database provides for analytical descriptions of all instances of such language in the narrative. Explicitly evaluative language was chosen because it removes the ambiguity inherent in implicitly evaluative language such as sarcasm or irony. Even though this choice follows the lead of source or redaction criticism and so may be erroneous at a fundamental level, it does allow the literary analyst to create a collection of data pertaining to the question of the narrator's evaluative perspective. Each instance of explicit evaluation is controlled by the narrator, who must show his agreement or disagreement if his narrative perspective is to remain under his control. The catalogue of evaluative discourse can be made to display all explicit correspondences and differences between the narrator and his characters. Even knowing the importance of implication in the economy of narratorial exposition, evaluative discourse seems a logical place to begin to examine the narrator's own evaluative point of view. Whenever a narrator rehearse the views of a character, in the context of his own discourse, he must always set those views in a context that allows the potential audience to know where he stands with respect to them. If strong views are simply reiterated with no conditioning context then the audience is inclined to see the speaker as agreeing with the reiterated views.

The occurrence of several key expressions of strong views within the Dtr narrative—the great orations—requires reexamination to see what, if any, conditioning context has been supplied to indicate the narrator's stance on those assertions. By studying the contextualization of all instances of explicit evaluation and amassing a regularized description of them, we can see if there are narrative contexts that relativize the inset evaluations and also whether there are any regular framing patterns that condition them.

The record structure of the database allows a description of the following items:

<u>Textual Location</u>

Fields:

book:
chapter:
verse:

<u>Evaluation and its Qualities</u>

Fields:

evaluation:	(positive, negative, or neutral)
evaluatee:	the person, place, or thing evaluated
tone:	the spirit in which evaluation is made (e.g. emotional, dispassionate, analytical)
register:	non-dialectic variations (e.g. evaluative standards from the spheres of covenant, or religion, or politics, or fundamental human concerns such as sex or territory)

<u>Contextualization of Evaluation</u>

Fields:

attribution:	who makes the evaluation
attributor:	who, if anyone, says that so and so makes this evaluation
ontological:	is the evaluation made from inside or outside the story world?
support:	does the context (literary and/or ontological) support the evaluation?
mitigation:	is there any obvious contextual mitigation of the evaluation?

The database reveals a remarkable degree of alignment between the evaluative spikes and the series of great orations identified as key expositional elements in the narrative:

Key Speeches	*Evaluative Spikes*
Josh 1:11–15	—
—	Josh 12
Josh 23	Josh 22–3
Judg 2:11–23	Judg 2:11–23
—	1 Sam 2:1–10
1 Sam 12	1 Sam 12
—	2 Sam 22
1 Kgs 8:14–61	1 Kgs 8:14–61
2 Kgs 17	2 Kgs 17
—	2 Kgs 19

The correlation between the great orations identified by scholarly readers and the evaluative spikes by the database suggests a relationship more than coincidental. The question is, what is the relationship and why have scholars included some of the evaluative spikes within the collection of orations while omitting others. It is reasonable to assume that explicit evaluation has been a key factor in forming scholarly readers' impressions that here we find mediated authorial opinion. The database, after all, with which the isolated "great orations" so frequently align, records only that feature of the narrative.

The "Spikes" and the Narrator's Point of View

Read in context, however, and with an awareness of the critical concept of narrative ontology, the great orations assume their inherently lower position on the scale of authority within the narrative. Samuel's speech, for example, is less the august oration of the detached author, more the carping censure of a deeply involved character. Samuel's rehearsal of events preceding is in glaring contradiction with prior events—events and a contradiction presented by the authoritative narrator—in an ill-concealed (thanks to narratorial privilege) effort to lord it over the Israelites who have nearly replaced God (and Samuel) with a human king. In no way can the narrator (and so the Dtr redactor) be understood to speak through the voice of Samuel in 1 Sam 12 when the narrative context so clearly undermines Samuel's speech. To assume that he does so is to ignore the hierarchical voice structure of the narrative in favour of assumptions about the function of the evaluative spikes in the narrative. This misreading is augmented by the lack of obvious explicit narratorial exposition. Only recently have biblical scholars begun to appreciate the fact that much or most exposition in biblical narrative is implicit (cf. Alter 1981:184).

Character Spikes

In every case of an evaluative spike that comes through the voice of a character in the story there are mitigating circumstances described in the narrative that explain, more or less, why the character made the evaluative remarks he or she did. The narrative contextualization provides a relative framework for the evaluations and it is within this framework that they have their primary relevance. To hear an extrapolation of their relevance beyond that framework, beyond the story world in which they are situated that is, one needs to see in the narrative context a construction that undercuts the context's own natural relativizing affect on the remarks contained in the frame. In other words, one needs to see and describe evidence that shows that the author/narrator allys himself and his overall narrative description with the views of the character voicing the evaluative remarks in question. Otherwise the normal framing effect of narrative discourse will limit and relativize the quoted material; this is a privilege that the narrative genre automatically accords to a narrator of the external, unconditioned type that we find in these narratives.

The Larger Overview

The most significant benefit of using a database to analyze literary problems in the Dtr narrative is that it allows the individual to keep in touch with all of the data chosen for study. Normally it is only possible to work in detail on a very limited portion of the narrative, unless of course one chooses to make the study of this narrative one's life's work. Even then, however, the comprehensive grasp of detail throughout the narrative will only come after years of study.

There are a total of 907 records in the database, 907 separate instances of evaluative language. The distribution of occurrences is as follows:

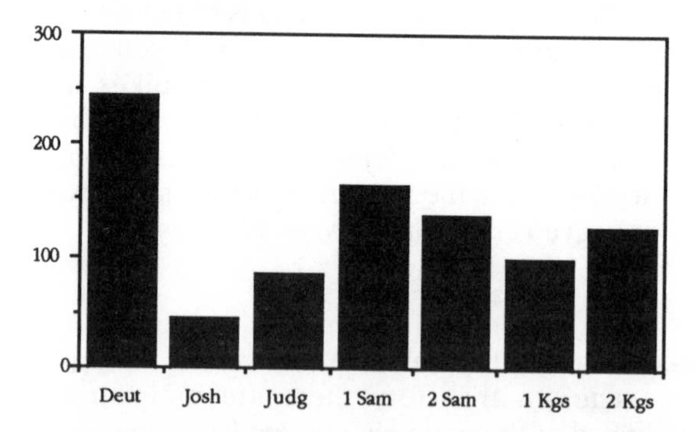

Aside from noting the exceptionally high quantity of evaluation in the book of Deuteronomy, a testimony to the charged rhetoric of Moses in that book, there are no great revelations to be had from a simple count of evaluative language by book. As soon as we subject each book to some finer analysis, however, some interesting patterns appear.

The "Normal Quantity" of Explicit Evaluation

The mean quantity of evaluation in most chapters of the narrative is relatively low—on the order of two or three occurrences in each chapter, with that total usually divided among several characters. By way of example, typical of all books but Deuteronomy, the following graph shows evaluative language in 1 Samuel:

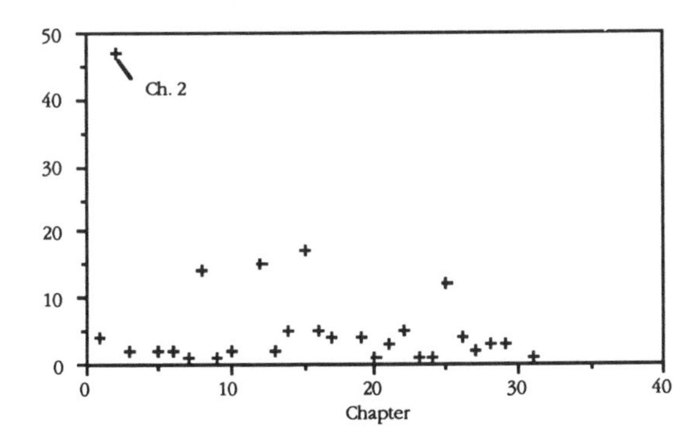

The mass of evaluative language in 1 Sam 2 becomes even more anomalous when we compare this graph to another that shows an attributional distribution in 1 Samuel—who is voicing all this evaluation?

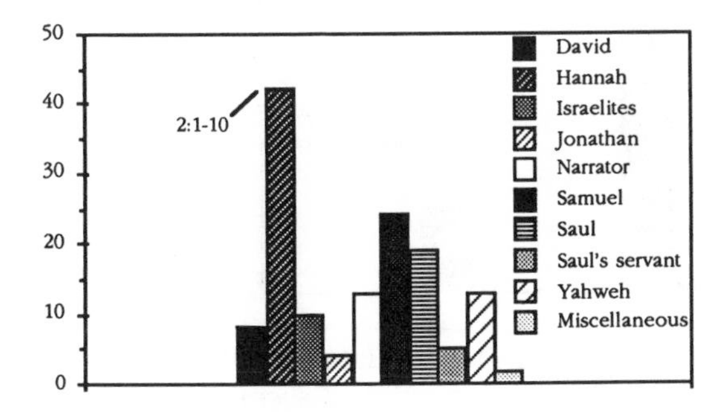

Here the anomaly that appeared first in the graph of simple distributions becomes more obvious.[10] Forty of the forty two

10 The miscellaneous category in this graph accounts for a variety of fifteen different evaluative voices in the narrative whose total number of evaluations amounts to twenty-

evaluations attributed to Hannah are located in 1 Sam 2. The result is an evaluative "spike" in the narrative, a localized concentration of evaluative discourse far above the norm.

Evaluative "Spikes"

In all books but Deuteronomy there are one or two outstanding passages in which the database reveals an abnormally high quantity of evaluative language. Deuteronomy, though laced with a heavy dose of evaluative discourse from one character, Moses, exhibits a more even profile. But Deuteronomy as a whole constitutes one such spike in comparison to the remainder of the Dtr narrative. The high profile of Mosaic rhetoric and evaluative discourse does not necessarily mean that the narrator agrees with Moses and gives him the floor. Moses is given the floor only so that the position he voices so strongly can be explored and understood in context in the subsequent narrative episodes.

Graphs by Book

The results, presented book by book, are as follows:

1. Deuteronomy

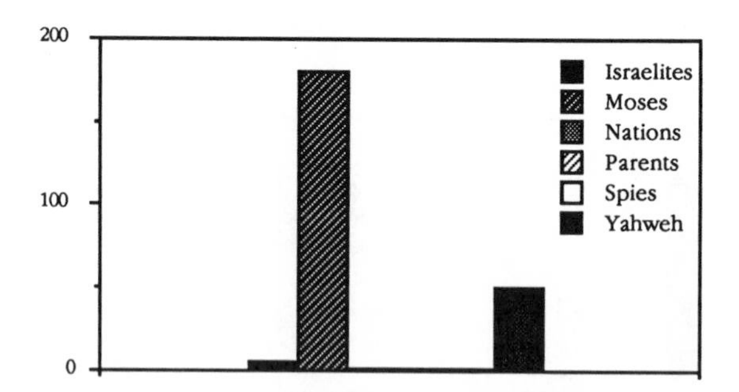

Moses is far the most vocal evaluator in the book of Deuteronomy, with Yahweh coming a distant second. A chapter by chapter breakdown is relatively insignificant in Deuteronomy, because Moses is so consistently vocal and others equally silent throughout the course of the speech. Polzin's detailed

six for an average value of 1.73.

observations about the voice structure and Moses' pride of place in the book of Deuteronomy are confirmed by the catalogue of evaluative language and Moses' relatively prominent place in it.[11] His interpretation of Moses' preeminence and the narrator's supposed attempt to borrow from the fount of Mosaic authority is, however, quite another matter. The narratorial situation from which the narrator represents Moses' rhetoric in the book of Deuteronomy grants him an immeasurably greater authority than any that any character in the story might have or offer.

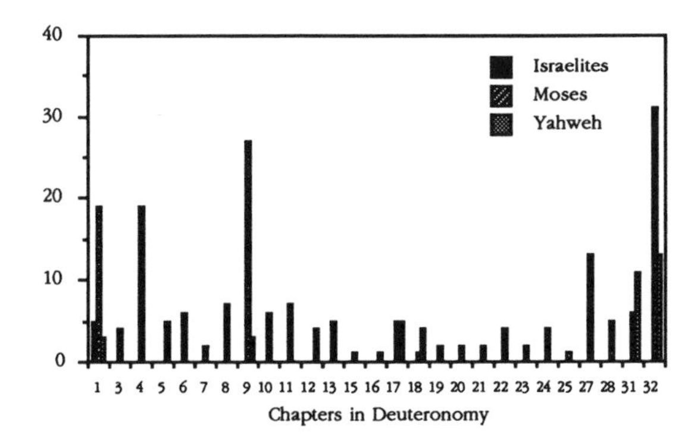

2. Joshua

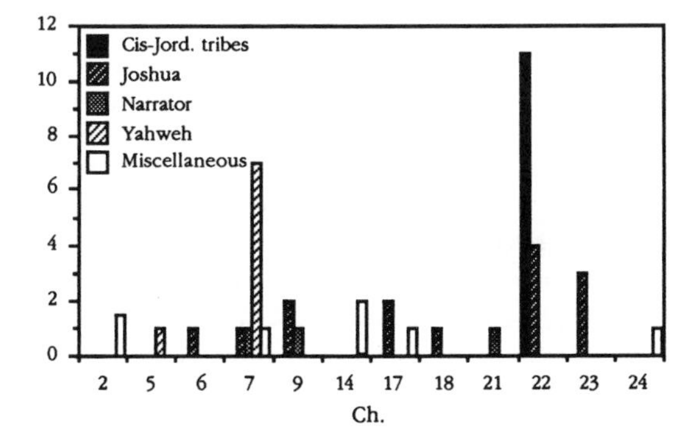

11 "The *overt* function of the narrator's direct utterances in Deuteronomy is to represent to his readers the word of Moses as pre-eminent, and Moses himself as the greatest prophet in Israel's history" (1980:30).

The graph shows two prominent spikes in the book of Joshua, one produced by Yahweh (ch. 7), the other by the Cis-Jordanian tribes (ch. 22).

Strangely, neither utterance has attracted much attention as a potential locus of authorial exposition disguised as character utterance. The reason for this neglect seems obvious enough: there are explicit conditions or situations in the context of the story world that anchor the evaluative remarks within that context. Yahweh's evaluations in ch. 7 are elicited in response to the sin of Achan. They are peculiarly relevant to that situation and suggest little in the way of global application, not the sort of far-reaching interpretations that scholars see in similar strong evaluative speeches such as Judg 2:11–23 or 1 Sam 12. The same is true of the Cis-Jordanian's protestations in Josh 22. Here all of the evaluative remarks do not seem able to bear the weight of authorial attribution because they appear as defensive utterances for the purpose of exonerating the Cis-Jordanian's actions. Consequently, scholarly readers have not seen them as having wider significance for the whole story.

In contrast, Samuel's speech in 1 Sam 12, though also a speech loaded with evaluative language defending Samuel and Yahweh, has been read as authorial exposition. There are at least three reasons for this difference. Most readers assume that the narrative defends God—it is a theodicy. If a prominent and pious character such as Samuel also defends God within the story world in the narrative, then his views must represent those of the author of the narrative. Second, Samuel's speech has a broad historical sweep to it. He includes wide expanses of Israel's history within his evaluations and this *seems* a more global, authoritative view than the limited defenses of the Cis-Jordanian tribes in Joshua 22. And third, scholars have found, in Samuel's speech, a fairly high count of so-called deuteronomistic language, the appearance of which in any sector of the narrative has been enough for redactional approaches to identify that section as representing the views of a deuteronomistic redactor. The example of Solomon's prayers (1 Kgs 8), however, is especially salutary in breaking that simplistic equation.

After the Cis-Jordanians' and Yahweh's evaluative peaks in the book of Joshua come those of the book's name-sake himself in chs. 22–3. As it happens, Joshua's speech in ch. 23 has been marked as one of the great orations in the Dtr narrative. Here the author is supposed to speak his own mind through the voice of a distinguished character. Quantity of evaluation and readers' perceptions of important, authoritative statements voiced by a hero of the story overlap. Needless to say the qualities of the accumulated evaluations and their supposedly heroic author (Joshua) have also promoted their authoritative reception in combination with the abnormal quantities.

3. Judges

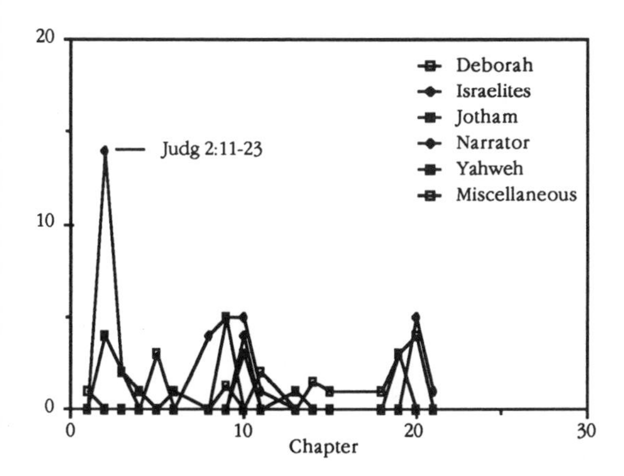

The graph shows a spike in ch. 2. In 2:11–23 the narrator offers his famous preview of the "cycles of the judges." The manner in which these evaluations of the Israelites stand out from other evaluative remarks in the book formally marks their pivotal role within the book and within the story of the conquest of the land. The evaluations look both forward and backward to appraise Israelite behaviour in both directions. It is no surprise scholarly readers have marked this section as an important one for understanding the authorial point of view in the narrative. The graph supports their perception; but the interpretation of the passage—the matter of how the reader is to take these evaluative comments—is another matter.

4. 1 Samuel

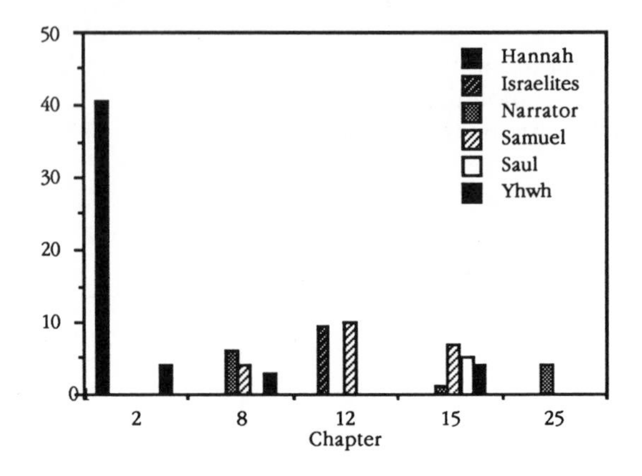

Hannah's emotional outburst in ch. 2 is far in excess of the norm for evaluative discourse in 1 Samuel. This evaluative spike is firmly contextualized in the circumstances of the story. Hannah's language is in praise of her lord, Yahweh, who has just demonstrated his power and goodwill by granting Hannah, a barren woman, a son. Hannah's song is another example of explicit evaluation in the narrative, like that of the special pleas of the Cis-Jordanian tribes in the book of Joshua, that is obviously relativized by its existential context in the story world.

Samuel's speech, on the other hand, has played a major role in scholarly theories about the perspective of the Dtr redactors. In terms of sheer quantity of evaluation it is 75% less significant than Hannah's prayer (40:10 ratio on a simple count comparison). Its pride of place, in scholarly theories about the narrator's views stems from three characteristics. First, Hannah's prayer aside, Samuel delivers the greatest quantity of his evaluative remarks in ch. 12. Second, his speech includes a sweeping historical review of Israel's covenantal history. By analogy with the narrative as a whole, scholars have associated this review with the sort of perspective one might expect of the historiographically inclined author/redactor. Finally, Samuel's evaluations in ch. 12 are strongly critical of Israel's behaviour, using covenantal language and categories for assessing that behaviour. Once again, because scholarly readers assume that this is the purpose of the narrative—to apprise Israel its responsibility for its exile, imminent or past—they have been prone to the assumption that Samuel's is the narrator's voice.

5. 2 Samuel

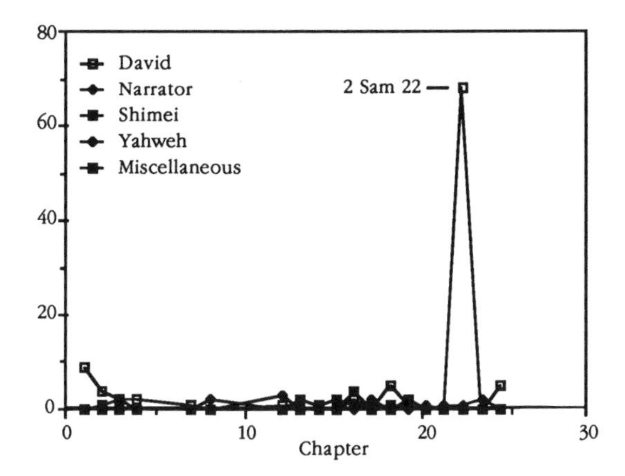

Once again, in 2 Samuel there is one strong evaluative spike, David's song of praise (ch. 22) in which a character gives vent to his emotions and the resulting peak is firmly contextualized and explained by its narrative context. Despite the large quantity of evaluative language used in the psalm and even though it is again a pious psalm of praise for Yahweh, scholarly readers have not identified the sentiments of the poem with those of the narrative's author. Though many factors influence reader-response, it is reasonable to presume that the firm contextual mooring of David's song has prevented scholarly readers from hearing in it the author's own sentiment in much the same fashion as Hannah's song has been treated. It is clear that the sorts of things—primarily praise for God's protection—that David has to say are not included in the agenda that scholars assume to lie behind the Dtr narrative. Last, but not least, the historical-critical bias against the "originality" of poetic sections inserted into "deuteronomistic" prose has contributed not a little to the poem's neglect.

6. 1 Kings

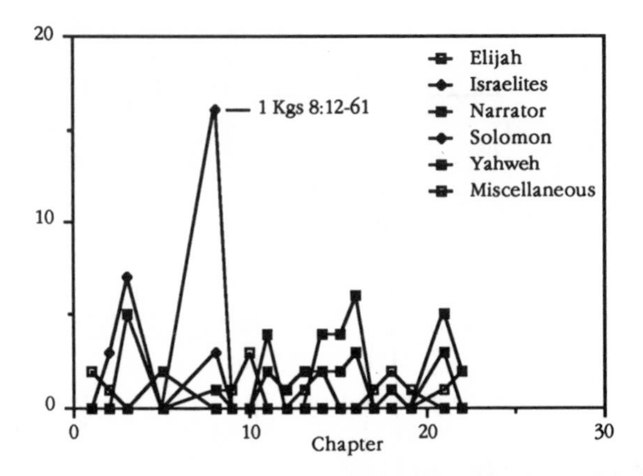

There is a high spike reflecting the florid rhetorical tones of Solomon's great prayers in 1 Kgs 8. Here again the evaluative spike coincides with one of the great orations that scholarly readers have identified as the views of the author disguised in the voice of one of the characters. The topics discussed by Solomon—sin, punishment for covenantal defection, and the possibility of divine forgiveness—seem admirably suited to a narrative and an author assumed to address the exile. And indeed, these should be matters of concern for both author and reader, both presumably looking back in retrospect to that disaster. It is not the perception that here, in the saturated evaluative discourse, we face an important moment or viewpoint in the narrative. It is, rather, the assumption that because Solomon voices such concerns he surely speaks on behalf the author that is dubious. The database, of course, cannot provide suggestions about how Solomon's prayers ought to be read in context; it only shows the unusual quality of the prayers and suggests one reason why the prayers have figured as they have in historical-critical readings of the narrative.

7. 2 Kings

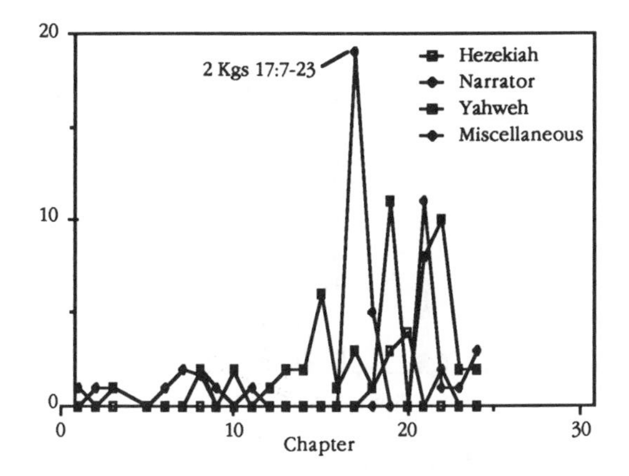

The most significant concentration of evaluative language in 2 Kings is, like the book of Judges, expressed by the narrating voice in ch. 17. Like many of the spikes, 2 Kgs 17:7–23 has been identified as a sincere expression of the views of the author/redactor. The difference between this passage (along with Judg 2) and most of the evaluative spikes/great orations is that here the author speaks in his own voice, supposedly because of the exigencies of tradition or the compulsion of convictions expressed at this point.

Here and in Judges 2 scholars are on firmest ground in their view that the great orations house the unadorned views of the author/redactor. But the seemingly obvious view—that here the author finally speaks in full candour, in his own narratorial voice—is complicated by contextual patterns like those surrounding the great character orations that undercut the evaluations by exposing their weakness and lack of correspondence with narrative reality. Evaluations in Judges 2 and 2 Kgs 17 are complicated by the fact of strong mitigating explanations or ironies that, once perceived, make it impossible for the reader to accept their valuations at face value. The situation in Judges 2—the generation gap—is unavoidable and the consequent apostasy, mitigated by the still stewing ironies of the book of Joshua. The apparent conclusiveness of 2 Kgs 17, to the detriment of the general Israelite populace, is extenuated by its lack of congruity with the narrative realities described throughout the preceding books about the kings and their adventures.

The Overall Picture

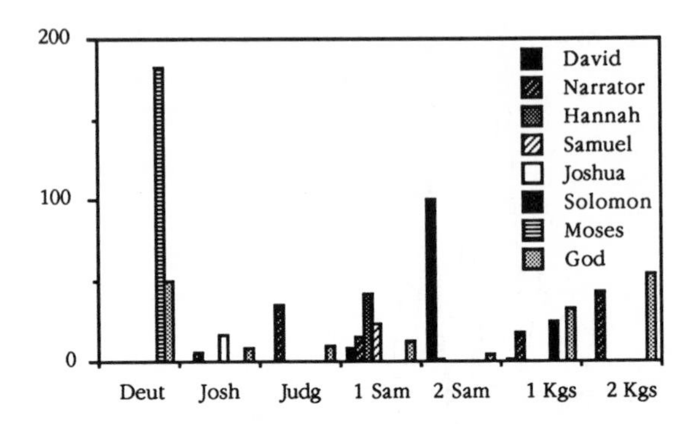

When the evaluative spikes are set against the background of the normal quantity of evaluative language found in any given chapter or book or expressed by any single voice in the narrative they only become more distinctive and pronounced. The relatively low level of evaluative discourse in the narrative accustoms the reader to a muted evaluative norm broken only a handful of times by these evaluative spikes. Little wonder that scholarly readers have reacted strongly to the evaluative spikes and interpreted some of these strong intrusions as the voice of the author/editor himself, regardless of whether he chose to speak in his own voice or through the agency of a character in the story. If the Dtr narrative is as hortatory as scholarship has said, where better to hear its preaching than in these evaluative pinnacles? The spikes do stand out—they are meant to—but they also stand out in contrast to the characteristic evaluative silence of the narrator and to his favourite expositional strategy: implicit commentary. The database reveals that the so-called key speeches or great orations in the narrative are closely aligned with these focal points of evaluation, confirming what Von Rad had said some time ago about the speeches: "Very much depends on the right understanding of these judgements" (1962:336).

BIBLIOGRAPHY

Abrams, M.H.
1981 *A Glossary of Literary Terms* (4th ed., Montreal: Holt, Rinehart and Winston).

Albright, W.F.
1938 "The Israelite Conquest of Canaan in the Light of Archaeology," *BASOR* 74, 11–23.

Alter, R.
1981 *The Art of Biblical Narrative* (NY: Basic Books).

Auerbach, E.
1975 *Moses* (tr. ed. R.A. Barclay, I.O. Lehman; Detroit: Wayne State UP).

Bakhtin, M.
1984 *Problems of Dostoevsky's Poetics* (THL 8; ed. tr. C. Emerson; Minneapolis: Minnesota UP).

Bal, M.
1977 *Narratologie. Essais sur la signification narrative dans quatre romans modernes* (Paris: Klincksieck).
1985 *Narratology. Introduction to the Theory of Narrative* (tr. C. van Boheemen; Toronto, Buffalo, London: Toronto UP).
1986 "The Bible As Literature: A Critical Escape," *Diacritics* 16, 71–9.

Baltzer, K.
1964 *Das Bundesformular* (2nd. ed.; WMANT 4; Neukirchen-Vluyn: Neukirchener).

Banfield, A.
1973 "Narrative Style and the Grammar of Direct and Indirect Speech," *Foundations of Language* 10, 1–39.
1978a "The Formal Coherence of Represented Speech and Thought," *Poetics and Theory of Literature* 3, 289–314.
1978b "Where Epistemology, Style, and Grammar Meet Literary History: the Development of Represented Speech and Thought," *New Literary History* 9, 415–54.

Bar-Efrat, S.
1989 *Narrative Art in the Bible* (BLS 17; Sheffield: Sheffield Academic Press).
Barr, J.
1961 *The Semantics of Biblical Language* (Oxford: Oxford UP).
1968 *Comparative Philology and the Text of the Old Testament* (Oxford: Oxford UP).
Benzinger, I.
1899 *Die Bücher der Könige* (KHAT 9; Leipzig & Tübingen: J.C.B. Mohr [P. Siebeck]).
Bickert, R.
1979 "Die Geschichte und das Handeln Jahwes," *Textgemäss* (eds. A.H.J. Gunneweg, O. Kaiser; Göttingen: Vandenhoeck & Ruprecht).
Birch, B. C.
1976 *The Rise of the Israelite Monarchy: The Growth and Development of I Samuel 7-15* (SBLDS 27; Missoula: Scholars Press).
Bloch, E.
1959 *Das Prinzip der Hoffnung* (Gesamtausgabe vol. 5; Frankfurt: Suhrkamp).
Boecker, H.–J.
1969 *Die Beurteilung der Anfänge des Königtums in den deuteronomistischen Abschnitten des I. Samuelbuches* (WMANT 31; Neukirchen–Vluyn: Neukirchener Ver).
Boling, R.G.
1975 *Judges* (*AB* 6A; Garden City, NY: Doubleday & Co.).
1982 *Joshua* (*AB* 6; Garden City: Doubleday & Co.).
Booth, W.
1961 *The Rhetoric of Fiction* (Chicago and London: Chicago UP).
Brueggemann, W.
1970 "The Triumphalist Tendency in Exegetical History," *JAAR* 38, 367–80.
Buber M.
1956 "Die Erzählung von Sauls Königswahl," *VT* 6, 113–73.
1964 "Die Sprache der Botschaft," *Werke II* (München: Kösel Ver.).

Budde, K.
1890 *Die Bücher Richter und Samuel: Ihre Quellen und ihr Aufbau* (Giessen: J. Ricker).
1902 *Die Bücher Samuel* (KHAT VIII; Tübingen: Mohr).

Campbell, A.F.
1986 *Of Prophets & Kings. A Late Ninth-Century Document (1 Samuel 1 – 2 Kings 10)* (CBQMS 17; Washington, DC: Catholic Biblical Assoc. of America).

Campbell, K.M.
1972 "Rahab's Covenant," *VT* 22, 243–4.

Carmichael, C.M.
1974 *The Laws of Deuteronomy* (Ithaca & London: Cornell UP).

Chatman, S.
1978 *Story and Discourse. Narrative Structure in Fiction and Film* (Ithaca & London: Cornell UP).

Childs, B.S.
1979 *Introduction to the Old Testament as Scripture* (Philadelphia: Fortress).

Coats, G.W.
1985 "An Exposition for the Conquest Theme," *CBQ* 47, 47–54.

Cohn, D.
1966 "Narrated Monologue: Definition of a Fictional Style," *Comparative Literature* 28, 97–112.
1978 *Transparent Minds: Narrative Modes for Presenting Consciousness in Fiction* (Princeton, NJ: Princeton UP).

Cross, F.M.
1973 *Canaanite Myth and Hebrew Epic. Essays in the History of the Religion of Israel* (Cambridge, Mass: Harvard UP).

Crüsemann, F.
1978 *Der Widerstand gegen das Königtum. Die antiköniglichen Texte des Alten Testamentes und der Kampf um den frühen Israelitischen Staat* (WMANT 49; Neukirchen-Vluyn: Neukirchener).

Damrosch, D.
1987 "Leviticus," *The Literary Guide to the Bible* (eds. R. Alter, F. Kermode; Cambridge, Mass.: Harvard UP).

De Vries, S.J.
1985 *1 Kings* (Vol. 12; Word Biblical Commentary; Waco, TX: Word Books).

Dhorme, E. P.
1910 *Les Livres de Samuel* (Études Bibliques; Paris: Gabalda).
Dietrich, W.
1972 *Prophetie und Geschichte* (FRLANT 108; Göttingen: Vandenhoeck & Ruprecht).
Doležel, L.
1967 "The Typology of the Narrator: Point of View in Fiction," *To Honor Roman Jakobson* (Vol. 1; The Hague: Mouton), 541–52.
1973 *Narrative Modes in Czech Literature* (Toronto: UP).
1980 "Truth and Authenticity in Narrative," *Poetics Today* 1:3, 7–25.
Driver, S.R.
1892 *A treatise on the Use of the Tenses in Hebrew* (Oxford: Oxford UP).
1913 *An Introduction to the Literature of the Old Testament* (9th ed.; Edinburgh: T. & T. Clark).
Dus, J.
1960 Gibeon—eine Kultstätte des Šmš und die Stadt des benjaminitischen Schicksals," *VT* 10, 353-74.
Ehrlich, A.B.
1910 *Randglossen zur hebräischen Bibel. Textkritisches, Sprachliches und Sachliches. III: Josua, Richter, I u. II Samuelis* (Leipzig: n.p.).
Eichrodt, W.
1961 *Theology of the Old Testament* (tr. J.A. Baker; 2 vols.; Philadelphia: Westminster).
Eslinger L.
1983 "Viewpoints and Point of View in 1 Samuel 8–12," *JSOT* 23, 61–76.
1985 *Kingship of God in Crisis. A Close Reading of 1 Samuel 1–12* (BLS 10; Sheffield: Almond).
1986 "Josiah and the Torah Book: Comparison of 2 Kgs 22:1–23:28 and 2 Chr 34:1–35:19," *The Hebrew Annual Review* 10, 37–62.
1988 "'A Change of Heart': 1 Samuel 16," *Ascribe To The Lord: Biblical and Other Studies In Memory of Peter C. Craigie* (JSOTSS 67; Sheffield: Sheffield Academic Press).
Ferry, A.
1963 *Milton's Epic Voice. The Narrator in Paradise Lost* (Chicago: Chicago UP).

Fitzmyer, J.A.
1981 *The Gospel According to LUKE (I–IX)* (*AB* 28; Garden City, NY: Doubleday & Co.).

Fokkelman
1981 *Narrative Art and Poetry in the Books of Samuel. Volume 1: King David (II Sam. 9–20 & I Kings 1–2)* (Assen: Van Gorcum).
1986 *Narrative Art and Poetry in the Books of Samuel. Volume 2: The Crossing Fates (I Sam. 13–31 & II Sam 1)* (Assen: Van Gorcum).

Fowler, A.
1982 *Kinds of Literature. An Introduction to the Theory of Genres and Modes* (Cambridge, MA: Harvard UP).

Friedemann, K.
1910 *Die Rolle des Erzählers in der Epik* (Leipzig: H. Hässel).

Friedman, N.
1955 "Point of View in Fiction: The Development of a Critical Concept," *PMLA* 70, 1160–84.

Friedman, R.E.
1981a *The Exile and Biblical Narrative* (HSM 22; Chico: Scholars Press).
1981b "From Egypt to Egypt: Dtr1 and Dtr2," *Traditions in Transformation* (eds. B. Halpern, J.D. Levenson; Winona Lk.: Eisenbrauns).

Fritz, V.
1976 "Die Deutung des Königtums Sauls in den Überlieferungen von seiner Entstehung I Sam. 9-11," *ZAW* 88: 346-62.

Gamper, A.
1963 "Die Heilsgeschichtliche Bedeutung des Salomonischen Tempelweihegebets," *ZTK* 85, 55–61.

Gehman, H.S.
Montgomery, J.A.
1951 *The Books of Kings* (ICC; Edinburgh: T. & T. Clark).

Genette, G.
1972 *Figures III* (Paris: Seuil).
1980 *Narrative Discourse. An Essay in Method* (tr. J.E. Lewis; Ithaca: Cornell UP).

Gerbrandt, G.E.
1986 *Kingship According to the Deuteronomistic History* SBLDS 87; Atlanta, GA: Scholars Press).

Gray, G.B.
1913 *A Critical Introduction to the Old Testament* (London: Duckworth).

Gray, J.
1970 *I & II Kings* (OTL; Philadelphia: Westminster).

Greenberg, M.
1969 *Understanding Exodus* (New York: Behrman House).

Gressmann, H.
1914 *Die Anfänge Israels* (SAT 1/2; Göttingen: Vandenhoeck & Ruprecht).

Gunkel, H.
1902 *Genesis* (Göttingen: Vandenhoeck & Ruprecht).

Gunn, D.M.
1980 *The Fate of King Saul. An Interpretation of a Biblical Story* (JSOTSS 14; Sheffield: JSOT).
1982 "The "Hardening of Pharaoh's Heart": Plot, Character and Theology in Exodus 1–14," *Art and Meaning: Rhetoric in Biblical Literature* (JSOTSS 19; eds. D.J.A. Clines, D.M. Gunn, A.J. Hauser; Sheffield: JSOT) 72–96.

Gutbrod, K.
1956 *Das Buch vom Könige: Das erste Buch Samuel* (Die Botschaft des alten Testaments XI/1; Stuttgart: Calwer).

Halpern, B.
1975 "Gibeon: Israelite Diplomacy in the Conquest Era," *CBQ* 37, 303–16.

Herrnstein Smith, B.
1978 *On The Margins of Discourse. The Relation of Literature to Language* (Chicago & London: Chicago UP).

Hertzberg, H.W.
1959 *Die Bücher Josua, Richter, Ruth* (2nd ed; ATD 9; Göttingen: Vandenhoeck & Ruprecht).
1964 *I and II Samuel. A Commentary* (tr. J. S. Bowden; OTL; Philadelphia: Westminster).

Hobbs, T.R.
1985 *2 Kings* (WBC 13; Waco, TX: Word Books).

Hughes, J.J.
1987 *Bits, Bytes and Biblical Studies* (Grand Rapids: Zondervan).

Hyatt, J.P.
1971 *Exodus* (NCB; Grand Rapids: Eerdmans, London: Marshall, Morgan and Scott).

Ingarden, R.
1973 *The Literary Work of Art* (tr. G.G. Grabowicz; Evanston: Northwestern University).

Isbell, C.
1982 "Exodus 1–2 in the Context of Exodus 1–14: Story Lines and Key Words," *Art and Meaning: Rhetoric in Biblical Narrative* (JSOTSS 19; eds. D.J.A. Clines, D.M. Gunn, A.J. Hauser; Sheffield: JSOT) 37–61.

Jepsen, A.
1956 *Die Quellen des Königsbuches* (Halle (Saale): Max Niemeyer).
1977 "batach," *TDOT* vol. 2, 88-94.

Jobling, D.
1986 *The Sense of Biblical Narrative: Structural Analyses in the Hebrew Bible II* (JSOTSS 39; Sheffield: JSOT).

Kasher, M.M.
1967 *Exodus* (Encyclopedia of Biblical Interpretation; Vol. VII; tr. ed. H. Freedman; New York: American Biblical Encyclopedia Society).
1970 *Exodus* (Encyclopedia of Biblical Interpretation; Vol. VIII; New York: American Biblical Encyclopedia Society).

Kaufer, D.S.
1983 "Irony, Interpretive Form and the Theory of Meaning," *Poetics Today* 4, 451–64.

Keil, C.F.
1982 *I & II Kings, I & II Chronicles, Ezra, Nehemiah, Esther* (Grand Rapids: W.B. Eerdmans [reprint]).

Keil, C. F. and Delitzsch, F.
1880 *The Books of Samuel* (tr. J. Martin. Edinburgh: T. & T. Clark).

Keller, C.A.
1956 "Über einige alttestamentliche Heiligtumslegenden II," *ZAW* 68, 85–97.

Kenik, H.A.
1983 *Design for Kingship. The Deuteronomistic Narrative Technique in 1 Kings 3:4–15* (SBLDS 69; Chico, CA: Scholars Press).

Kitchen, K.A.
1989 "Where Did Solomon's Gold Go?" *BAR* 15, 30–31.
1989 "Shishak's Military Campaign in Israel Confirmed," *BAR* 15, 32–33.

Klein, R.W.
1983 *1 Samuel* (WBC 10; Waco, TX: Word Books).
König, F.E.
1897 *Historisch-kritisches Lehregebäude der hebräischen Sprache. Vol. 2: Syntax* (Leipzig: J.C. Hinrichs).
Kuhl, K.
1962 "Die "Wiederaufnahme"— ein literarkritisches Prinzip?" *ZAW* 64, 1–11.
Labuschagne, C. J.
1973 "The Particles "hen" and "hinneh," *OTS* 18, 1–14.
Langlamet, F.
1970 "Les récits de l'institution de la royauté (I Sam. VIII-XII)," *RB* 77, 161–200.
Leech, G.N.
1974 *Semantics* (Markham: Penguin Books of Canada).
Levenson, J.D.
1975 "Who inserted the Book of the Torah?" *HTR* 68, 203–33.
1981 "From Temple to Synagogue: 1 Kings 8," *Traditions in Transformation* (eds. B. Halpern, J.D. Levenson; Winona Lk.: Eisenbrauns) 143–66.
Lind, M.C.
1980 *Yahweh Is a Warrior. The Theology of Warfare in Ancient Israel* (Kitchener: Herald Press).
Liver, J.
1963 "The Literary History of Joshua 9," *JSS* 8, 227–43.
Long, B.O.
1987 "Framing Repetitions in Biblical Historiography," *JBL* 106, 385–99.
Malamat, A.
1955 "Doctrines of Causality in Hittite and Biblical Historiography: A Parallel," *VT* 5, 1–12.
Mayes, A. D. H.
1978 "The Rise of the Israelite Monarchy," *ZAW* 90, 1–19.
McCarthy, D.J.
1971 "The Theology of Leadership in Joshua 1–9," *Bib* 52, 165–71.
1973 "The Inauguration of Monarchy in Israel: A Form-Critical Study of I Samuel 8–12," *Int* 27, 401–12.
1974 "The Wrath of Yahweh and the Structural Unity of the Deuteronomistic History," *Essays in Old Testament*

Ethics (J. P. Hyatt memorial vol.; eds. J.L. Crenshaw, J.T. Willis; New York: KTAV), 99–110.

1978 *Treaty and Covenant* (Analecta Biblica 21; Rome: Pontifical Biblical Institute).

McHale, B.

1978 "Free Indirect Discourse: A Survey of Recent Accounts," *Poetics and Theory of Literature* 3, 249–87.

Mettinger, T.N.D.

1976 *King and Messiah. The Civil and Sacral Legitimation of the Israelite Kings* (Lund: C.W.K. Gleerup).

Meyers, C.

1987 "The Israelite Empire: In Defense of King Solomon," *Backgrounds for the Bible* (Winona Lk.: Eisenbrauns), 181–97.

Milgrom, J.

1976 "Profane Slaughter and a Formulaic Key to the Composition of Deuteronomy," *HUCA* 47, 1–17.

Millard, A.

1989 "Does The Bible Exaggerate King Solomon's Golden Wealth?" *BAR* 15, 20–29, 34.

Miller, J.M.

1974 "Saul's Rise to Power: Some Observations Concerning 1 Sam. 9.1–10.16; 10.26–11.15 and 13.2–14.46," *CBQ* 36, 157–74.

1977 "The Israelite Occupation of Canaan," *Israelite and Judean History* (eds. J.H. Hayes, J.M. Miller; Philadelphia: Westminster) 213–84.

Miller, P.D.

1973 *The Divine Warrior in Early Israel* (Cambridge, Mass.: Harvard UP).

Möhlenbrink, K.

1938 "Die Landnahmesagen des Buches Josua," *ZAW* 56, 238–68.

Moesnner, D.P.

1983 "Luke 9:1–50: Luke's Preview of the Journey of the Prophet Like Moses of Deuteronomy," *JBL* 102, 575–605.

Montgomery, J.A.

Gehman, H.S.

1951 *The Books of Kings* (ICC; Edinburgh: T. & T. Clark).

Moore, G.F.

1895 *Judges* (ICC; Edinburgh: T. & T. Clark).

Moulton, R.G.
1908 *The Literary Study of the Bible* (rev. ed. of original, 1895; Boston: D.C. Heath & Co.).
Mowinckel, S.
1964 *Tetrateuch — Pentateuch — Hexateuch* (BZAW 90; Berlin: A. Töpelmann).
Muilenburg, J.
1959 "The Form and Structure of the Covenantal Formulations," *VT* 9, 347–65.
1968 "The Intercession of the Covenant Mediator (Exodus 33.1a, 12-17)," *Words and Meanings* (D. W.Thomas vol.; eds. P.R. Ackroyd, B. Lindars; Cambridge: UP) 159–81.
Nelson, R.D.
1981 *The Double Redaction of the Deuteronomistic History* (JSOTSS 18; Sheffield: JSOT).
Noth, M.
1967 *Überlieferungsgeschichtliche Studien* (Tübingen: M. Niemeyer Ver).
1968 *Könige* (Neukirchen-Vluyn: Neukirchener Ver).
1981 *The Deuteronomistic History* (2nd ed. [1957]; tr. J. Doull, J. Barton, M.D. Rutter, D.R. Ap-Thomas; ed. D.J.A. Clines; JSOTSS 15; Sheffield: JSOT).
Olson, D.T.
1985 *The Death of the Old and the Birth of the New. The Framework of the Book of Numbers and the Pentateuch* (BJS 71; Chico, CA: Scholars Press).
Parker, K.I.
1988 "Repetition as a Structuring Device in 1 Kings 1–11," *JSOT* 42, 19–27.
Payne, J.B.
1972 "Saul and the Changing Will of God," *Bibliotheca Sacra* 129/#516, 321–5.
Peckham, B.
1984 "The Composition of Joshua 3–4," *CBQ* 46, 413–31.
Pedersen, J.
1926 *Israel. Its Life and Culture* (vol. 1; Copenhagen: Povl Brauner).
Perry, M.
1979 "Literary Dynamics: How the Order of a Text Creates Its Meanings," *Poetics Today* 1:1–2, 35–64, 311–61.

Person, R.
1986 *Reflex Tips, Tricks, and Traps* (Indianapolis, IN: Que Corp.).

Polzin, R.
1980 *Moses and the Deuteronomist. A Literary Study of the Deuteronomistic History* (New York: Seabury).
1981 "Reporting Speech in the Book of Deuteronomy: Toward A Compositional Analysis of the Deuteronomic History," *Traditions In Transformation: Turning Points in Biblical Faith* (eds. B. Halpern, J.D. Levenson; Winona Lk.: Eisenbrauns) 193–211.

Porten, B.
1967 "The Structure and Theme of the Solomon Narrative (1 Kings 3–11)," *HUCA* 38, 93–128.

Pratt, M.L.
1977 *Toward a Speech–Act Theory of Literary Discourse* (Bloomington, IN: Indiana UP).

Press, R.
1938 "Der Prophet Samuel," *ZAW* 56, 177-225.

Prince, G.
1984 Review of G. Genette, *Nouveau discours du récit*, *Poetics Today* 5:4, 867–8.

Rabinowitz I.
1984 "ʾAZ followed by imperfect verb–form in preterite contexts: a redactional device in biblical Hebrew," *VT* 34, 53–62.

Von Rad, G.
1962 *Old Testament Theology. The Theology of Israel's Historical Traditions* (Vol. 1; tr. D.M.G. Stalker; New York: Harper & Row).

Rimmon-Kenan, S.
1983 *Narrative Fiction. Contemporary Poetics* (London & New York: Methuen).

Rost, L.
1982 *The Succession to the Throne of David* (tr. M.D. Rutter, D.M. Gunn; Sheffield: Almond Press).

Šanda, A.
1911 *Die Bücher der Könige* (HAT 9; Münster i. Wesf.: Aschendorffsche Ver).

Sandmel, S.
1972 "The Ancient Mind and Ours," *Understanding The Sacred Text* (ed. J. Reumann; Valley Forge: Judson) 29–44.
Sawyer, J.F.A.
1967 "Context of Situation and Sitz im Leben," *Proceedings of the Newcastle upon Tyne Philosophical Society* 1, 137–47.
1972 *Semantics in Biblical Research* (SBT 24; London: SCM).
Schneidau, H.N.
1976 *Sacred Discontent. The Bible and Western Tradition* (Berkeley: U. of Calif. Press).
Schulz, A.
1919 *Die Bücher Samuel* (HAT VIII/1; Münster: Aschendorff).
Seebass, H.
1965 "Traditionsgeschichte von I Sam. 8, 10:17ff.,und 12," *ZAW* 77, 286–96.
Segal, N.
1988 "Review of M. Sternberg, *The Poetics of Biblical Narrative*," *VT* 38, 243–9.
Smend, R.
1971 "Das Gesetz und die Völker," *Probleme biblischer Theologie* (ed. H.W. Wolff; München: Chr. Kaiser Ver) 494–509.
1978 *Die Entstehung des Alten Testaments* (Stuttgart: Kohlhammer).
Smith, G. A.
1900 *The Historical Geography of the Holy Land* (7th ed.; London: Hodder & Stoughton).
Smith, H. P.
1899 *A Critical and Exegetical Commentary on the Books of Samuel* (ICC; Edinburgh: T. & T. Clark).
Soggin, J.A.
1972 *Joshua* (OTL; Philadelphia: Westminster).
Speiser, E. A.
1971 "The Manner of the King," *WHJP* vol. 3, 280–7.
Stalker, D.M.G.
1962 "Exodus," *Peake's Commentary on the Bible* (eds. M. Black, H.H. Rowley; Don Mills, Ont.: Nelson) 208–40.
Stanzel, F.K.
1971 *Narrative Situations in the Novel* (tr. J.P. Pusack; Baltimore & London: Johns Hopkins UP).

1979 *Theorie des Erzählens* (UTB 904; Göttingen: Vandenhoeck & Ruprecht).
1981 "Teller-Characters and Reflector-Characters In Narrative Theory," *PT* 2:2, 5–15.
1984 *A Theory of Narrative* (tr. C. Goedsche, Cambridge: Cambridge UP).

Sternberg, M.
1978 *Expositional Modes and Temporal Ordering in Fiction* (Baltimore & London: Johns Hopkins UP).
1985 *The Poetics of Biblical Narrative. Ideological Literature and the Drama of Reading* (Bloomington: Indiana UP).

Stoebe, H.J.
1973 *Das erste Buch Samuelis* (KAT VIII/1; Gütersloh: Gerd Mohn).

Talmon S.
1978 "The Presentation of Synchroneity and Simultaneity in Biblical Narrative," *SH* 27, 12–25.

Thenius, O.
1864 *Die Bücher Samuels* (2nd edn.; KHAT 4; Leipzig: Hirzel).

Tucker, G.M.
1972 "The Rahab Saga (Joshua 2): Some Form-Critical and Traditio-Historical Observations," *The Use of the Old Testament in the New and Other Essays: Studies in Honor of William Franklin Stinespring* (ed. J.M. Efird; Durham, NC: Duke UP) 66–86.

Uspensky, B.
1973 *A Poetics of Composition* (tr. V. Zavarin, S. Wittig; Berkeley: U. of Calif.).

Van Seters, J.
1983 *In Search of History. Historiography in the Ancient World and the Origins of Biblical History* (New Haven, CT & London: Yale UP).

Vannoy, J. R.
1978 *Covenant Renewal at Gilgal. A Study of 1 Samuel 11.14-12.25* (Cherry Hill: Mack Pub. Co).

Veijola, T.
1975 *Die ewige Dynastie* (Helsinki: Suomalainen Tiedeakatemia).
1977 *Das Königtum in der Beurteilung der deuteronomistischen Historiographie* (Helsinki: Suomalainen Tiedeakatemia).

Visser, N.W.
1977 "Temporal Vantage Point in the Novel," *Journal of Narrative Technique* 7, 81–93.

Vogt, E.
1965 "Die Erzählung vom Jordanübergang. Josue 3–4," *Bib* 46, 125–48.

Vriezen, Th.C.
1967 "Exodusstudien Exodus I," *VT* 17, 334–44.

Webb, B.G.
1987 *The Book of Judges. An Integrated Reading* (JSOTSS 46; Sheffield: Sheffield Academic Press).

Weinfeld, M.
1972 *Deuteronomy and the Deuteronomic School* (Oxford: Clarendon Press).

Weingreen, J.
1976 *From Bible to Mishnah* (Manchester: Manchester UP).

Weiser, A.
1961 *The Old Testament: Its Formation and Development* (tr. D. M. Barton; New York: Associated).
1962 *Samuel: seine geschichtliche Aufgabe und religiöse Bedeutung. Traditions-geschichtliche Untersuchungen zu 1. Samuel 7–12* (FRLANT 81; Göttingen: Vandenhoeck & Ruprecht).

Wellhausen, J.
1973 *Prolegomena to the History of Ancient Israel* ([reprint] Gloucester, Mass.: Peter Smith).

Wenham, G.J.
1971 "The Deuteronomic Theology of the Book of Joshua," *JBL* 90, 140–8.

Westermann, C.
1982 *Elements of Old Testament Theology* (tr. D.W. Stott; Atlanta: John Knox).

Wiener H.M.
1929 *The Composition of Judges II 11 to 1 Kings II 46* (Leipzig: Hinrichs).

Wright G.E.
1946 "The Literary and Historical Problems of Joshua 10 and Judges 1," *JNES* 5, 105–14.
1982 "Introduction," *Judges* (*AB* 6; R. Boling; Garden City, NY: Doubleday & Co.) 3–88.
1982 *Joshua* (AB 6; Garden City, N.Y.:Doubleday & Co.).

Würthwein, E.
1977 *Die Bücher der Könige. 1. Könige 1–16* (Göttingen: Vandenhoeck & Ruprecht).

Zakovitch, Y.
1972 "*ypth = bdn*," *VT* 22, 123–5.

Zimmerli, W.
1968 *Der Mensch und seine Hoffnung in alten Testament* (Göttingen: Vandenhoeck & Ruprecht).
1978 *Old Testament Theology in Outline* (tr. D.E. Green; Atlanta: John Knox).
1982 "Knowledge of God According to the Book of Ezekiel," *I am Yahweh* (tr. D.W. Stott; Atlanta: John Knox) 29–98, 143–54.

INDEX OF AUTHORS

❑ T

❑ U

❑ V

❑ W

❑ Z

INDEX OF SUBJECTS

❑ S

❑ T

❑ V

❑ W

INDEX OF CITATIONS

❑ Judges

❑ 1 Samuel

❑ 2 Samuel

❑ 1 Kings

❑ 2 Kings

❑ Job

❑ Nehemiah

❑ 1 Chronicles

❑ 2 Chronicles

INDEX OF HEBREW TERMS